D0948759

THE DISCOVERY
OF DEATH
IN CHILDHOOD
AND AFTER

SYLVIA ANTHONY

THE DISCOVERY
OF DEATH
IN CHILDHOOD
AND AFTER

BASIC BOOKS, Inc., Publishers
New York

FIRST AMERICAN EDITION: 1972

© 1971 by Sylvia Anthony
Library of Congress Catalog Card Number: 73-180283
SBN 465-01671-5

PRINTED IN THE UNITED STATES OF AMERICA

CONTENTS

CHAPTER I

INTRODUCTION

ONE summer afternoon before the Second World War, a small group of friends were having tea in a London garden, and after the children had run off to play, I said I thought of writing something on the development of the concept of death in childhood. A guest, Franz Borkenau, said he thought it a good idea. Later I suggested to Professor Burt that I should make it the subject of a Ph.D. thesis (a degree I failed to achieve), and he sent me for advice to Professor J. C. Flugel who, happily for me, and I like to think also for him, consented to act as a supervisor. Flugel was an academic psychologist – a former pupil of Mc-Dougall – and also a Freudian of early vintage, which was an uncommon combination; he was not a physician, but an experienced and well-qualified psychoanalyst, which I was not and did not seek to be.

An abstract of the thesis was published in 1939. Later, the thesis was expanded into a book, *The Child's Discovery of Death*, for which Professor Flugel wrote an introduction. In this he touched on a fact which I had scarcely considered: that the subject of death was generally taboo. His observation was not only true and important but in a sense prophetic, for a taboo may be attacked, even with cheers from onlookers, without necessarily disappearing. What tends to disappear, at least temporarily, is the missile launched against it.

In this case, the cheers were represented by encouraging reviews from eminent *littérateurs* – Desmond McCarthy, G. W. Stonier, Rosamond Lehmann – and others whose work I heard of but had no chance to read, because the publishing house from which press cuttings were dispatched was bombed soon after the book came out. The partakers of tea in the garden had meanwhile dispersed over three continents, some never to meet again, though all survived the war.

Flugel had written in his introduction:

Living organisms die and they reproduce, and these two aspects of life exercise upon us an uncanny fascination ... We all of us believe today that sexual problems and the way in which they are solved have some very real importance for the development and mental health of the individual. Hence the great number of books on the psychology of sex that have appeared in recent years ...

There is no corresponding literature on the psychology of death – and this in spite of the fact that psychoanalysis has shown that in many important respects our attitude towards death is similar to that towards sex. Both subjects are often unpleasant, inasmuch as they tend to arouse anxiety (though at bottom the anxiety may be differently motivated); we often react to both forms of unpleasure and anxiety by the same devices of flight, repression, taboo and symbolism (we talk of a 'departed' friend as we talk of a 'fallen' woman, shunning in both cases the greater affect that a more direct expression might involve); both subjects may be intimately bound together in ideas of widespread or indeed of universal significance ...

He congratulated me 'on having had the courage to overcome the resistances and taboos which have hitherto surrounded this difficult and delicate subject – a courage comparable to that of the writers who braved the corresponding sexual taboos a decade or two ago'.

In a sociological study published in 1965, to which I shall refer again, Geoffrey Gorer wrote: 'In 1955 I put into words my awareness that death had superseded sex as a taboo subject.' Flugel had shown awareness of this phenomenon fifteen years earlier, but Gorer made no reference to this, nor to *The Child's Discovery of Death*, which had been very widely reviewed at the time of its appearance. But it had appeared in 1940, when Englishmen were more concerned with organizing and defending themselves against sudden death than in pondering its psychology or sociology. Yet the 1955 statement was one of many

instances of the way we practise the taboos we are challenging.
To lead in breaking a taboo may appear brave and bold, but
probably the true innovators are hardly conscious of the courage
others see in them. Focusing intensely on the object studied, one
is unaware of the intangible barriers around it, even surprised
that it seems so delightfully untouched and unexploited. That
impression may be a delusion. One may not be a solitary adven-
turer. At any rate let me explain in this way any similar omissions
of my own.

It was in 1955 also that Borkenau published in *The Twentieth
Century* a paper on the concept of death, in which he linked
Freud's treatment of the idea with a philosophic-historical argument embracing palaeolithic ritual and modern totalitarianism
in one masterly sweep. Using as the basis of his theme the
contradictoriness which Freud found in man's experience of
death – that he was unconsciously immortal but consciously
well aware of death's inevitability – Borkenau traced these conflicting attitudes at work within every human culture, and
argued, on Hegelian lines, that civilizations which begin as
death-denying end as death-affirming, and vice versa.

A psychologist is perhaps by training relatively myopic in
discerning patterns in history. An Hegelian repetition of cultural
attitudes to the idea of death or the ritual relating to it seems to
me too neat to represent the actualities of human behaviour over
the ages. It must be left to historians and archaeologists to rebut
or develop elegant theories on such a time-scale. This is not to
suggest that elegance in science is not a virtue, or that we do not
need hypotheses of man's history both large and small-scale.

In the later 1950s the taboo began to be more generally lifted.
I. E. Alexander wrote an article in 1957 entitled 'Is death a
matter of indifference?', in the *American Journal of Psychology*,
and followed it up with some research on children and adolescents to which I shall refer again later.

Medicine men in every culture have a special relation to
taboos. They are necessarily aware of cultural conventions, and
usually support and share them, but it is their function to touch,

and verbally to touch upon, what is otherwise deemed untouchable. When Dr Hermann Feifel published in 1959 a collection of essays by various authors entitled *The Meaning of Death*, the contributors were mostly medical practitioners. But among other things the psychological problems of the profession itself in this context were treated with frankness and perspicacity, and the inclusion of an eminent psychologist among the contributors, by recognizing the involvement of workers in other disciplines, came like a breath of fresh air.

The function of the primitive medicine man is divided in civilized communities between the physician and the priest. Both may, indeed must, breach the taboo on the subject of death. In a standard work published in 1962, *Man and his Destiny in the Great Religions*, Professor S. G. F. Brandon refers to the 'discoveries which each person makes of the facts of death and birth'. He proceeds:

They are advisedly placed in this order, since the discovery of death is usually prior in individual experience to that of birth and it is by its nature calculated to produce the profounder impression. The child, when it first learns that people die, quickly draws out the personal implications of the fact, and, although in most instances the effect of the original shock quickly disappears before the pressure of more immediate interests, the fact is duly registered by the mind and realization of its fuller significance steadily grows.[1]

At this point he refers to *The Child's Discovery of Death*, which naturally pleased me, but also illustrated the extent of the taboo, for in the twenty-two years since that work was published there had been a flood of authoritative volumes on the psychology of the child, yet apparently this work by a writer otherwise unknown was the theologian's only reference for the topic.

I have said, partly in my own defence, that we may practise the taboos we think we are challenging. One further example will be given, nearer the present date:

It is possible that certain conflicts are uniquely adapted to produce

[1] *op. cit.*, p. 6

nightmares. This holds for conflicts which have at their core a concern with death. It is possible to cite innumerable historical and anthropological examples which indicate that death is of paramount concern to mankind. Yet until the rather recent impact of existentialist writings, for example, May, Angel and Ellenberger (1958), such concern seems to have been subject to a curious repression or at least an avoidance by American psychologists.[1]

As this statement referred only to American psychologists one cannot suppose that the writers would have intended to refer to work originating elsewhere, but the very relevant studies of Alexander and his colleagues and of Feifel and his contributors had been carried out and published in the United States within the previous decade. An article immediately following in the same journal refers to the measurement of anxiety about death, based on a study of the reactions of medical students, and it also omits reference to Alexander's or Feifel's studies, but in this case the relevance would be less obvious and omission could be attributed to a laudable intention not to multiply references beyond necessity.

Not being a medicine man myself in either sense, I had for many years no opportunity to follow up the earlier studies in this field, until, during the 1960s, three events impelled me to take them up again. First, I learned, by chance contact with an American Fulbright Fellow, while on a visit to Australia in 1961, that The Child's Discovery of Death was known to psychologists in the States, largely through Dr Feifel's book. Secondly, in 1965 I was asked to contribute a chapter from The Child's Discovery of Death to a collection to be published in the United States, entitled The World of the Child. Thirdly, in 1969, when much of the present book had already been written, Dr Sula Wolff published Children under Stress and, in connection with it, wrote an article in New Society with extensive reference to the findings of my 1940 book. Again it seemed that it had not been superseded, but

[1] M. J. Feldman and M. Hersen, 'Attitudes towards death in nightmare subjects', Journal of Abnormal Psychology, 1967, 77, 5

THE DISCOVERY OF DEATH

it was almost unobtainable, and I did not want to have it re-printed, being aware of weaknesses.

The plan was therefore for another book, repeating and adding to earlier observations, relating them to later researches in kindred fields, placing the whole in the sort of setting such a subject deserves. These were ambitious objectives. Achievement was bound to fall short of full success. The literature on the psychological development of children is very extensive, so that I cannot fail to miss relevant and important items, the more since my professional work after publication of *The Child's Discovery of Death* has not been mainly among children. As for what I have called the setting, the matter is so limitless that what has been covered was determined more by the necessity of design and the restrictions of personal knowledge and ability than by the nature of the subject. Moreover, a taboo which does not apply to medicine men permits them to quote from the work of laymen in this field, but does not necessarily allow laymen to speak for themselves untaboo'd. Their work (until quoted) is likely to be considered unprofessional.

Among modern British writers two, Arthur Koestler and Geoffrey Gorer, are especially notable for writings or lectures on the concept of death. Koestler is concerned with the enormity of man's aggressive propensities and the inadequacy of his death concept; Gorer with the lack of support which British (and other Protestant) cultures offer to the bereaved. To both these subjects I shall return, though I shall not repeat, and therefore cannot do full justice to, the authors' arguments.

In the final plan, two topics have been set aside and hardly touched upon: the idea of death in adolescence, and suicide. They demand separate treatment.

Gorer began his 1965 study with an autobiographical statement of great value in the development of his sociological theme. If I could, I should do the same, but I cannot: not for lack of experience of bereavement and grief. I can, however, make the negative statement that no member of my immediate family died while I was a young child, except an infant brother whom

I had not seen. He was born at home, but we older children were sent away for the occasion, and my mother took the baby away, before our return, in the hope of a cure for a congenital illness. On our parents' return after three weeks without the baby, we others, aged seven, five and four, were deeply disappointed, but I, the five-year-old, cannot remember being puzzled about the meaning of death.

During the last decade a large number of researches have been published, with somewhat contradictory results, on the association between separation and bereavement in childhood and mental illness or disorder in later life. Fuller reference will be made to this subject later. In medical journals reference is made to the broken heart, which used to be the province of the poet. The effect of separation from the mother in early childhood, and of death of the father then or later, may both, it seems, be long-lasting and damaging if the need of the individual sufferer is not recognized and relieved. Yet the campaign to secure pensions for widows was long (1912–25 in England)[1] and the bitterness of the opposition now seems almost unbelievable, when it is realized from Peter Marris's[2] study after the Second World War, how much widows and their children still suffer socially and economically although pensions have become statutory provision. Men seem to want those they left behind to have good reason to mourn. We are more used to admitting mixed motives nowadays than in the pre-Freudian era.

Reason to mourn – of course the statement is superficial and absurd. Mourning is super-rational: a natural imperative.

'May she rest in peace. It's a fine funeral.' . . . the grave was filled hurriedly by four spades. A mound grew up on it, and a ten-year-old boy climbed on top. . . . His snub-nosed face was contorted. He stretched out his neck. If a wolf cub had done this it would have been obvious it was about to howl. The boy covered his face with his hands and burst into sobs.[3]

[1] See M. D. Stocks, *Eleanor Rathbone*, 1949
[2] P. Marris, *Widows and their Families*, 1958
[3] B. Pasternak, *Doctor Zhivago*, 1958

The social ritual is also imperative. In England during the period before the Second World War when there was widespread unemployment with bitter poverty, a campaign began for cheaper funerals. Yet people who could scarcely afford sufficient food would pay for mourning ceremonies. I myself knew a small farmer in Monmouthshire who took his van every Saturday at this period round the mining valleys of the Rhondda; he could sell flowers for graves to people who could not pay for eggs or vegetables. There was a contemporary popular song with the refrain, how fine it would be 'to be blooming well dead' and in a coffin 'with knobs on'. The last words, quoted in Parliament, invaded the language and stayed, after the reference to the coffin had been forgotten and the men who had fancied a slap-up funeral as better than the dead greyness of life had gone into the army. Have the words of that song been reprinted? Whoever wrote it, it was genuine English working-class satire, a joke and no joke.

Only after the end of the Second World War did two English writers, Evelyn Waugh[1] in fiction and Jessica Mitford[2] factually, describe with implicit horror funerary customs common in the United States. The distaste commonly felt by English and Scottish people for the practices described is partly, but by no means entirely, I believe, due to the commercialism which fattens on grief. It may also be due to the dictates of a culture which disapproves the display of private emotion and senses hypocrisy in any public ritual expressive of it. Nevertheless, apart from the commercialism, the American customs Waugh and Mitford described, repulsive as they may be to us, represent more closely the ways, so far as we can judge, of the earliest human ancestors of whom we have record, than do the brief, restrained, relatively frugal rites commonly prescribed in Britain today, or even the more prolonged ceremonies of our State funerals.

Long before the Egyptians learned how to embalm the royal corpse, palaeolithic man coloured his dead, apparently to imitate, or in fantasy or ritual to maintain in them, the hue of life, and he

---

[1] E. Waugh, *The Loved One*, 1948
[2] J. Mitford, *The American Way of Death*, 1963

expended in the burial goods which must still have had a value for the living. Americans who are not very wealthy may spend more than they can well afford on the funeral of one of their family, and the rites accorded to Sir Winston Churchill may have cost England a considerable sum, but the value, economic and aesthetic, of the material buried with a pharaoh, or centuries later at Sutton Hoo in East Anglia, must have been far greater, relative to the size and wealth of the earlier community.

Thus in discussing burial customs one leaps millennia, and the barriers between scientific disciplines. Burial customs surely throw light on the concept of death of those who take part in them. But if, in our own day, it is a flickering and uncertain light, leaving much in each individual participant still hidden, perhaps even from himself, that may be no less true of our ancestors.

Skeletons found on the threshold of caves on Mount Carmel in Palestine were at one time thought to be the earliest ritual burials discovered. They surprised the scientific world because the skeletons seemed to combine characteristics of Homo sapiens and of Neanderthal man, previously assumed to be a distinct, earlier species.[1] It was with reference to these burials that the anthropologist, Marett, wrote at the time of their discovery:

Instead of succumbing to a fear so everlasting in its enmity, man for many thousands of years has met it squarely with the aid of a no less everlasting hope. . . . He will be immortal; he will overcome the time process and see it out. Thus, then, so far as force of will could do it, Neanderthal man, to whom we grudge the name of Homo sapiens, achieved a future life.[2]

Marett's statements may not have represented the views of all his fellow anthropologists, nor are the Mount Carmel burials now believed to be the earliest discovered human interments. But it is clear that a complex concept of death–life relationship developed very early and was very widespread in the cultural history of man,

[1] D. A. E. Garrod and D. M. A. Bate (vol. 1) and T. D. McCown and A. Keith (vol. 2), The Stone Age of Mount Carmel, 1937, 1939
[2] R. R. Marett, Faith, Hope and Charity in Primitive Religion, 1932, p. 25

and that an eminent man in the twentieth century identified himself imaginatively with those remote predecessors in respect of it. Marett suggests and illustrates the persistence of an attitude to death which underlies the dynamic of the ritual, namely, the denial of its finality.

Historical records provide evidence of persistent denial of the denial. Prehistory, by the nature of its data, does not and probably cannot do this. Hastings, a contemporary of Marett, was compassionate rather than sympathetic about the denial of death's finality. He judged that human reactions to the horror of death were universal among mankind. This horror, he wrote,

has given rise to an obstinate disbelief in the necessity of death, and to attempts, continually repeated in spite of invariably disastrous experience of failure, to escape it. . . . The picture thus presented of the desperate refusal of mankind to accept a cardinal condition of existence is one of the most pathetic in the history of the race.[1]

The process of denial, which seemed to defy rational explanation, is explicable by Freudian theory. Negation may be a stage whereby a painful idea is permitted to enter consciousness.[2] Examples will be given of the operation of this psychological process in the thinking of children about death. Whether the manner of early burials should bear the whole weight of Marett's interpretation is uncertain. The placing of the body in a position like that of the foetus in the womb, and the warm colouring of which traces are sometimes found on it, also suggest the thought that Goethe put into the mouth of Mephistopheles: on departing,

all phantoms must obey a law
To use the way they entered in before.[3]

Hastings and Marett both attribute to early and to contemporary primitive man conceptions of death in which they themselves participate. Yet eminent archaeologists such as Professor

[1] J. Hastings, 'Death', *Encyclopaedia of Religion and Ethics*, 1908
[2] S. Ferenczi, 'The problem of the acceptance of unpleasant ideas', *Further Contributions to Psychoanalysis*, 1926
[3] J. W. Goethe, *Faust*, 1949

Frankfort tell us that a great gulf separates our habits of thought from those of even the earliest civilization of which we have extant records, in relation to the perennial problems of man's place in nature, his fate and death. If this is so, one would suppose that the gulf separating us psychologically from prehistoric man would be at least as wide.

Consistent with this view of the gulf between the thinking of early and modern man is Comte's theory of successive stages of human culture from the early theological to the modern rational positivist. The great French physiologist, Claude Bernard, disagreed with Comte, holding that the theological stage persisted in the individual alongside the scientific rational, and would continue to do so as long as man longed to know the beginning and the end of things.

Tout doit avoir nécessairement un commencement et une fin. Or nous ne pouvons pas concevoir ni le commencement ni la fin. Nous ne pouvons saisir que le milieu des choses, c'est là le domaine scientifique. . . . Mais cela n'empêche pas que le commencement et la fin nous tourmenteront toujours et nous tourmenteront surtout.[1]

This longing, he wrote, was of the heart, not of the head; man would never renounce it; indeed it is the desire to know such unknowns that leads men to scientific inquiry.

Bernard's view echoes Pascal, and is consistent with Freudian theory of the function of the irrational unconscious, although in some respects Freud might have accepted the views of Comte more readily than those of Bernard.

Does the thinking of children provide for modern man a track across the gulf that otherwise separates a modern adult from early or from modern primitive man? 'It is not possible for everyone to go and study savages,' Reinach wrote, 'but we have almost an equivalent at hand in children.'[2] Jung, in a relatively early work,

[1] C. Bernard, *Philosophie (MS inédit)*, J. Chevalier (ed.), 1937. 'Everything has to have a beginning and an end. Yet we can conceive neither the beginning nor the end. We can only grasp the middle of things: that is the province of science. . . . But that does not prevent us being constantly tormented by the beginning and the end, more than by anything else.'

[2] S. Reinach, *Orpheus*, 1960

suggested 'that we draw a parallel between the phantastical, mythological thinking of antiquity and the similar thinking of children, between the lower human races and dreams. This train of thought,' he continues,

is familiar through our knowledge of comparative anatomy . . . which shows us how the structure and function of the human body are the results of a series of embryonic changes which correspond to similar changes in the history of the race. Therefore, the supposition is justified that ontogenesis corresponds in psychology to phylogenesis. . . . The state of infantile thinking is nothing but a re-echo of the prehistoric and the ancient.[1]

The recapitulation theory to which Jung referred, which had been developed in detail by Stanley Hall and J. M. Baldwin, American psychologists, was at the time Jung wrote accepted also by Freud, Rank, Abraham and other psychoanalysts. It is not accepted by psychologists today. Margaret Mead suggested in 1954 that it still lay behind much psychoanalytic thinking. The concept of 'the primitive', she wrote, is of a synthetic personality 'built up from a hybrid of sociological, pseudo-biological theory' and then supposed to be an analogue of 'the child' or 'the psychotic' in later psychological research. 'A fully acculturated member of a living culture differs in every respect and systematically from members of any other culture.'[2]

Children, however, are nowhere fully acculturated, or perhaps it would be as correct to say that there is everywhere a subculture of childhood. When children's reactions to the observation of death, or reference to it, resemble those recorded of members of cultures remote from their own in time or space, there is a problem which the psychologist cannot dismiss. In Chapter 2 examples will be given of behaviour in which such similarities appear. In Chapter 3 an explanatory theory will be discussed.

[1] C. G. Jung, *The Psychology of the Unconscious*, 1915 (1951 edn), pp. 14ff.

[2] M. Mead, 'Research on primitive children', L. Carmichael (ed.), *Manual of Child Psychology*, 1954

RECAPITULATION?

It used to be held as a general law of psychology that children in the stages of their mental development followed the developmental stages of the human race. That theory is now rejected. Yet it is a theory of great interest when we are studying the development of the child's concept of death, because we have archaeological and anthropological information about human cultural development of this concept, more perhaps than of any other. Before rejecting the theory it is worthwhile considering and illustrating on what grounds it might rationally arise. What behaviour of modern children resembles – and in what way – behaviour reported of ancient, or modern pre-industrial, man in the face of death?

Primitive thought, we are told by Frankfort,

looks, not for the *how* but for the *who*, when it looks for a cause. . . . It looks for a purposeful will committing an act. . . . We understand phenomena, not by what makes them peculiar, but by what makes them manifestations of general laws. But a general law cannot do justice to the individual character of each event . . . which is what early man experiences most strongly. . . . To him, death is *willed*. The question, then, turns once more from the *why* to the *who*, not to the *how*.[1]

Some young children in our sample, and some older children of low intelligence, were found to think in this way. When given a series of English words (in a research programme to be described more fully later) and asked to say what each word meant, these

[1] H. and H. A. Frankfort *et al.*, *Before Philosophy*, 1946 (1949 edn), pp. 24-5

children said that *dead* meant *killed* or *murdered*. The condition, for them, involved *who*, an animate agent, essentially.

Professor Piaget's studies of the child's conception of causality present evidence of the operation of thinking which may be described in the terms Professor Frankfort has used of early man. The definition of *dead* as *killed* or *murdered* shows a double leap in the child's thinking; he not only leaps to the assumption of the purposeful will as cause, but avoids direct attention to the *what*, the fact or object.

Generalizations about ways of thinking, early or modern, childish or adult, should not blind us to variations within societies at all levels of sophistication and within individuals at different stages of development; science looks not only at general laws which may be presented simply, but at laws governing complex variances also. 'Even among the most primitive peoples,' wrote Malinowski, 'the attitude to death is infinitely more complex and, I may add, more akin to our own than is usually assumed.'[1] Among the Pacific (Trobriand) islanders whom he studied, death was rarely supposed to occur without the intervention of an evil spirit, and death from natural causes was not recognized in their institutions, yet there seemed to be some conception of the possibility that very insignificant people might die simply of old age. There is no exclusion of contradictions and uncertainties in primitive thinking on such subjects, nor, as we shall see, among children in our own culture.

Let me give a second example of resemblance. In this case a child suggested an activity with reference to his own death, similar to that which would have been undertaken on his behalf by surviving relatives in earlier times. Jeremy was one of a small number whose parents had undertaken to keep records for me of their references or reactions to death. In this case the mother wrote the report, but was not present when the event occurred:

[H.R.1.]* Time, 6.15 p.m. Jeremy (5:10) in the bathroom, being put to

[1] B. Malinowski, *Magic, Science and Religion*, 1948, pp. 133, 30, 312

* Quotations from the home records will be numbered sequentially [H.R.]. In each case the parent dated the record; the child's birth date was recorded in

bed, said quite suddenly to the nursemaid Margaret – he was alone with her – that he was going to die, but he wouldn't die without Booby (his toy rabbit). For a moment he looked sad, but almost immediately was quite cheerful again.

The elaborate arrangements made for the continued life after death of the Egyptian pharaohs have been frequently described. An ancient Assyrian king, recounting his virtuous deeds, included the pious burial of his father, and used the present tense to record: 'His royal ornaments *which he loves*, I displayed before [the god] Shamash and placed in the grave with my father.'[1] Such objects are found in graves very widely dispersed in place and time; it is only the evidence for the psychological attitude motivating the practice which is comparatively rare.

The third example of resemblance between the thinking of children in our own culture and that accepted in other cultures concerns the idea of reincarnation. Francis's mother supplied the following:

[H.R.2.] Francis (5:1) saw a coffin being carried into a house and arrived for his bath full of excitement. There was some conversation about the coffin, why it had to be nailed down, etc. Then: F: 'Of course the person who went away [i.e. in the coffin] will become a baby, won't he?' M: 'What makes you think so?' F: 'Of course he will, won't he?' M: 'I don't know.' F: 'When John [F's baby brother] was born, someone must have died.' All this was said in a tone of conviction, as though there were no doubt about it. The conversation then changed to the subject of the dripping taps. He was having his bath while the recorded incident took place.

Susan Isaacs[2] records a similar conviction on the part of a girl aged five, and Jung provides another example, though in that case complicated by the fact that the child, Anna, had been told that her grandmother at death would become an angel, and that

---

the record book, and his age has been added in the quotation; otherwise the words are in each case as written by the child's relative

[1] A. Heidel, *The Gilgamesh Epic and Old Testament Parallels*, 1946, p. 139
[2] S. Isaacs, *The Social Development of Young Children*, 1930, p. 161

babies are little angels brought by the stork.[1] The stork is perhaps less familiar to British than to German children, but we shall find angels cropping up later, in the home records, though not in support of reincarnation.

The fourth example is concerned with a gruesome feature of primitive funerary ritual which the child's imagination embroidered with conscious fantasy and fun. It was the custom, indeed a sacred duty, among the Melanesians of New Guinea, which continued to be performed in secret even after it was severely penalized by the white government, to partake of the flesh of the dead person. 'It is done with extreme repugnance and dread and usually followed by a violent vomiting fit. At the same time it is felt to be a supreme act of reverence, love and devotion.'[2] Herodotus knew of the custom as practised by tribes distant from Greece, far east, perhaps on the borders of China; it was reported to have persisted until the thirteenth century A.D. among the people living in what is now Tibet. They were said to be in the habit of eating the carcases of their deceased parents, 'that for pity's sake they might make no other sepulture for them than their own bowels'.[3]

The child is reported as follows:

[H.R.3.] Ben (6:4): 'Why can't you keep cream to the next day?' (The family had no refrigerator.) M: 'Because it goes bad. Most things do that have been alive. If you don't eat them soon, you can't eat them at all.' B: 'Do you think when we die we go up to the shops in heaven, and then God buys us and puts us in his larder and eats us?'

The fifth example, though it also has some gruesome features in early ritual, carries with it in the behaviour of the child no implication of insensitive cruelty, but only of the fear of separation from loved ones which was doubtless also the main motive in the original practice. In early tombs of rulers not only food,

[1] C. G. Jung, *The Development of Personality*, 1954
[2] Malinowski, *op. cit.*, p. 32
[3] Herodotus, *The History* (1935 edn), III, 38 and note to IV, 26

ornaments and furniture are provided but also servants. The pharaohs were believed immortal, and sharing their tomb may have been a coveted privilege. Hindu widows have, within living memory, chosen to join their husbands on the pyre. The practice of *sati* was not narrowly local, nor can one suppose that the death was always suicidal or voluntary. 'It is found ... at Ur in Sumeria, in the Neolithic of eastern Siberia, and, quite recently, among the Banyoro of Uganda, who buried their king in a grave lined with the living bodies of his wives and retainers, whose arms and legs were broken to prevent their escape.'[1]

[P.R.1.]* The Norwegian psychologist, V. Rasmussen, reports his daughter S (6:8) saying to her mother: 'You must stay with me every day, and when I die, you must be in the coffin with me.'

The ritual sacrifice of children was also a widespread and long-lasting practice. In ancient Palestine they immolated children in honour of the king-god Moloch or Melek or to Baal, god of war; reference is made to such rituals in Deuteronomy and the historical books of the Old Testament, and they are constantly denounced by the Hebrew prophets.[2] Manasseh was only one of the kings who 'reared up altars for Baal ... and worshipped all the host of heaven ... and made his son pass through the fire, and observed times, and used enchantments, and dealt with familiar spirits and wizards'. The denunciations of Jeremiah show indirectly that, even to Jews, such sacrifices had in earlier days appeared to have religious sanction, as indeed the story of Abraham clearly suggests.

The firstborn was in the greatest danger. Ezekiel refers to the passing through fire of 'all that openeth the womb'. Recognition of divine claim to the firstborn male was made at the Passover,

[1] S. Cole, *The Prehistory of East Africa*, 1954, p. 107

* Records of children's sayings directly quoted from scientific publications will be sequentially numbered [P.R.]. The application may be extended to biographical data or restricted when the reference is general or indirect

[2] Deuteronomy xviii, 9–10; II Kings xvi, 3; xxi, 6; II Chronicles xxviii, 3; Isaiah lvii, 5; Jeremiah vii, 31; xix, 3–9; xxxii, 30–6; Ezekiel xxiii, 36–9; Micah vi, 7. See also S. A. Cook, 'Israel before the Prophets', *Cambridge Ancient History*, vol. 3, ch. 9

when firstborn males of both man and beast were sanctified, but not sacrificed if redeemed.

> Every firstling of an ass thou shalt redeem with a lamb; and if thou wilt not redeem it, then thou shalt break his neck; and all the first-born of man among thy children shalt thou redeem . . .[1]

Frazer[2] records that the practice of killing the firstborn, and in some instances eating them, was originally prevalent in Australia, China, India, Africa, Russia and Ireland. Among the ancient Greeks the sex of the victim does not appear to have been important. Agamemnon had vowed his firstborn to the goddess before the child's birth. In Greek legend there is frequent repetition of the theme of child murder followed by the serving up of the child to the unwitting father; it was the eater rather than the murderer who was most guilty of sacrilege. In Arcadia, human sacrifice to Zeus persisted until the second century A.D.,[3] and also in Carthage, colonized from Phoenicia (Canaan). Plutarch records that the Greeks made it a condition of a victorious peace treaty that sacrifices of children to Baal should stop, but the Carthaginians later refused to carry out the *diktat*.

The attitude of the child to the risk of ritual sacrifice is suggested with the utmost literary economy in the Hebrew stories of Abraham and Isaac and of Jephthah's daughter.[4] In other legends the parent's motive does not appear so pure nor the child's reactions so noble. The anxiety aroused in the performers of a deed socially approved but biologically so offensive – aroused, perhaps, either by compliance or non-compliance with custom – was rationalized in the drama of Oedipus as menace *from* the babe, and both mother and father were supplied with a powerful ethical motive.[5] When the murdered child was female, however, the

[1] Exodus xiii, 13
[2] J. G. Frazer, *The Golden Bough*, Part 3, 'The Dying God', 1966, p. 179 ff.
[3] W. R. Halliday, 'The religion and mythology of the Greeks', *Cambridge Ancient History*, vol. 3, ch. 22
[4] Genesis xxii, 1; Judges xi, 30–40
[5] Oedipus was exposed, not ritually sacrificed; a practice, according to Gibbon, 'sometimes prescribed, often permitted, almost always practised with

mother had no such motive. The sacrifice of Iphigenia, like the intended murder of Oedipus, set up an unholy chain-reaction of unsanctified mating and slaughter.

Did children in such societies suffer anxiety? We do not know. A child may believe that he may die mysteriously any night, and yet show no anxiety:

[H.R.4.] Francis (4:11): 'Flowers die and we die, don't we, Mummie?' M: 'Yes.' F: 'Who kills us in the night? Does Jesus?'

The mother recording this added: 'The reference to Jesus killing us in the night is due, I think, to the fact that Francis has recently had read to him the nursery rhyme about Matthew, Mark, Luke and John, in which the following lines occur:

> Before I lay me down to sleep
> I give my soul to Christ to keep,
> And if I die before I wake
> I pray that Christ my soul will take.

No comment was made at the time.'

Another example shows a child associating death of human beings with that observed of plants in the garden, following a conversation about beginnings:

[H.R.5.] Ben (3:4), in his home garden with his mother, after she had been greeted by a passing friend with whom she had been at school, asked her where he was when she was at school. M: 'You weren't anywhere at all.' B: 'Yes, I were inside you.' M: 'No, I don't think you were anywhere.' B: 'I were under your feet.'

A few days later, Ben asked how plants come up in the spring, after not showing above ground in the winter, and after being answered, inquired:

[H.R.6.] Ben (3:4): 'When shall we all be dead and gone, and then come back again?'

---

impunity ... and the Roman empire was stained with the blood of infants, till such murders were included by Valentinian ... in the Cornelian law' [A.D. 530–33], *Decline and Fall of the Roman Empire*, 1776, ch. 44

In many mythologies the afterlife and the underworld are associated with cycles of vegetation and fertility. The goddesses of fertility and the moon, Ishtar (Ashtoreth, Astarte) and Demeter the mother goddess, mourn the departure of the young ones, Tammuz or Persephone, and seek them in a dark underworld, from which they may only temporarily return to sunlight. The annual renewal of life depended on the ritual union of the male and female principles; in some cults, human sacrifice was associated with this rite. The prophet Ezekiel, who denounced his people for sacrificing their children by fire, also recorded among their heresies rites carried out in the dark, under ground, in caves with beasts painted on the walls; and above ground, women weeping for Tammuz, looking towards the north, where the unchanging Pole star symbolized eternal life.[1] Yet another heresy was displayed by a company of men who turned their backs on the temple, standing between the porch and the altar, and worshipped the sun towards the east, the mythological source of resurrection.

Frazer traced a connection between the Tammuz cult and the legends about the golden bough that Aeneas had to pluck before making his way to the underworld to visit his dead father.[2] Gold, as a symbol of immortality, still keeps its mystique.[3] Virgil wrote that the bough resembled mistletoe which bears a golden berry in the frosty woods in winter, borne on another tree.[4] The association of mistletoe with holy renewal of life, with the winter solstice, and with permission to kiss anyone of the other sex, which children learn at Christmas time, clearly goes back long before the birth of Christ.

The leaves of many deciduous trees turn golden at the death of

[1] Ezekiel viii, 7-16

[2] J. G. Frazer, *The Golden Bough*, 1966; Virgil, *Aeneid*, VI, 136-48 and 205-9

[3] On gold as symbol of immortality see R. B. Onians, *The Origins of European Thought about the Body, the Mind, the Soul, the World, Time and Fate*, 1954

[4] H. E. Butler, in *Introduction to Aeneid Book VI*, 1920, points out that the golden-berried mistletoe of southern Europe does not fruit in winter; Virgil, however, may have been aware of this, but used poetic licence to combine two mythical attributes in the golden bough

the year, so that golden boughs may suggest death without reference to Virgil or Sir James Frazer. The poet G. M. Hopkins wrote of a child who wept at 'Goldengrove unleaving', that 'as the heart grows older/It will come to such sights colder', but then, when Margaret weeps, she will know why:

> Now no matter, child, the name;
> Sorrow's springs are the same,
> Nor mouth had, no nor mind, expressed
> What heart heard of, ghost guessed;
> It is the blight man was born for,
> It is Margaret you mourn for.

Our home records provide no reference to gold or golden leaves, but there is a curious echo of the *Aeneid* in a reference to reincarnation:

[H.R.7.] Ben (9:2), in a long conversation with his father and his younger brother: 'Mother says you get born again about every thousand years.'

The fertility of monarchs influenced the fate of their people for centuries after it had ceased, in Europe, to be popularly associated with the fertility of herds and crops. As royal power diminished politically, popular concern might have been expected to cease, but in England the reduction of the political power of the Crown seemed to lead its subjects to identify themselves more closely with the royal family. When George V died, children in England heard simultaneously about death and about the matrimonial affairs of the heir, Edward VIII. Richard found both puzzling, and finally summed up the situation as follows:

[H.R.8.] Richard (3:11): 'The old king's dead and he's married; the new king's not dead and he's not married.'

This demonstrates the vagueness still surrounding the meaning of 'dead' for a child under four years old. It also demonstrates certain associations which have their counterpart through the ages and in the distant past of mankind. In the last and the previous example the child's thought had been directly communicated by adults; in other examples, children seem to have spontaneously expressed ideas and beliefs similar to those recorded of members of cultures remote from their own. Reference has been made above to a theory, now generally discredited, that the individual passes through a succession of psychological stages representative of cultural stages in the evolution of the species. Not only does observation of individual development throw doubt upon this theory: it is difficult, in following the record of any particular human culture, to interpret it as a consistent evolutionary process over a long period of time, in respect of the conception of death. It seems as though in both modern and ancient, primitive and civilized societies there exist side by side the believer in an after-life, the sceptic, and the indifferent; and most men find each represented also within themselves. In the history of a culture such variations may be found to hold the field not in simple succession but in a kind of long-term fluctuation. Reference has been made to Borkenau's theory of successive civilizations which rise to prominence on the basis of a death-denying or death-affirming thesis moving towards its antithesis at their close.

As an example of the process of general cultural change of this kind one may take a scholar's[1] account of the early religious history of the Hebrews, whose translated literature, foundation of Western culture, is the most readily available to us. The form of burials in the land and time of the Hebrew patriarchs (Abraham, Isaac, Jacob) shows that there was belief in an after-life in the tomb, though the graves of Israelites of this period cannot be distinguished from the rest. Such belief was consistently rejected by the writers of Genesis, Exodus, Joshua and other early books of the Old Testament. Mortuary practices presupposing belief in survival were explicitly prohibited, and there was silence about the individual's destiny after death. Yet the belief persisted in spite

[1] S. G. F. Brandon, *Man and his Destiny in the Great Religions*, 1962, ch. 4 *passim*. The passage in the Book of Job which inspired Handel's magnificent aria 'I know that my Redeemer liveth' is apparently too obscure to permit interpretation as a belief in bodily resurrection

of priestly orthodoxy and prophetic denunciation. Pronounce-ments that under the One God reward and punishment were justly meted out to men during their lifetime were found at vari-ance with fact, and fact with equity. Job when afflicted could only plead:

> Are not my days few? cease then
> And let me alone, that I may take comfort a little,
> Before I go whence I shall not return,
> Even to the land of darkness and the shadow of death.

Job did not deny the finality of death; the problem was to see it as consistent with the omnipotence and benevolence of God. Holding fast to the latter creed, later canonical and apocryphal texts show the abandonment of the former position. In Ezekiel the dry bones live, the graves are opened. In Daniel it is prophesied that 'many of them that sleep in the dust shall awake, some to everlasting life, and some to shame and everlasting contempt'. Belief in bodily resurrection first appears in the extant Hebrew documents during the second century B.C.[1] The Christians in the first century A.D. were not the only Jewish sect among whom this belief was orthodox and its denial heresy.

Biblical scholarship thus shows, in the development of Hebrew religion on which that of Western culture is grafted, not a simple evolution of the conception of death but an accepted line set like a melody, sometimes discordant, above a bass of traditional prac-tice, and counterpoint voice or voices which in due time take over the melodic line. A recapitulatory theory of child psychological development would be difficult to frame on such a basis, but neither the prevalent attitude of the culture in which he is reared nor variations within the culture seem to provide an adequate answer to the question how it happens that a child's thoughts on death, often clearly spontaneous, may resemble those of cultures remote from his own.

[1] Apocrypha, II Maccabees. xii; see Brandon, *op. cit.*, p. 137

CHAPTER 3

EXPLANATORY PRINCIPLE

IF things our children say and do about death resemble the behaviour recorded of men far distant in place and time, and if
theories of recapitulation and of a racial unconscious are rejected,
on what principle is such behaviour to be explained?

On the same principle, it is suggested, as Onians uses to explain
his observations in his study of *The Origins of European Thought
about the Body, the Soul, the World, Time and Fate* (1954). Onians
found that Greek and Roman thought on these matters resembled, with slight variations in detail, that of Celtic, Slavonic,
Germanic and other Indo-European peoples, and also of early
Egyptians, Babylonians and Jews. He infers that, although influence cannot be excluded entirely, *the same phenomena led to the
same conclusions.* The inference is strengthened and the chance of
influence reduced, when similar observations are recorded of
early Chinese or South American indigenous peoples.

In order to present this simple principle as a psychological
explanation, its terms must be expanded. *The same conclusions*
refers to the beliefs and behaviour recorded in Onians's text of the
peoples he studied, with reference to the themes listed in his title.
It seems justifiable to add to the list the theme of death, and to
study in the same way the sayings of children.

Conclusions are reached by cogitative or reasoning processes;
that is, not by immediate perception, sensory apprehension, conditioning, external compulsion or, except incidentally and addi-
tionally, by other psychological processes.

The same phenomena. A phenomenon has been defined as a
possible datum of experience at any given moment. *Experience*
assumes an experiencer or subject. The data of experience includes

what is perceived, as one's own affect or as object or quasi-object, whether or not assumed to be independently real or knowable. At this point we must avoid entanglement in the philosophical questions such as Berkeley raised 200 years ago and phenomenologists discuss today. We observe that for many persons, phenomena at a given moment may appear (to keep Onians's terminology) sufficiently *the same* to permit communication with agreed conceptual reference. We observe also that such communication with agreed reference tends to persist beyond the moments of immediate experience. Things or events thus described may then be accepted as *the same phenomena*, without consideration of whether objective components or subjective selection and organization of experience are the main source of the similarity in consequence of which the experience became communicable.

Origins. Onians does not suggest that for all men the same phenomena lead to the same conclusions about the subjects he has studied, but that this tends to happen in respect of the speculations and explanations worked out in the early history of cultures which later became more sophisticated. Men at such a cultural stage are shown to be as capable of logical reasoning as at later stages, and moved in the same way by threat to personal survival, but the knowledge at their command is less extensive. Psychologists and physiologists who study the effects of stress find that men vary greatly in manner and degree of arousal and reaction under threatening conditions; only perceived threat to life itself arouses all men in discernibly similar ways or to a similar extent. Phenomena which induce, in men of widely separated cultures, reasoning leading to similar conclusions are: the body perceived as separable from the soul, the world independent of the self, fate inexorable, time which goes only one way for man, and surely life under threat of death.

It is now our aim to show that the young child, ignorant like early man of many facts known to modern adults, capable like early man of logical reasoning, and like him unwilling to accept separation and non-existence, dissolution and decay, is led by the same phenomena as they to similar conclusions.

The psyche or soul was associated by the Greeks, and following them the Romans, with the head, and many other peoples have considered the head peculiarly sacred as the seat of the soul. The psyche had faculties dissociated from consciousness. Importance was attached to the sneeze as a strange happening, traced to something within the head, and regarded as a spontaneous expression of that something, independent of the body and the conscious will. So it was customary for a Greek who sneezed to say 'Zeus, save me!' Jewish bystanders uttered a prayer for the sneezer's life, and Hindus said 'Live!' A writer on English folklore a century ago noted that in County Durham a blessing was invoked on children when they sneezed; he evidently did not think the custom general in England, but added that in the Duchy of Wurttemberg 'a fit of sneezing in which one of the professors indulged was responded to by a cry from all the pupils of "*Gesundheit!*"', which he seemed to expect as much as the Emperor Tiberius, who was extremely particular in requiring it from his courtiers'.[1]

The custom of saying 'Bless you!' on hearing a sneeze was not followed in the home of the child of whom the following was recorded:

[H.R.9.] Ben (6:7) with his mother in the kitchen; he was doing up his shoes; his mother sneezed. B: 'Funny how you can't remember your life before at all.' M: 'Yes. What made you think of that?' B: 'Because you can't imitate a hitchoo.' (The word 'hitchoo' was only heard on this occasion.) This was the end of the conversation. Ben went out to play. The subject of sneezing was not referred to again.

References by Ben to recurrent lives have been given in [H.R.6.], three years earlier than the above, and [H.R.7.], three years later. Here imitation is evidently viewed by Ben as essentially a voluntary act, and sneezing as 'a spontaneous expression of something within a person, independent of the body and the conscious will'.[2] Independence of the body is independence of the present incarnation. The differing functions of will and psyche

[1] W. Henderson, *Folklore of the Northern Counties*, 1879
[2] Onians, *op. cit.*

are demonstrated by the inability to imitate a sneeze, and confirm the fact of previous existence; what is left for the child to wonder at is the inability to remember it.

The psyche, as immortal soul and vital principle, was located by the Greeks in the head, and possibly as cause or consequence they identified cerebro-spinal with seminal fluid.[1] The Chinese also identified the soul responsible for vitality and strength with the seed or sperm. This view encouraged a positive attitude to male continence as a means of conserving vitality and the immortal soul. It seems to be within this same complex of thought that a child may suppose the act of procreation dangerous to the father. In families to whom a child is born posthumously, the event may be associated with anxiety either later on the part of the posthumous child, or at the time of the birth on the part of an elder brother. The scientist, Gustav Fechner, suffered in this way. His father died, after a long illness, when he was five years old. The youngest daughter was born the day after the father's death. Gustav took this to mean that the father had died in giving another life, associating the event with a strong feeling of guilt, according to the account given by the psychoanalyst, Dr Hermann.[2]

Our own records [H.R.2.] show Francis, aged five, associating one individual's death with another's birth, and our later school records show the powerful sense of guilt felt by a boy (Bernard N) on the death of his father. In the following record no personal anxiety was involved, but the boy's train of thought involves association between semen, coitus and danger to the father by loss of vitality. Frazer, in *The Golden Bough*, collected records of the belief that the father, being actually incarnate in the child, died or was in danger when his wife conceived.[3]

[H.R.10.] Ben (8:10) and Richard (5:8), at tea with M, were talking about who was the youngest king ever, and R was interested and

[1] *ibid.*, pp. 189 ff.
[2] I. Hermann, 'A study of G. T. Fechner', abstract in *Psychoanalytic Review*, 24, 1937
[3] *op. cit.*, 1966, vol. 2, p. 188 ff.

amused to hear of the king of Spain who was king before he was born. B then said something which showed that he thought the father died as a result of begetting the child. M said she did not think the two things would be connected with each other. B: 'But mothers sometimes die when the children are born.' M said that she did not think anyone died as a result of making a baby begin. B said that he thought something might come out of the father's inside that oughtn't to, and so he might die.

The view that male continence conserves vitality and the immortal soul, and that complete celibacy offers a means of ensuring immortality, is clearly a potential source of psychological conflict, since procreation also offers a means of extending the man's *blood* and personality through future time. 'Their sons they gave, their immortality', was written of the young men who went to war in 1914.[1] Shakespeare, to persuade a young heir to marry, urged that:

> nothing 'gainst Time's scythe can make defence
> Save breed, to brave him when he takes thee hence.[2]

Over two thousand years earlier, the theme is the same; Orestes and Electra appeal, at their father's grave-side:

ORESTES: We are the seed of Pelops; let us not be blotted out.
            You are the dead – and yet not dead: still you can live in us.
ELECTRA: Children preserve alive a dead man's name and fame.
            They are like corks that hold the fisherman's net, and keep
            His knotted lines from sinking to the ocean bed.[3]

'Posterity is for the philosopher what the other world is for the religious man.'[4] The aphorism, a little too slick in the distinction between religion and philosophy, does indicate a deep rift between two ways of thinking. 'The thought of *posterity*', it has been

[1] R. Brooke, *1914 and Other Poems*, 1917
[2] Sonnet 12
[3] Aeschylus, *The Choephori* (1961 edn.)
[4] Diderot, quoted by J. Baillie, *The Belief in Progress*, 1950

said, 'attained its greatest significance in that period of ancient Israelite thought when history was already conceived according to a forward-moving pattern, but belief in the resurrection of the dead had not yet emerged.'[1] In this period of intense religious development and in this culture the significance of posterity was religious as much as philosophical. The blessing upon Abraham, that his seed should be as the stars in number, was contingent upon the maintenance by that seed of a covenant and a distinctive code of behaviour, the covenant being made with One God.[2]

Belief in immortality through the seed or germ-plasm may be found in a secular or a religious context. But this defence by 'breed' does not seem alone to satisfy man's desire for immortality, or perhaps it is more correct to say that in transmission between generations, nature is so seldom divorced from nurture that 'breed' is not thought of as operating only biologically. It tends to be strengthened by the teaching of genealogies, instances of which abound in Homer, both Testaments of the Bible, and the work of the College of Heralds. The Maori of New Zealand, before the coming of the white man, were taught to memorize 'immense genealogies which make the Bourbons, to say nothing of the Mountbattens, appear a pack of parvenus'.[3] The Maori was intensely proud, resenting the least affront not merely to his own dignity but to that of his remoter kinsmen and ancestors.

Since women as well as men secrete cerebro-spinal fluid, the question whether, on this view of the psyche, they also have immortal souls was not necessarily answered in the negative. Neither chastity nor procreation, however, offered women immortality of the kind offered to men, though the early Church stressed the association of virginity and eternal blessedness for both sexes. But the mother was supposed to be only the host of the seed. According to Aristotelian teaching the male contributes form, the female only substance to the embryo. The fact that both

[1] Baillie, *op. cit.*, p. 95 ff.
[2] Genesis xv, 5; xvii, 6-7
[3] E. H. McCormick, in K. Sinclair (ed.), *Distance Looks our Way*, 1961, p. 99

sperm and ovum contribute substances determining form was not established until the modern era, by Wolff (1733–94) and von Baer (1792–1876). Among Jews, however, inheritance was valued culturally as well as biologically. Endogamy provided a safeguard for the transmission of culture. From the canonical stories of Isaac and Jacob to the apocryphal story of Tobit and Tobias, Jewish fathers bade their sons take a wife of their own kindred, even if they had to go far to find her, and recent disputes about the identity of the Jew have publicized the long-accepted doctrine that Judaism is inherited through the mother.

The importance of cerebro-spinal and seminal fluid for immortality may be related to *the importance of moisture and dryness* in the transition of the psyche from stage to stage of existence. In Greek thought, immortality was associated with that part of the body remaining after initial decomposition, namely the skeleton.[1] At different periods cremation and burial were practised. The burning of the corpse set the psyche free to join the shades, while the bones retained the genius and potency of the dead, as a seed holds the fertility of the plant. The seed is dried before being sown. For germination, rebirth, the dry seed needs dampness. To pour a libation therefore signifies a hope for the resurrection of the dead, though as Kitto[2] points out with reference to the Hyacinth ritual, the practice may have developed from earlier cults half forgotten. In the times of the Hebrew patriarchs and the lands over which they wandered, some tombs were built equipped with conduits leading in from ground level, through which libations could be poured to nourish the dead in their after-life.[3]

Susan Isaacs[4] reports instances of children suggesting revival of dead animals by putting them in water:

[P.R.2.] When the children went to feed the chickens, they found that

---

[1] Onians, *op. cit.*, pp. 254 ff. and 272

[2] H. D. F. Kitto, *The Greeks*, 1951, p. 198. cf. 'Was it too much to break a jar of wine upon my ashes, strew them with cheap hyacinths?' Propertius, IV, 7 (trans. G. Highet, *Poets in a Landscape*, 1959)

[3] W. F. Albright, *The Old Testament and the Archaeology of Palestine*, 1949

[4] S. Isaacs, *Intellectual Growth in Young Children*, 1931, pp. 182, 188

one of them had died in the nest, probably having been trodden on by the hen. Dan (4:1) saw this and at once said, 'Oh, it's dead.' He was very concerned, and took it to one of the maids to ask her to 'put it in water to keep it'.

[P.R.3.] Having far too many mice now, Mrs I chloroformed a family of young ones. Christopher, Dan and Priscilla dissected one each [during which] Priscilla and Dan carried on a play . . . with the dead mice as children. . . . There were many inquiries and answers as to whether it was 'better'. . . . Presently Dan said, 'Now I'm going to put some water on it, and make it come alive again.' Priscilla joined in this. It was clear that for Dan this was pure play and fantasy – not a belief that it *would* come alive again.

The earlier record [P.R.2.] was not of fantasy, but the child was probably thinking of reviving an animal as one might revive a cut flower or a drooping pot plant. There may be no analogy here between the thoughts of the children and those of rebirth in early cultures, or only a very remote analogy.

The significance of burial. When the thinking of the child is an intellectual exercise relatively untouched by emotion, the resemblance to that of earlier man may be deep and startling, as were Ben's deductions from 'a hitchoo'. When children organize a funeral, as they often love to do, either for a pet animal or a fantasied object, although the parallel of motivation and action may again be striking (as will be recorded), the behaviour tends to be shallow, frivolous and superficial compared with that of adults who, in earlier as in later ages, were faced with the need to dispose of their dead. I shall discuss the adult behaviour first, and shall use as examples three records from much later ages than those of the origins Onians recorded. The reason why it seems admissible to do this is stated in the latest of the three, the *Aeneid*.

When Aeneas was led by the sibyl on his visit to the underworld, he saw on the banks of the Styx a crowd of ghosts vainly imploring passage, and asked her why this should be. 'The deep marshes of Cocytus and the Stygian swamp you are looking at,' she replied, 'represent *a sanction [numen] which the gods, having sworn to maintain it, dare not disregard.* All this hapless crowd whom you are viewing remain unburied; the ferryman is the famous Charon; the wave bears across those who have had sepulture.'[1] Only the buried reached the fields of peace. The sibyl's words suggested that the gods were reluctantly bound to observe the maintenance of the barrier between the buried and unburied dead, hence that the obligation was independent of and prior to the current dispensation.

It was a feature of very ancient myths, that after burial the man's spirit would go on a journey over water, below the earth of everyday. In the Egyptian and the Sumerian mythology the setting sun was followed, from west to east; Gilgamesh (c. 2,000 B.C.) goes this way, in deep darkness 'along the sun's path, with the north wind in his face, until dawn breaks'.[2] Over this subterranean ocean a boat was needed, and some kind of oar or pole.[3] For the cremation of Patroclus in the *Iliad* everything is to be provided 'that a dead man ought to have with him when he travels into the western gloom'.[4] The Hebrew Sheol was a dark, dry, dusty underworld, reached through a chaos of waters or ringed by many walls.[5]

Whatever the journey anticipated for the soul, reverent treatment of the body after death seems to have been the due of the clan-member in many communities from prehistoric ages, and though from time immemorial it had apparently been associated with some reference to an after-life, it is also found among Greeks, Romans and Hebrews independent of any accepted concept of immortality.

The importance attached to the mode of disposal of the corpse from the point of view of the dead person is shown by the state

[1] *Aeneid*, VI. The lines translated are 323-6:
Cocyti stagna alta vides Stygiamque paludem,
di cuius iurare timent et fallere numen.
haec omnis, quam cernis, inops inhumataque turba est;
portitor ille Charon; his, quos vehit unda, sepulti.
[2] A. Heidel, *The Gilgamesh Epic and Old Testament Parallels*, 1946
[3] W. F. Jackson Knight, *Cumaean Gates*, 1936
[4] *Iliad*, XXIII
[5] Psalm lxxxviii

of mind of those who perpetrate or plan to perpetrate the slaughter not only of the body but also of the soul of their enemy. In ancient Assyria to be left unburied was part of a legal punishment.[1] Achilles threatened to give the body of Hector not to the flames but to the dogs, but the gods prevented the sacrilege. In Judea, Jehu commanded that Jezebel should be given burial, 'for she is a king's daughter', but Elisha had prophesied that the dogs should eat her carcase, 'so that [after her death] they shall not say, This is Jezebel', and so it was, according to the book.[2] Many centuries later, the Roman emperor Commodus left unburied the bodies of murdered senators; his cruelty, wrote Gibbon, 'endeavoured to extend itself beyond death'.[3]

At the time of the prophets, immortality of the soul was not orthodox doctrine, but (and here it is of no importance whether the record is of fact or fiction) one can scarcely doubt that the motives and death-concept of those who gave Jezebel to the dogs were the same as those of Achilles in his plan for Hector; the prophet's reason is a gloss.

Attitude to burial or cremation is relatively independent of the ritual which accompanies it or the myths which explain the ritual. Even in ancient times, it is clear that the rites seemed vitally important to those who had no thought or assurance of after-life. As examples of this divorce, and the wide ramifications of the attitude to burial, let us examine in some detail a Greek and a Jewish text: Sophocles's *Antigone* and the apocryphal Book of Tobit.

Antigone's brother has been killed in a rebellion against the ruler, his uncle Creon, and Creon refuses to allow him to be buried. Antigone tells her sister:

> I will bury my brother,
> And if I die for it, what happiness,
> Convicted of reverence. . . . Live, if you will,
> Live, and defy the holiest laws of heaven.

[1] Heidel, *op. cit.*, p. 155, and *Cambridge Ancient History*, vol. 3, ch. 4
[2] I Kings xxi, 23 and II ix, 36–7
[3] Gibbon, *Decline and Fall of the Roman Empire*, 1776, ch. 4

ISMENE: I do not defy them; but I cannot act
    Against the State. I am not strong enough.
ANTIGONE: Let that be your excuse, then.

*　　*　　*

ANTIGONE: We have a duty to the dead.
CREON: Not to give equal honour to good and bad.
ANTIGONE: Who knows? In the country of the dead, that may be the
    law.
CREON: An enemy can't be a friend, even when dead.
ANTIGONE: My way is to share my love, not share my hate.[1]

There is no clear denial of the finality of death in the *Antigone*.
The sacred obligation to bury rests nevertheless on the kin of the
dead. The question *Who is my kin; who may make this claim on me?*
is raised by Creon, who would exclude rebels even when of the
immediate family. It is not answered unequivocally by Antigone
herself, for on being led to her death she says that she would not
have disobeyed on behalf of a husband or a son. Some critics have
supposed these lines to be an interpolation (which in itself would
provide evidence of cultural conflict), but it is noted that in other
cultures the ritual obligation is strictly limited. An Indian quoted
to Professor Carstairs[2] a Sanskrit text which defined a son as 'he
who rescues a man from hell', because the son alone can perform
the funeral rites without which nirvana is unattainable.

　　In the Book of Tobit[3] the same sacred obligation is a major
theme of a more rambling story. Tobit, like Antigone, persisted
in burying his dead in defiance of the political *force majeure*. The
identity of the kin is in no doubt here; it is the Jewish nation. The
story gathers into a naïve unity a number of themes relevant to
our subject. The writer, probably a Jew living in Aswan (Elephan-
tine) in the third to the second century B.C., laid the scene in

[1] Sophocles, *Antigone* (1947 edn)
[2] G. M. Carstairs, *The Twice-Born*, 1957
[3] The Book of Tobit (trans. and ed. D. C. Simpson), in *The Apocrypha of the
Old Testament in English*, R. H. Charles (ed.), 1913. (The Authorized Version has
also been quoted)

Assyria and Media some 500 years earlier. Tobit, the hero, with his wife Anna and son Tobias, is carried away captive from Galilee to Nineveh by the Assyrians. There he rises to a position at court which involves travel in Media, where he leaves some money in trust. At home in Nineveh he lives as a good orthodox Jew until his royal patron dies. Under the new king, Sennacherib, the state is troubled. Tobit cannot go into Media. Judea is invaded, and in Nineveh many Jews are slain.

And whomsoever Sennacherib slew . . . I buried. And Sennacherib sought them and found them not. And one of the Ninevites went and informed the king concerning me . . . and when I perceived that I was sought for to be put to death, I was afraid, and ran away. Then all my goods were seized, neither was there anything left me which was not taken to the royal treasury, save my wife Anna and my son Tobias.

Within two months Sennacherib is killed by his own sons. His successor appoints as chancellor Tobit's nephew, Achiacharus,[1] by whose intercession Tobit is pardoned. At the next Pentecostal feast Tobit tells Tobias to go out and find a poor, worthy Jew to share their dinner. Tobias returns with a report of a Jew murdered in the market-place. Tobit buries the man, for which his neighbours mock him, asking if he wants to be proscribed again. He goes blind, which he interprets as a judgement of God for his sins, and prays for death. With this he remembers the money left in Media, so he calls Tobias and delivers a long homily: live uprightly, give alms, take a wife of the seed of your fathers, pay servants' wages promptly, don't get drunk, 'pour out thy bread on the burial of the just but give nothing to the wicked', and finally, go and collect the money from Media; here is the trust-document; find a guide and be off together.

Seeking a guide, Tobias 'found Raphael, that was an angel'. His father approved the arrangement because the unrecognized angel claimed to be one of his own tribe. So the two set off, together

[1] In Arabic Ahikar, hero of an earlier story which survived in many languages and was the source of a Gospel parable. F. C. Conybeare et al., *The Story of Ahikar from the Aramaic, Syriac, Arabic, Armenian, Ethiopic, Old Turkish, Greek and Slavonic Versions*, 1913

THE DISCOVERY OF DEATH

with Tobias's dog, though Anna wept and told Tobit he was too greedy for money, which was of no value compared with their child.

The angel had an additional commission, to rescue from suicidal sorrow a girl-cousin of Tobias's in Media, whose seven husbands had in succession been killed by an evil spirit on the wedding night before they had lain with her. Tobias had heard of this, and when Raphael suggested he should marry her he was reluctant, saying his death would grieve his parents. But Raphael told him how to frighten away the evil spirit, and the wedding took place. The father-in-law quietly prepared a grave overnight, but found in the morning that it was not needed; the bridegroom was still alive.

The marriage delays the travellers a fortnight. Tobit, counting the days, gets anxious, and Anna quite desperate. However, Tobias and the angel eventually return with the bride and the funds, the dog running ahead gaily wagging its tail (in a Latin version), and Raphael instructs Tobias how to cure his father's blindness. Offered generous wages, Raphael quietly reveals his angelic nature, tells them to write the whole story in a book, and disappears.

The tradition of the sacred right of kin to burial was evidently independent of belief in a future life. Powerful men were constantly tempted to defy the tradition, thereby claiming arbitrary power, i.e. power above divine laws.[1] The tradition therefore provided a basis for opposition to overweening ambition. It survived not only the scepticism, widespread in the ancient world as today, about an after-life, but also the question of the range of the obligation. The Roman poet Horace (in an unusually obscure ode) begs the passing sailor to throw three handfuls of earth, at

---

[1] The argument that the sacredness of human life depends on divine laws was expressed by Donne in our own age:
> Men do not stand
> In so ill case, that God hath with His hand
> Signed kings blank-charters, to kill whom they hate.
>
> *Poems, Satire III*

least, on the corpse of a stranger lying on the shore, if only to save himself from the danger of neglecting such a sacred duty. Having been nearly shipwrecked off the coast described, Horace was perhaps imagining himself as the corpse, or thinking of the legendary helmsman Palinurus, murdered there when he escaped the waves.[1]

When the survival of the spirit of the dead is no longer accepted as a fact of life, *not to kill* and *to keep alive* absorb the ethical and sacred significance which earlier accompanied the ritual disposal of the corpse. In both systems of thought the promotion of existence of fellow men is seen as an outstanding social obligation, superseding the petty concerns and emotional demands of everyday life; both are functions of the concept of death. Issues which arise primarily in the clash between sacred tradition and arbitrary power tend to expand into the further problem of range of fellowship. Tobit made no question about the range of kinship involved in his burial-duty; other Jews were less assured. A problem was set in terms of a Jew who had been attacked and left *half*-dead.[2] One after another two righteous members of his own people passed by but did nothing to help him. A member of another tribe followed, and by the exercise of much care and expense saved the man's life. The problem to which this story by counter-question supplied the answer was of range of fellowship, but to inquirers steeped in the ancient tradition of the sanctity of burial obligations it clearly presented a further query: should not the living and the half-dead be treated with as much care and kindness as the dead?

Ancient ways of thinking about the obligations of the living to the dead lead to moral and political questions very much alive today. The uncertainties about death and the thought that the dead should be treated with a concern which is not perhaps rationally justified, exemplified in these ancient ways, have also been observed in the behaviour of children:

[1] Horace, *Odes*, I, 28. See also *Carminum Libri*, IV, and C. Connolly, *The Unquiet Grave* Epilogue, 1961,
[2] Luke x, 30–37

[P.R.4.] Harold found a dead rat in the garden. He and Frank stamped on it, but Dan said, 'Don't hurt it.' Harold then said, 'Shall we bury it?' and all joined in doing so. Frank asked, 'Will that make it come alive again?' Another child said, 'Does the rat like it?'

[P.R.5.] The children found the young rabbit lying outside the hutch dead . . . and decided that it must have been killed, either by a cat or a rat. Jane (10:9) said, 'Shall we cut it up?' and Mrs I replied, 'If you wish to.' Later in the day, however, they announced that they had decided not to cut it up, but to bury it instead. Priscilla (7:5) said, 'It's so pretty, we don't want to cut it up, we want to keep it.' They buried it in a hole, and nailed together two pieces of wood in the form of a cross, to put over it, writing on this, 'To Whiskers, child of Benjie and Bernard. Born . . . Killed . . .'[1]

The cross and inscription were obviously borrowings from adult ceremonial, which had dramatic value. The preference for burial over dissection, however, because of affection for the individual animal suggests the operation of an impulse which we may assume originally contributed to the ritual disposal of human dead, and has in recent years become a source of moral conflict in civilized society, through the demand for dismemberment of the dead to furnish substitute organs for the living.

The children spontaneously chose between two forms of action the one which seemed to them to express affection the more appropriately. The form they chose was, in detail, obviously culturally learned. In terms of the explanatory principle, the impulse of affection, or rather, the consciousness of it, is the phenomenon, and the action of burial the conclusion, in respect of which the children resembled men of other cultures. Clearly the phenomenal function included more than affection: one may surmise there was also a desire to respect the integrity of the being loved, and an unconscious identification of earth with that which holds living things hidden and close, motherhood. Our records of the children, however, provide no direct evidence of this.

Fantastic elaboration about death and after-life. Even in translation,

[1] Isaacs, *op. cit.*, pp. 180, 196

early myths may intrigue us by their power and fantastic detail. One of our subjects, aged eight, was found to be reading his elder brother's schoolbook of Norse mythology, and gave it up reluctantly, saying, 'They're very good myths.' In the elaboration of detail about death and after-life, children are found to develop fantasies like those of men of distant cultures.

[H.R.11.] Catherine (9:0), returning from a walk with M, a younger sister and a baby brother, asked, apparently à propos of nothing: 'What happens to people when they are dead? Are they eaten by worms? Or do they go and dance about in heaven? I'll tell you all about it when I'm born again! Are you born again?' M said some people said so. The subject was then dropped. The tone was flippant until the last four words.

[H.R.12.] Richard (5:5), on a summer holiday, walking up from the beach with M – a thunderstorm obviously approaching – talked at great length, beginning with rational discussion of bad weather, and then: 'thunder is drums of soldiers in the sky – we shall go up in the sky if a war comes, so you needn't mind – the angels will let down a long rope with a hook on the end and catch you up on the hook [this was addressed to M personally] and then you'll turn into an angel, and it will be lovely, because you'll be able to fly, because angels can fly, they have wings . . .'

It has been reported by Raymond Firth[1] of the Tikopian people that in their view there is eating and drinking in the heavens, and some spirits go and work in the cultivations, but the great occupation is dancing. In the view of the Tikopians, thunder is made by spirits. Richard's fantasy of the thunder as military drums may have been suggested by an adult; the existence and habits of angels had certainly been communicated to him in this way. The rope with the hook on the end, however, seems to have been a spontaneous elaboration: the child, having heard of heaven as far above, had thought out the means by which people might be transported there. Neither he nor his mother knew that some primitive peoples, when they bury their dead, furnish them with ladders or plaited thongs on which to climb to heaven. The same

---

[1] R. Firth, *The Fate of the Soul*, 1955, pp. 18–21

idea, however, occurred to American children, as reported by the psychologist, Stanley Hall,[1] in 1921. He found that several in a sample of school children believed that when people die, they may go up to God on a ladder or rope.

Heaven and deity. The final example to be given, perhaps because we have no information about the child's background, is the most mysterious in its conclusions about the nature of the forces that rule the universe: from what phenomena did the child come to the conclusion he so emphatically expresses? The example is from Wallon,[2] whose honesty and competence as a psychologist will not be questioned.

[P.R.6.] C . . . vin (7) was asked: 'Where is the sun today?' C: 'In God.' (*'Dans le bon Dieu.'*) Q: 'How can the sun be in God?' C: 'Because it [He?] moves quickly.' (*'Parce qu'il va vite.'*) Q: 'Where is God?' C: 'In heaven.' (*'Au ciel.'*) Q: 'What is He like?' (*'Comment est-il fait?'*) C: 'Like an animal.' (*'En bête.'*) Q: 'Have you seen him?' C: 'No.' Q: 'How do you know what He is like?' C: 'Like an animal.'

In what animal form, we wonder, did this child see God? As the lamb or dove of Christianity? The Hindu cow? The inscrutable cat of the Egyptians? The sacred bull or golden calf? The imperial eagle soaring with the sun? To children long ago their culture would have offered such images as not fantastic, but how or whence the French boy received the idea we do not know; only that he had accepted and developed it.

In sum, when we seek to explain the thoughts of children on death by the principle which Onians used to explain the origins of European thought on the soul, time, fate, etc. – that the same phenomena led to the same conclusions – we find indeed the same *conclusions,* but are left with conjectures, tantalizing clues or groping ignorance about the *phenomena,* perceived and interpreted, which led to these conclusions.

[1] G. Stanley Hall *et al., Aspects of Child Life and Education,* 1921
[2] H. Wallon, *Les Origines de la pensée chez l'enfant,* 1945, vol. 1, p. 159

CHAPTER 4

KNOWING

STUDY of the development of a particular concept, thought or idea may suggest ignorance or disregard of the fact that general laws of conceptual development have been established. This is not so. Some ideas have a fundamental position in the conceptual structure, or exceptional power during historical periods, as *justice* had in ancient Greece, *piety* in ancient Rome and *liberty* in sixteenth- to nineteenth-century Western civilization. Whitehead wrote of such concepts in *Adventures of Ideas*; they are traced in the *Journal of the History of Ideas*. The idea of death, it is our theme, has this kind of exceptional position and power in the life of the individual; has had throughout human history, and will continue to do so.

In this chapter the aim is to show how the concept develops in individual children by age and intelligence, and how its development may be related to that of other concepts such as *life* and *cause*. In the first part, I shall quote mainly from my own researches, including those published in 1940, long out of print; in the second part from researches carried out more recently, in America, China, France, Sweden and Switzerland as well as England.

Three methods were used in the earlier English investigation: (1) *Records made systematically by parents* (a) for the specific research project and (b) published by other psychologists; (2) *Definition of the word 'dead'* inserted with due precaution into the vocabulary scale of a test of general intelligence (the English revision of the Terman-Merrill form of the Binet scale); (3) *A story-completion test*, translated from the French form designed in Geneva.

Discussion of results obtained from the third method is deferred to the next chapter, because the stories, being fictions, stimulated fantasy, whereas methods (1) and (2) were designed for the observation of children's apprehension and description of fact.

The total number of children studied in the 1940 publication was relatively small, 128. The majority were city children, Londoners from different areas – dockside, rather higher status working class, and middle class – and from child guidance clinics serving western and south-eastern areas of London and a special school for the subnormal with wide catchment. The rural minority lived in a small English-Midlands village untouched by tourism and several miles from the nearest town. Like the Londoners (except some of the educationally subnormal), the village children were of primary school age, but as the school was closed for summer holidays they were interviewed when they came by general invitation to play with the writer's children, also of primary school age.

The intention was to study equal numbers of boys and girls, but it will be seen from Table 1 below that boys preponderated.

TABLE 1: *Distribution of the English sample by place of interview and sex*

Place of interview	Primary school London	Primary school Rural	Home London	Special school London	Clinic London	Total N	Total %
Sex						N	%
Boys	31	8	7	8	17	71	55·5
Girls	39	2	4	3	9	57	44·5
Total N	70	10	11	11	26	128	
Total %	54·7	7·8	8·6	8·6	20·3	—	100·0

By chance, boys were over-represented in the home-records sample. Their preponderance in the clinic quota was to be expected because more boys than girls were referred to child guidance clinics in England; the disproportion in the special school was partly due to the same tendency, partly chance. With the village children a different social factor led to a similar result: the boys had bicycles, the girls had not; the boys therefore came to play from a wider area. An attempt was made to redress the balance by interviewing in the London primary school more girls than boys.

The relation of the death-concept to age was studied most precisely by the second method. Responses to the word were found to fall into five categories:

A   Apparent ignorance of the meaning of the word *dead*.
B   Interest in word or fact combined with limited or erroneous concept.
C   No evidence of non-comprehension of the meaning of *dead*, but definition by reference to (a) associated phenomena not biologically or logically essential, or (b) humanity specifically.
D   Correct, essential but limited reference.
E   General, logical or biological definition or description.

Of the seventy children not educationally subnormal, two thirds gave answers placed in C-category. Their age ranged from 5:0 to under 12:0, with average age 8:0. No child under 5:0 answered in C-category, no child under 8:0 gave a response above C-category. The highest mental age in B-category was 6:7, the lowest in D-category was 8:9.

The age distribution of the children responding in each of these categories is shown in the Appendix (Table A1). Definitions had been given in the course of administration of an intelligence test. It was therefore possible to range the responses in each category by mental age also, and this distribution is shown in the Appendix (Table A2).

The total number of children entered in Table 1 is forty-five more than those entered in Tables A1 and A2. Omissions include the eleven home-records children and all other children who had previously been tested on the same scale, including thirteen of the educationally subnormal children. As the former tended to be of high intelligence level, the mental age distribution was presumably cut off at both ends.

The general pattern of Tables A1 and A2 shows that as the child grows older, his concept of *dead* changes in the manner shown by the order and the qualitative differences of the A–E classification. There is positive association between age and the specific conceptual development. The association is somewhat closer with 'mental age' (change in general intellectual development) than with 'chronological age' (increment of months since birth).

The age 7:0–8:0 appears as a pivot of change. Every child of this age-range gave a response in C-category. This finding is fully in accordance with psychological and educational theory. In many countries serious or compulsory schooling begins at age 7. The conceptual conformity we have found at this age, however, cannot be attributed to schooling, since in England school attendance is compulsory from the age of five years.

Examples of responses, classified A–E

A CATEGORY. Ignorance is the characteristic of this category. Inability to respond to the word in the vocabulary list is not sufficient evidence that the child's thinking is at this level. Lack of concern or interest in situations involving death may provide non-verbal evidence. Imitation of ritual behaviour associated with death may indicate lack of comprehension.

Examples

A.1. [P.R.7.] Ruth, when just two years old, made herself noticed by repeating the speech, 'Pip is dead.' (Pip was the name given to a little girl she knew.) This amused her for several days, and she said the words with the deepest pathos like a wailing woman. She lowered her head, drew up her eyebrows, half closed her eyes, and spoke with a lugubrious, subdued voice.[1]

A.2. (Reported by school teacher.) Marlene (2:11) was brought to school by her father, who had found her lying asleep beside her dead

[1] V. Rasmussen, *Child Psychology*, 1921, vol. 1, p. 22

mother on the floor by a half-made bed. The mother had apparently suffered a heart attack. On arrival at school, Marlene said quite happily to the teacher, 'Mother lay down on the floor and went to sleep, so I went to sleep too.' (Tested by the writer at age 3:3, Marlene was assessed as of mental age 2:8; her mental age at her mother's death may therefore be estimated as 2:5.)

A.3. [P.R.8.] A little boy (2:2), after nearly killing a fly on the window-pane, seemed surprised and disturbed, looking round for an explanation, then gave it himself: 'Mr F'y dom [gone] to by-by [sleep].' But he would not touch it or another fly again – a doubt evidently remained and he continued uneasy about it.[1]

A.4. [H.R.13.] Ben (3:2), in the garden with his father, asked why we had no dog. F said we had one once, but it was dead. B asked what happened to it; F tried to explain. B went into the house to M and tried to get her to explain it to him, having meanwhile forgotten the word.

A.5. [H.R.14.] Ben (3:3), in the garden with M. B: 'Are you a old lady, Mother?' M: 'No, not yet.' B: 'When will you be a old lady?' M: 'When I'm seventy.' B: 'What will you be after you're a old lady?' M: 'I shall die, some time.' B: 'And what will you be then?' (After some further talk, M discovers that B means what age will she be then. She explains that one does not increase in age after death, but withers like flowers, or perhaps goes on a bonfire, like withered plants.) B: 'I don't want you to be a old lady, Mother.'

A.6. [P.R.9.] Ursula (3:4) with M found a dead moth in the garden and discovered that it could not move. U: 'Like the crab at St Leonards, and there was a boy took the pail and got water and put it in to see if it would move and it didn't move. Why didn't it move, Mummie?'[2]

B CATEGORY. The characteristic features of behaviour at this stage are (a) interest, combined with (b) a limited concept, which may be (c) erroneous. Inability to respond to the word in the vocabulary list is not sufficient evidence that thinking is at this level.

[1] J. Sully, *Studies of Childhood*, 1895, p. 240
[2] S. Isaacs, *Intellectual Growth in Young Children*, 1931, p. 359

Examples

B.1. [P.R.10.] Phineas (3:9) had not before seen the others cut dead animals up, and was puzzled. He has no clear idea of death, and asked several times, 'Why are you killing it?' The other children laughed and assured him . . . that it was dead. Presently he said, 'Is it dead, nearly?'[1]

B.2. [P.R.11.] Phineas (4:0) was cutting his orange, and said, 'I'm killing the orange. I'm cutting it – that is killing it, isn't it?'[2]

B.3. [P.R.12.] Julius (3:10) and Theodor (5:5). J: 'If people don't go out for a walk, they die.' T: 'People don't die if they don't go out for a walk, but they grow pale.'[3]

B.4. [H.R.15.] Edward (2:5) and Stephen (4:10). M reports: 'Edward, of course, hasn't appreciated [death] yet, but Stephen quite frequently comes up against it and puzzles for a few minutes. . . . At present he thinks that we all turn into statues when we die, owing to the fact that he first met Queen Victoria as a statue in Kensington Gardens and then was told that she had been dead some time. The dead birds in poultry shops obviously puzzle him, and at first he thought they were asleep.'

B.5. [H.R.16.] Francis (4:5), examining a pictorial Bible, was particularly interested in a picture of the death of Moses, which represented Moses kneeling on a mountain with a bright light directed on him. He asked what the picture was about, and M read the title. He exclaimed in surprise: 'Is that how you die?' M explained that we all did not die like that. He remained puzzled, and afterwards the picture seemed to have a great fascination for him, for he turned to it whenever he had the opportunity.

B.6. Daphne (4:8, mental age 3:11). *Definition:* 'It don't go on.'

B.7. Henry (5:2, mental age 6:2). *Definition response:* 'I think I don't know dead.' When told a brief, absurd story about a dog which died, he said, 'It died, 'cos it ate too much bones.'

B.8. Chloe (5:5, mental age 5:0). *Definition:* 'To go asleep.' Later, giving a reason why a little girl was sad, and having heard the absurd

---

[1] *ibid.*, p. 194
[2] *ibid.*, p. 199
[3] D. and R. Katz, *Conversations with Children*, 1936, p. 127

story about the dog, C said, 'She was sorry abou' t' li'l doggie.' (Why
was she sorry about the little doggie?) C, after a long pause: 'Because
... because he was in hospital.'

B.9. Joan (6:9, mental age 5:8). *Definition:* 'Send it in hospital.'

B.10. Alfred (6:6, mental age 5:8). *Definition:* 'Hadn't had no dinner.'

C CATEGORY. The child does not show or express inability to
understand the word or observed fact. Reference is made to (a)
humanity only or (b) associated phenomena not logically or
biologically essential.

Examples

C.1. Sheila (5:7, mental age 8:3). *Definition:* 'When people get dead.'
(And then?) 'They go in their grave.'

C.2. Rose (5:9, mental age 7:2). *Definition:* 'Sometimes you're dead'
(laughing). (And then?) 'Then you go in heaven, if you're good.'

C.3. [H.R.17.] Stephen (4:10) and others about a year older. M reports:
'They were taking off outdoor clothes before school. S: "My daddy
has a bad cold." Small girl: "He won't get better until he's dead"
(frivolously). Small boy: "Stephen won't be dead for a long time."
S (very gay, in a high, squeaky, excited voice): "Edward won't be dead
for longer still. He won't be dead for a hundred years, 'cause he's only
two and a half." Small boy: "Everybody'll be dead when they're a
hundred." ' Conversation faded out as the other children went into
class. S turned to putting shoes on apparently quite unmoved, as though
the whole matter had slipped from his thoughts.

C.4. Fred M (7:5, mental age 7:5). *Definition:* 'When you're in your
coffin and you're layin' in it' (waving his hand horizontally).

C.5. Margaret F (7:8, mental age 9:8). *Definition:* 'Somebody what's
been killed.'

C.6. Alfred J (8:2, mental age 8:7). *Definition:* 'When you die.' (And
then?) 'All the beetles eat your eyes out.'

C.7. Pamela Q (10:11, mental age 10:5). *Definition:* 'When you're in
your coffin. When you don't know where you are.'

C.8. Joe Y (12:7, mental age 6:6). *Definition:* 'When people get murdered.'

D CATEGORY. Characteristically there is no apparent inability to understand the word or the event. Reference to humanity only or specifically, as in C-category, may be combined with logical or biological essentials or with generalization.

Examples

D.1. Betty N (10:3, mental age 10:1): 'When a person doesn't live any more.'

D.2. Fred J (9:8, mental age 10:6): 'When you're dead, you can't come alive again.'

E CATEGORY. Definition or description refers to logical or biological essentials.

Examples

E.1. Patrick (8:10, mental age 11:11): 'A body that has no life in it.'

E.2. Marian (10:9, mental age 14:6): 'When you have no pulse and no temperature and can't breathe.'

E.3. [H.R.17b.] Richard (11:10). Letter to M. After an unfinished sentence under date Saturday, the letter continues, on Sunday: 'A boy named [L.B.] got a heart attack on Friday evening. He was running around gym, and suddenly he fell down, he was blue in the face. Somebody ran for Mr J who carried him to the infirmary. He was unconsious [*sic*]. There were lots of rumours: 1. David P dragged him around the floor. 2. Dixon had kicked him. (Dixon wasn't in the gym!) 3. Dennis T knocked him on the head. None of these were true. Mr B said on Saturday that he was dead. He said the infirmary had done all they could. He said [he] hoped we could take it better than he'd done. He was almost crying. He said that L had something missing out of his heart. The doctor said it was a wonder he didn't die sooner. . . . He was about eleven I think. The chapel tonight is going to be about him. Mr S said it was a part of life to see other people die. They sent us to [a] movie. It was awfully good . . . I am very well. How are you?'

Only above the age of seven do we find definition of *dead* as the negation of *living*. Before beginning to consider in more detail the psychological development which the A–E sequence illustrates, let us study the parallel development of the concept of *life*. Not, of course, that *living* is the sole antithesis of *dead*; as an intelligent child stated, *dead* means a *body* that has no life in it. The more full antithesis, which covers all the inorganic, is generally outside the child's verbal range, though not in every case outside its means of expression by reference to objects.

[P.R.13a.] Sully noted long ago that all apparently spontaneous movements are taken by young children to be a sign of life. 'When children in the infant department of a London board school [the primary school of today] were asked what things in the room were alive, they promptly replied the smoke and the fire.'[1] Piaget is the exponent of a theory of childhood animism which has inspired many researches over the last thirty years.[2] In his earlier work, anthropological interpretation of the mentality of primitive man was used in the interpretation of the mentality of the child. The latter was described as differing structurally from that of the civilized adult in being animist and pre-logical, though the childish mentality was not identified with that of the primitive described in the same terms.

Disagreements among anthropologists in this field have tended to be reproduced among psychologists. Lévy-Bruhl's view of the mentality of primitive man as pre-logical was countered by Malinowski's observations of the skill and reasoning powers applied by Trobriand Islanders to the practical concerns of their daily lives, and Susan Isaacs demonstrated personally to Piaget how children showed understanding of mechanical operations at an earlier age than he hypothesized and argued their own interests with impeccable logicality.[3] Margaret Mead holds that *primitive man* is an abstraction without unitary objective existence, and

[1] Sully, *op. cit.*, p. 96
[2] J. Piaget, *The Child's Conception of the World*, 1929. See also W. Dennis, 'Historical notes on child animism', *Psychology Review*, 45, 1938
[3] Isaacs, *op. cit.*, pp. 43–4

evidence accumulates that animism is not characteristic only of 'primitive' or children's thinking. According to Bertrand Russell[1] every philosopher, in addition to the formal system he offers the world, has another, much simpler, of which he may be quite unaware, and it is these imaginative preconceptions that provide the positive basis of his system. The imaginative preconceptions of Plato and Aristotle were to a great extent animistic. Anaxagoras, philosopher and friend of Pericles, was prosecuted for impiety because he taught that the sun and moon were not alive. The animism of the ancient world, like that which Tylor described as characteristic of primitive man, was not simply a philosophic theory or a system of religious belief but also a basis of physics. Not until Newton were all traces of animism removed from the laws of motion. If the imaginative preconceptions of modern man tend to be mechanical, it is a relatively recent development in the long history of human thought.

The animism of the child, according to Piaget, falls into four stages. In the first, life and will are attributed to inanimate objects generally. In the second (from about the beginning of the seventh year) life is attributed to everything that moves. In the third stage (from eight to twelve years) life is attributed to things which appear to move by themselves; and thenceforward the child's view increasingly approximates to that of the adult. Researches on the basis of this theory and of allied formulations set out by Piaget in the study of concepts of causality have been undertaken notably by Deutsche and by Roger Russell and his colleagues using English-speaking subjects; by Huang and Lee using Chinese subjects; by Dennis with Amerindian children, Margaret Mead with Manus children, Klingberg with Swedish children, and by many others.

Roger Russell,[2] critical of Piaget's technique, designed a standardized procedure by which hundreds of children were questioned with reference to twenty objects, as to whether these were

[1] *A History of Western Philosophy*, 1940, pp. 226, 227

[2] R. W. Russell *et al.*, 'Studies in animism', *Journal of Genetic Psychology*, 55, 1939; 56, 1940

living and could feel. The questioning opened: 'You know what living means? A cat is living, but if an automobile runs over it, it is dead.' This approach (as was later recognized) tends to confuse the issue, for even if cats in America have not proverbially nine lives as in England, and even if none survive being run over, the suggestion that *dead* is the sole antithesis of *living* raises doubt about the validity of findings referring to inorganic inanimate objects. This difficulty does not apply, however, to that section of Russell's results in which no such introductory example was given. In general his investigation supported Piaget in respect of successive stages of decreasing animism, without altogether confirming the ages found in the Swiss studies.

Dennis's Amerindian studies also offered corroboration. Margaret Mead's[1] did not, and although her technical approach was different, this does not appear fully to explain the variation of results, to which I shall refer again later. The need for technical subtlety of approach comes out clearly in the work of Huang and Lee and of Klingberg. The child may call an object *living* to which he does not attribute animate or anthropomorphic character or even life. The behaviour of Chinese and Swedish children was remarkably similar in this respect, as appears in the results shown in Table 2.[2]

Comparing by and large the responses to the two questions, it is clear that children were more likely to attribute *living* than *life* to objects *animate or inanimate*. One cannot comment further on this strange finding (which appears to have a semantic basis in the relation between forms of meaning and conceptualization) without knowledge of the languages used by the children. Some of the differences between the Chinese and the Swedish children, such as the former's early certainty about the dog, may be due to

[1] M. Mead, 'An investigation of the thought of primitive children', *Journal of the Royal Anthropological Institute of Great Britain*, 62, 1932

[2] Data from (i) I. Huang and H. W. Lee, 'Experimental analysis of children's animism', *Journal of Genetic Psychology*, 66, 1945, and (ii) G. Klingberg, 'The distinction between living and non-living among 7- to 10-year-old children', *Journal of Genetic Psychology*, 90, 1957

differences in language usage, such as we shall note in a difference between English and Hungarian children later. The resemblance provides an unsolved problem.

TABLE 2: *Concepts of 'life' and 'living' at successive age levels of Chinese and Swedish children. Affirmative, per cent*

Question	Is it living?		Has it life?	
Animate objects	Dog	Tree	Dog	Tree
Children				
Chinese				
under 6:0	100	52·4	100	33·3
6:0–8:7	100	36·8	100	26·3
Swedish				
7:0–8:11	94	88	92·5	74·5
9:0–10:11	97	100	97·0	97·0

Inanimate objects	Moon	River	Ball	Stone	Moon	River	Ball	Stone
Swedish								
7:0–8:11	67	35·5	16·5	6·0	61	25·5	10·5	4·5
9:0–10:11	43	23·0	3·0	3·0	30	20·0	0·0	0·0

With increasing age the percentage of children attributing life to inanimate objects steadily diminishes; this generalization, shown in detail in Table 2 for the Swedish children only, applies also to the Chinese children, for whom less detail is available.

As the attribution of life to inanimate objects diminishes with increasing age, there is found a period in which the attribution of life to animate objects also diminishes. The process is initiated while the criteria are still uncertain. Thus Chinese children between age 6:0 and 8:7 are *less* likely to think a tree is living or has life than their juniors, and even above the age of 9:0 some Swedish children do not attribute living or life to a dog, who do attribute it to a tree. These anomalies may be due to fluctuation in the individual child in the use of spontaneous movement as the main criterion of living.

But what does the child mean when he attributes life to an object? Is he also endowing it with animate or anthropomorphic characteristics? The data collected by Huang and Lee and by Klingberg are more extensive than that quoted above. Some of Klingberg's fuller detail is presented in Table 3 below, and shows that children may say that an object is living yet not attribute to it certain functions of life.

TABLE 3: *Further analysis of responses of 7- to 8-year-old Swedish children*

RESPONSE

	Lives and feels	Lives, does not feel	Does not live, feels	Does not live or feel	Total number of children
OBJECT					
Tree	24	33	0	8	65
Moon	30	12	2	15	59
River	1	23	0	41	65
Watch	3	21	0	42	66

The adult observer may not generally realize how traditional usage in his own culture leads to uncertainty, in the child, of the meaning and boundaries of life. The child may not hear politicians refer to a live issue or stockbrokers to a live share, but he may be alerted to the danger of a live wire or the nuisance of a dead end; the telephone wire may go dead; the ground is alive with ants; clouds race across the sky; the moon peeps in at the window; the telegraph wires sing between the posts. The pathetic fallacy riots in the literature of languages living and dead. 'The mountains skipped like rams, and the little hills like lambs.' Doubtless something of the same kind happens in China. Nor is the child confused only by language. Few children fail to be presented with a doll or mechanical toy in which the simulation of life by form, colour, texture and motion is calculated to deceive.

It is not to be doubted that semantic ignorance and confusion contribute to animism of both adult and child in many cultures, but they cannot be supposed a sufficient explanation of it. Wallon has demonstrated that the young child's way of thinking differs from that of the adult not merely by ignorance or characteristic system but by a readiness to tolerate antinomies even when verbally expressed. The following, from his examples, bear especially on the child's thinking about life and death:

[P.R.13b.] Q 'Are your eyes alive?' (*'Est-ce que tes yeux sont vivants?'*) A 'Yes, Madam.' Q 'Your nose?' A 'No ... yes, yes.' Q 'Why [do you say] your eyes are alive?' A 'Because one can make them move.' (*'Parce qu'on les fait marcher.'*) Q 'Do they move all the time?' A 'Yes ... at night they don't move, because one is asleep.' Q 'When you are asleep, are your eyes alive?' A 'No, Madam, because one is not moving them.' Q 'And your nose? ... when is that alive?' A 'Only in the day-time.' Q 'How do you know it is alive in the day-time?' A 'Because one makes it move. Little babies make their nose move too.' Q 'Do dead people move?' A 'No.' Q 'Are the dead alive?' A 'No, Madam, when they are not dead, they are alive.' Q 'When you are asleep, you don't move; are you dead?' A 'No, Madam, I am sleeping.' Q 'But are you not alive when you are sleeping?' A 'No, Madam.'[1]

This child has apparently based his concept of life on the theme of movement, which many other observations suggest as being common practice. His response also demonstrates Wallon's observation that concepts which are unitary for the adult may not consistently draw upon a single theme for the child. Another child considers as living everything that may be used as a means or tool by the living human being, though he is clearly confused about it:

[P.R.14.] L . . ard (7:6):[2] Q 'Are there things not alive?' A 'Yes.' Q 'What things?' A 'Animals that are dead.' Q 'Can anything be made from dead animals?' A 'Coats, with their skins.' Q 'Are the skins alive?' A 'No.' Q '. . . and the hats, are they alive?' A 'Yes . . .' Q 'Are the coats alive too?' A 'Yes.' Q 'The animals' skins are living and the animals are dead?' A 'Yes.'

The way children classify objects, according to Wallon, de-

[1] H. Wallon, *Les Origines de la pensée chez l'enfant,* 1945, vol. I, p. 174 ff.
[2] *ibid.,* p. 279

pends on the current theme of their thinking or the way they are having to handle things; this he believes to be a more general difference between the usual thought-processes of the child and the adult than the animist differentiation. Moreover he holds (and this idea anticipates discussion on creativity begun after Wallon's death) that the attribution by the child of stable invariant properties to perceptual reality is not altogether propitious for the development of knowledge, for the invariant forms are then held to be reality itself, original, primitive, necessary, absolute or *a priori*, whereas the history of thought shows that it has never been possible to express reality in its totality. So in the development of the individual, the persistence of a certain degree of syncretic thought (*un mélange de l'être et de la connaissance*) beneath the routine formalism of collective perception and knowledge is undoubtedly the condition of really original artistic or scientific discovery.

This subtle and brilliant interpretation of the immature stage and the developmental process provides also a psychological explanation of certain inconsistencies in research findings on animism. Conclusions about the child's animism tend to differ with the rigidity of the psychologist's theory either of the way children think or the way adults do. Jahoda[1] has pointed out that both Huang and Klingberg (whose researches have been quoted above) show some lack of appreciation of Piaget's theoretical position regarding childish thought; that although their researches add much to knowledge they do not upset Piaget's theory of child animism. Klingberg holds that the thinking of children, even before the age of seven, is a function of a mental structure not differing fundamentally from that of the adult. This argument may finally turn upon the definition of *structure* in this context. In Freudian terms (or those of Plato or St Paul) the thinking of both child and adult must be conceived as organized in depth,

[1] G. Jahoda, 'Child animism: a critical survey of cross-cultural research', *Journal of Social Psychology*, 47, 1958, pp. 213–22. Animistic responses by adults have also been shown to be a function of sentence contexts and instructions, by A. J. Simmons and A. E. Goss, *Journal of Genetic Psychology*, 91, 1957, pp. 181–9

with relatively distinct levels, differently structured. The child's thought appears to move with greater flexibility between these levels; the work of the poet and of the original thinker in any field may depend upon a similar facility. The study of language and of philosophical systems suggests that the thinking of normal and also of unusually intelligent adults, below the conscious level, may be animistic. Moreover it has been shown that at the conscious level, adult students in America may be confused about 'what it means to be alive'. Dennis[1] found a large percentage to maintain that a lighted match was alive, that the sun has life, and also the ocean. The adult with whom the child has been compared may thus prove an abstraction as much as the Economic Man of early political theorists, or the primitive man whose general existence Dr Mead denies. 'Childish' thinking similar to that of Dennis's American students was also found by Zazzo among adult students in Paris when they were faced with problems of physics such as Piaget had presented to children.[2]

The general observation stands, illuminated in detail in many researches, that the way of thinking of children tends to be more animistic – to attribute some kind of animate quality more widely – in earlier than in later years. This tendency we may hypothetically derive from two developmental processes, one general to all children and one varying with the culture in which they are reared. In the developmental process, it seems that there is initially no differentiation between self and object, and the self is animate. Other persons provide for the infant the earliest basis for generalization of phenomena as persistent objects other than self, and so as the basis of his earliest concepts. Among objective phenomena, the inanimate becomes a separate category at a later stage, before the acquisition of speech, through handling and locomotion, not, of course, through being consciously classified as different from animate.

[1] W. Dennis, quoted in N. L. Munn (ed.), *The Evolution and Growth of Human Behaviour*, 1955, pp. 321–4

[2] R. Zazzo in J. M. Tanner and B. Inhelder (eds.), *Discussions on Child Development*, 1956, vol. 2, pp. 257–60

The second cultural process is linked with the first in so far as animistic behaviour or suggestion by adults will be readily accepted by the child. If what is suggested is actually not accepted among the adults of the culture as rational or credible, the child's logical development may be retarded; if it is generally accepted in his culture, his animism is simply a part of his acculturation and maturation. If the child is reared in a culture in which it is particularly important for his survival that he should *not* entertain animistic notions, the adult may actually teach the child to be less animistic, *within an area of danger*, than the adult is himself in the general concerns of life. This is broadly the explanation suggested by Margaret Mead for her findings among Manus children.

The child's concepts of *living* and *dead* develop partly through the discovery of what in his experience corresponds to the usage of the words and partly through the search for words which correspond to an apprehended differentiation of percepts; or rather, for the means of conceptualizing a category of objects which he perceives as differentiated within a previously apprehended whole. How communicate the idea of *things that don't move of themselves*? If this is the criterion for the *not alive*, then the sun and moon are alive but a tree is not. An adult may at times find gaps in language for the expression of a concept describing not a novel objective occurrence but a novel subjective classification of experience. The child, whose command of language is still relatively and consciously inadequate, cannot be sure whether in the language of his culture there is an expression for his way of thinking, or whether the expression he is using actually denotes a conceptual category with different frontiers. Gradually he adjusts his way of thinking to the current adult usage of the available words, and learns to perceive 'reality' in accordance with the appropriate cultural conceptual scheme.

Except for Roger Russell's deceased cat, the child's animism has usually been studied with reference to the development of differentiation between the animate and the inorganic inanimate. The introduction of this cat, which seems at first sight an extraordinary lapse in an experimental plan, may in fact have been due to an unconscious understanding of the child's way of thinking. The records quoted above under B-category show how children in their fourth year may observe the difference between living and dead animals and ask for explanation. The actual uncertainty about criteria, and the importance of movement in this connection, are illustrated in the following incident reported by Isaacs:[1]

[P.R.15.] The rabbit had died in the night. Dan (4:0) found it and said, 'It's dead – its tummy doesn't move up and down now.' Paul (4:2) said, 'My daddy says that if we put it into water, it will get alive again.' Mrs I said, 'Shall we do so and see?' They put it into a bath of water. Some of them said, 'It's alive.' Duncan (7:1) said, 'If it floats, it's dead, and if it sinks, it's alive.' It floated. . . . One of them said, 'It's alive, because it's moving.' This was a circular movement, due to the currents in the water. Mrs I therefore put in a small stick which also moved round and round, and they agreed that the stick was not alive. They then suggested that they should bury the rabbit.

During their sixth year, children whom we studied for our research showed in their play spontaneous and persistent interest in phenomena illustrating movement due to physical properties and relationships. (I do not think this was more marked in the boys than the girls, but the home-records sample included a lesser number of girls, and their records were restricted to death references.) Thus of Richard (5:5) it is reported:

[H.R.18.] He loves to bury a little wooden boat in the sand in a pool, then gradually take handfuls of sand away until suddenly the boat seems to shake itself free, and springs to the surface. He discovered this game for himself. Two months later he invented a game showing how his head could be moved as though it were inanimate: 'Look how I pull my head up and down' (all smiles). He gripped the corner of a handkerchief in his teeth, holding the opposite corner in his hand, and pulled his head down rhythmically, letting it bob back again as though released, between each pull. We laughed, and copied him. Then R took the handkerchief and pretended it was a clock key, wound up his face and said, 'Ting!'

[1] Isaacs, *op. cit.*, pp. 182–3

Thus the child, experimenting with the objects presented in his immediate world, recognizes that things which do not ordinarily appear able to move of themselves, and are therefore excluded from the primary undifferentiated category based on persons as objects, may nevertheless move through physical interrelationships independently of persons; also that being moved by external force is not an exclusive condition of *not* being a person or alive. His activities are not an outcome of fully conscious, logical thought and planned experiment, but flow directly from his interest at this stage.

In the face of physical problems to which he cannot know the answer the child may produce animistic fantasies, or attempt to work out a rational theory, or refuse to abandon an agnosticism which he considers it is the function of the adult to dispel. Piaget has reported how young children, going out for a walk when the moon is high, think the moon, animate, is following them, and Richard's behaviour (aged 5:9) seemed to support this view, but further analysis of the record showed this was not so. He did indeed think that the moon was moving on a track parallel to his own, independently of himself, but earlier (aged 5:0) he had remarked of a girl who, in a song, 'wanted the moon to play with', that 'the moon would be a silly thing to have, because it would squash up in your hand, because it's only air'. [H.R.19.] It seems unlikely that he thought it animate, therefore, in any full sense.

[H.R.20.] The same child, Richard (aged 5:4), was asked a question from one of Piaget's researches: 'How did the sun begin?' He replied, 'What do you mean, how did it begin?' and pressed for further explanation of the question, which was not supplied. At length he said, '*I* don't know. It's *you* that ought to tell *me* that! How *did* it begin? And why does it shine more on one side of the house than on the other?' From this encounter the psychologist concluded that questions designed to test the extent and quality of childish animism should not be presented except in an environment in which the child feels free to respond, 'I don't know! It's you that ought to tell me that!'

A common process of conceptual development lies behind the changes in the child's concepts of *alive* and *dead*. The gradient of change is roughly measured by that of the average age levels at the foot of Table A2 in the Appendix. In Table 2 the developmental process and rate of change are shown in more detail by comparison of the percentages of children in the 7–9 and 9–11 age groups who think of inanimate objects as animate. In the younger sample already few children thought animate balls and stones which they could handle, and in the older sample none thought these objects had life. But the moon and the river, animate to many of the younger sample, were still animate to many, though invariably less, of the older children. Let us examine more closely the psychological characteristics of the successive A–E categories of Table A2.

In A-stage, a child does not imagine her mother as dead even when she actually witnesses the event, as Marlene did; he hears the word and can attach no meaning to it, as happened to Ben. These are negatives; what is positive at this stage?

An intense interest in elementary classification of objects may be observed from the end of the second year or earlier, simultaneous with or preceding the early acquisition of speech. In his study of the growth of concepts of number, Piaget refers to a child of 1:10 whose behaviour indicated the activity of colligation, basic to addition, by his saying 'and another' of further items to be added to a grouping. In our own records [H.R.21.] Ben (2:2½) whose total spoken vocabulary of thirty-nine words was below the average reported by Smith[1] for that age, frequently said 'There's another there', pointing to or touching similar things such as dining-room chairs. At this stage a child taken for a walk may call every man he sees 'Dada', which is found the more surprising as he has shown for several months that he can distinguish his father from strangers. Sully[2] notes [P.R.16.] this of his own child, who at eighteen months 'proceeded after the manner

[1] See D. McCarthy, 'Language development in young children', L. Carmichael (ed.), *Handbook of Child Psychology*, 1954, p. 424
[2] Sully, *op. cit.*

of other children to embrace within the term "papa" all male
adults, whether known to him or not'. An example with reference
to animals is given by Lorenz: a child 'whose parents were quite
desperate because he couldn't tell the difference between a dog
and . . . a horse, said "bow-wow" to both, but not to a goose.
It was clear . . . that bow-wow simply meant mammal.' [P.R.17.][1]
Again Sully anticipates this observation, giving the fifteenth
month as the age when 'this word [bow-wow] was thrown about
in the most reckless way . . .'.

There is thus ample evidence that during the second year the
child's catalogue of verbal symbols lags behind his conceptualizing achievements, and also that the concepts he works out – the
objects he takes together for generalized labelling – may not
correspond correctly with those of his culture. Concepts in our
culture are most commonly determined by visual presentation.
An exception is, of course, in the naming of parents, where the
verbal symbol refers not to a generalized visual phenomenon but
to a particular instance of a functional relationship. If 'the child,
misled by some rough resemblance in form, clothes, etc. applies
to the stranger the tender name of father'[2] the reason is not lack
of discrimination but ignorance that this case is an exception to
the rule of classification by generalized visual appearance. This is
the stage when recognition of resemblances is important and
exciting; the dominant intellectual activity is to classify and name
by generalization. The characteristic question is 'What's that?' In
a sample of two-year-olds, one fifth of all questions demanded
the name of an object or person.[3]

At this stage the use or function of an object is not conceptually
distinguished, but is bound up with its appearance, as total phenomenon. The child asks 'What?' before he begins to ask 'Why?'
As Wallon says, there is [at the A-stage] inability to break down
the object as phenomenon (*décomposer la représentation de l'objet*)

[1] See Tanner and Inhelder, *op. cit.*, vol. 1, p. 99
[2] Maine de Biran (1803 edn), quoted Dennis, 'Historical notes on child
animisms'
[3] McCarthy, *op. cit.*

67

into those properties which serve as fundaments of relationship with other objects. And Piaget speaks of the stage at which the child 'still conceives of causes as merely a function of perceived objects'.[1]

The transition from A-stage to B-stage is marked, then, by the substitution of 'Why?' as more prevalent than 'What?' questions. The transition involves development of the *concept of cause*. It is at B-stage, not at A-stage, that a concept of death emerges. In order to understand what lies behind that emergence it is necessary to consider the development of the apprehension of causality.

Hume, in his famous theory of causation, argued that whereas philosophers had been unable to present a satisfactory solution of the relations of cause and effect, every infant, 'nay even brute beasts', acted as though familiar with it. 'And if I be wrong, I must acknowledge myself to be indeed a very backward scholar; since I cannot now discover an argument which, it seems, was perfectly familiar to me long before I was out of my cradle.'[2] Briefly, Hume's theory is that *post hoc* becomes *propter hoc* by association and habit: 'The necessary connection between causes and effects is the foundation of our inference from one to the other. The foundation of our inference is the transition arising from the accustomed union. These, therefore, are the same.'[3] The repeated objective, external association of events by contiguity in time and/or space effects a subjective, psychological association between the ideas of these events, which is the foundation for an inference of necessary (causal) connection between them.

The philosophical discussions to which this theory has given rise lie outside our scope. For psychologists it has a double interest, first in respect of the empirical evidence of its validity within a restricted field and its extraordinary strength as a technique for further discovery within that field; second, in respect of the modifications which later observations demand. As for the first

[1] J. Piaget, *The Child's Construction of Reality* (1955 edn), p. 291

[2] D. Hume, *An Inquiry Concerning Human Understanding*, vol. 4, ch. 2

[3] D. G. C. McNabb, *David Hume* (quoting *The Treatise of Human Nature*, vol. 1), 1951, p. 163

point: from the Soviet Union, and indeed from pre-Soviet Russia[1] to the United States, and at stations between, the brute beast in the laboratory is nowadays to be observed acting upon Humean principles, by reacting to the *accustomed union* of bell and dinner, or their equivalents, as though there were a *necessary connection* between them. As to the second point: two modifications of the theory seem to be required. The first is due to the rejection of the associationist psychology prevalent in Hume's time and for over a century later. So far from weakening Hume's scepticism, however, this development actually carries it further. Hume denied that the causal relationship had its foundation in objective events, placing it rather in the association of *ideas* of events *perceived* as contiguous in space and/or time. Later psychological theory adds scepticism of the objectivity of the perception. 'Regularities are only found because they are sought. But it is in the seeking that the category of causal unity is primarily involved.'[2]

The second modification is suggested by observation of the development of the child – remembering that Hume himself referred to the behaviour of the child and the 'brute beast'. For there is a stage in the child's development, made clear because he is able to speak, when he does not separate phenomenon and function. This has been noted by psychologists of childhood, and examples will be given below from the home records. But if we suppose that the animal which cannot speak is not further developed in respect of the conception of causality than the child who can, then we must suppose that the dog conditioned to salivate by the accustomed transition from first event, bell-sound, to second event, presentation of dinner, is *not* inferring that the bell causes the appearance of the dinner, or that there is a functional relationship, but that there is a pre-dinner-bell-sound.

This is a matter on which there have been volumes written, and are many yet to come, particularly following up the recent work

[1] In particular the well-known work of I. P. Pavlov
[2] G. F. Stout and C. A. Mace, *Manual of Psychology*, 1932, p. 421

of Neal Miller.[1] I have only stated a case here, not argued it. One example from our records of the child's confusion of phenomenon and function is as follows:

[H.R.22.] Ben (2:5) wants things that appear to be falling down, in pictures, to be put straight, and seeing a picture of ships, said he would go in the ship, and put his foot on the picture, on the floor. (He had travelled in a ship two months previously.)

When the function and phenomenon are inseparable a thing *is* what it *does* and does what it is or is seen as. The question why any action is or is not performed cannot therefore arise at this stage. Hence although Stephen (4:10) is puzzled about the dead poultry in the shop, and thinks they may be asleep, Edward (2:5) finds nothing to question. Edward's reaction is of A-category, Stephen's of B.

This is the psychological background for the fact that the child does not usually ask *why* questions as soon as he begins to speak, and shows no concern about death before he reaches the stage of questions about reasons, causes, motives and necessary connections between events.

When the child acquires names for objects, the name represents the phenomenon as a whole, both function and appearance. When the function is more general than the appearance, he may define the object by reference to function, as indeed an older subject may also do. The manner of reference, however, tends to be characteristic of the developmental stage. Asked 'What is a chair?', a characteristic response of the young child is 'to sit on'. Terman, in an early commentary on the Binet tests, noted the immaturity of this type of response.[2] The functional definitions commonly given by children, he wrote, 'show two grammatical forms which correlate significantly with mental age; the use of the infinitive and impersonal is the earlier. A child of higher mental age will reply "you sit on it".' The difference corresponds to successive

[1] N. E. Miller, 'Learning of visceral and glandular responses', *Science*, 163, 1969, p. 3,866
[2] L. Terman, *The Measurement of Intelligence*, 1917

stages of liberation of phenomenon from function. The function of being a seat is the property of the chair; sitting, in the earlier formulation, is not yet fully apprehended as a relationship between two independent objects. The more mature reply shows that mutuality of relationships has become part of the general conceptual scheme. The more mature reply often seems to the adult less advanced than the earlier impersonal one, the more because it is itself succeeded by a third stage in which impersonality is combined with the awareness of functional separateness; the chair may then be defined as *a piece of furniture to be sat upon*. In the same way, the impersonality of typical definitions of *dead* in B-category ('to go asleep, it don't go on') seem superficially more mature than 'somebody's killed' or 'when people's dead' of C-category, which correspond to the more mature form, 'you sit on it'.

B-category corresponds to the stage when *why* questions come in spate. This verbal search for causes suggests an activity previously dammed by concentration on the process of acquiring names for phenomena. Noun learning involves colligation, or in Spearman's[1] formulation, the eduction of correlates. The verbal eduction of relationships is initiated in the *why* stage.

In the suggested revision of Hume's theory of causation, the accustomed union of experienced events provides, first, the foundation for the reflex responses of the cradle infant, and then the foundation for inference of necessary connection, that is, of cause-effect relationship. But how is the transition mediated?

The German psychologist, Wilhelm Stern,[2] some half century ago, criticized Hume's theory on the basis of his observation of children's behaviour. He maintained that it is not expectation derived from habitual experience that gives rise in children to the idea of cause, but the non-occurrence of the expected; that the concept originates in wonder or surprise. Nor, he added, would the non-occurrence of accustomed union of events fully account for the observed behaviour of children, since they will also seek

[1] C. Spearman, *The Nature of 'Intelligence' and the Principles of Cognition*, 1932
[2] W. Stern, *The Psychology of Childhood*, 1914-27

to find causes for events and phenomena which are new in their experience. He quoted Helmholtz's suggestion that such behaviour arises from the child's *unconscious conclusions*. Helmholtz was using the word *unconscious* before Freud gave it its present psychoanalytic significance; Stern in following him may wish to suggest that we cannot know what union of events is new in a child's experience. The accustomed coming of a mother to comfort a child who cries may provide an embryonic inference of necessary connection and so a psychogenetic code for the conception of cause.

Stern did not solve the problem, but I think he provided the clue. Certainly expectation derived from habitual experience is not sufficient to originate a concept of cause, and although such a concept's origin seems to be associated with surprise at the breakdown of such expectation, that also is insufficient. Indeed such breakdown is frequently arranged in laboratory experiments with animals, with the result that the conditioned reflex response is extinguished. Pre-dinner-bell-sound becomes a-bell-sound. By Humean theory a connection inferred as necessary between events has been severed. By alternative theory a phenomenon (is-does) has changed its character, change being in the nature of phenomena. The only necessity is that of subjective adjustment to the nature of the phenomenon, which is a biological necessity, not a cognized inference. The experimenter sometimes reports that the animal is extinguished, though in fact it comes to no harm. Nor does it apparently develop a concept of cause.

The clue is, that such a breakdown of expectation may be necessary for the origination of the causal-concept, but it is not sufficient until the child has reached the stage of separating function from object-totality. The concept of cause is then generated not by habitual experience of association between events, nor by the cessation of such association, but by change in an expected relationship between function and appearance of a phenomenon. In connection with the concept of death, the function is frequently that of movement, but this is not necessarily so. Piaget gives an example referring to plant life.

[P.R.18.] Del (6 plus): 'They [the roses on a rose-bush] are all withered – why? They shouldn't die, because they are still on the tree.'[1]

An example of the frequent early association of death with immobility was given in the record of Ursula (quoted above [P.R.9.]), who asked why the crab did not move. The child had evidently reached the stage of separating phenomenon from function before this question was asked. In one recorded example the concept of dead appears to have preceded the first recorded *why* question. This record, by G. Scupin, has been quoted by Piaget[2] and by Nathan Isaacs.[3] It identifies death with immobility.

Piaget noted the preoccupation of a boy of 6–7 years old with the subject of death, and considered that this is of importance in the development of mature concepts of causality from earlier thinking in which (in his view) motivation is the source and explanation of the existence of things. Everything seems well regulated, Piaget suggests, until the child becomes aware of the difference between life and death. 'From this moment, the idea of death sets the child's curiosity in motion, precisely because, if every cause is coupled with a motive, then death calls for a special explanation.' Clearly death cannot be explained in terms of motive of the being that dies, for in the case of animals the question of suicide does not arise, nor does it occur to the child in the case of human beings. If death is attributed to the activity of other persons, a causal explanation may still be given. Obviously such cases occur, as when animals are killed for food, or when animals harmful to man are killed in order to safeguard human life. There are also occasions when men are killed by men – and, as we have seen, some children will define *dead* as *killed* or *murdered*. Wallon[4] has reported a response from a child

---

[1] *The Language and Thought of the Child*, 1959, p. 175. Clearly Del already had a concept of death as separation, but not as general inevitable occurrence

[2] *ibid.*, p. 33

[3] 'Children's why questions' (in S. Isaacs, *op. cit.*, p. 310). [P.R.19.] 'The child's mother was lying on the ground. The boy wants her to get up: "*Du bis ya nicht tot, warum stehste nicht immersu auf?*" '

[4] Wallon, *op. cit.*

who had found a logical solution to the problem of causality, death and motivation in accordance with what he had been taught of the laws of God and man:

[P.R.20.] M (7:0) said of the storm that it was due to a ball of fire. Q: 'Who made this ball of fire?' M: 'The devil . . .' Q: 'Where is he?' M: 'In heaven.' ('*Au ciel.*') Q: 'What else does the devil do?' M: 'He makes people die.' ('*Il fait mourir du monde.*') Q: 'If there were no devil, would old people not die?' M: 'That is so.' ('*Si.*')

Lacking some such mythology, human mortality, unlike that of animals (or even like that of animals in some cases, as Clifford Sully insisted), cannot be explained in terms of motivation consistently with any rule of social law and propriety, the decorous organization of life in society which the young child generally shows himself so well aware of, and so much concerned to have surrounding him, even if only that he may sometimes break out of it. The law that permits death must be a law of nature; a law uniform and impersonal.

The steps by which children come intellectually to the conception of laws of nature, and of causality operating in accordance with such laws, may then start from those reactions which lead them to the thought, traditionally opening the study of classical logic, that all men are mortal. This intellectual ascent may be painful. But like the storied *Pilgrim's Progress*, there is an early stage at which a former burden is cast off. This burden is a sense of guilt for sins which the child earlier wished but was in fact powerless to commit; those impulses which psychoanalysts call death-wishes even when they precede the concept of death. Normally, intellectual maturity brings humility; the child finds that he, like all other living beings, has no magical power against death or to procure it. If love cannot save, neither can hate of itself destroy, and if death is inevitable for all, then indeed love cannot save. His 'death-wishes' were powerless.

Actual bereavement during this stage of growth may distressfully interfere with this intellectual-affective development, as will be shown in the next chapter.

74

The B-stage is one of cognitive exploration. The child discovers the fact of death and, in a limited way, what it implies. The C-stage is one of elaboration. The child becomes preoccupied with personal and cultural concomitants of the death process. It is thought of in terms of human experience, without biological generality. Burial, coffins, graves fill the picture; ghosts hover in the background. Ceremonial burials of dead animals are organized and enjoyed.

The C-stage is marked by interest in the ritual surrounding the idea of death. Consequently it is at this stage that we may expect to find differences between children of different cultures, as well as resemblances. A research[1] conducted in Budapest before the Second World War, using the Hungarian language in which the words for *dead* and *death* have different roots, found that the younger children did not use the latter term at all, and owing to the common pictorial representation of Death as a reaper in white, the older children tended to personify the abstraction. This personification doubtless corresponds to the almost invariable human reference of the English-speaking children in C-category, but the personification of death by English children was not found. It appears to be a function of the language and general environment of the Hungarian children.

The attitude of the children who carried out the ceremonial burial of the baby rabbit, Whiskers, as reported by Dr Isaacs, was serious but not tragic. In other social situations the attitude of children to the idea of death, if not the event, is often observed to be the reverse. Greek comedy, we are told, developed from the jesting of those lining the road along which the mourning women passed in the funeral procession for Tammuz or Persephone. Primitive funeral rites concluded with feasting and obscenities. Some songs of wartime strike this note – 'The bells of hell go ting-a-ling-a-ling for you but not for me.' Schoolchildren traditionally make a mock of death. In their study of the lore and

---

[1] M. Nagy, 'The child's theories concerning death', *Journal of Genetic Psychology*, 73, 1948

language of schoolchildren in modern Britain the Opies[1] state:

When they are about ten years old, children enter a period in which the outward material facts about death seem extraordinarily funny. They ask each other: 'You going to be burnt or buried?' They have mock laments:

> Little Willie's dead,
> Jam him in the coffin,
> For you don't get the chance,
> Of a funeral of'en.

They inscribe their names on the flyleaf of their schoolbooks, adding, 'When I am dead and in my grave and all my bones are rotten, This little book will tell my name when I am quite forgotten', a version of which is found on a sampler of 1736. Certain songs like Whyte-Melville's 'Wrap me up in my tarpaulin jacket', Montrose's 'Clementine', and the popular song, 'When I die, don't bury me at all, Just pickle my bones in alcohol', become an obsession, chorused over and over again. Death, which when they were younger, they may have regarded as a frightening and private subject, has now come out into the open. They have found that it is still a long way off, and these songs are a sign of their emancipation.

The Opies' interpretation of this behaviour gains support from a research on affective responses to the concept of death among children and adolescents by Alexander and Adlerstein.[2] They tested the degree of emotion aroused by the concept, and found that the concept aroused emotion in all the age groups (5–8, 9–12 and 13–16) when verbal response was required, but when tested by GSR (electrical arousal) the middle age-group was not found to be significantly aroused, and the young children less than the adolescents.

Although therefore the Opies' psychological interpretation of children's behaviour may be over-simplified, the description is

---

[1] I. and P. Opie, *The Lore and Language of Schoolchildren*, 1959
[2] I. E. Alexander and A. M. Adlerstein, 'Affective responses to the concept of death in a population of children and early adolescents', *Journal of Genetic Psychology*, 93, 1958

widely based and fully to be trusted. Yet an obsessed individual is not wholly free from anxiety; it would appear from their behaviour that the children are still on the defensive, and glad of the company of their fellows in the defiance and mockery of death.

CHAPTER 5

IMAGINING

NURSERY rhymes and old fairy stories are full of allusions to death and horrors. What could be more grim or poetically gruesome than the giant's song in *Jack and the Beanstalk*:

Fee Fie Foe Fum!
I smell the blood of an English man.
Be he alive or be he dead
I'll grind his bones to make my bread!

Such stories, rather than innocuous tales in which passion 'is turned to favour and to prettiness', have been nursery fare for centuries in many lands.

In this chapter death will be studied as it appears in children's fantasy. Of course we should have little to study (unless we broach the subject) if children do not spontaneously think or speak about death. It used to be supposed that this was so. However, in a research carried out in Geneva[1] to discover the emotional problems of disturbed children the investigators reported their surprise at the frequency of references to death in children's completions of story openings in which no such reference was made.

The first thing for us to find out, therefore, was whether English children, emotionally disturbed or not considered so, would also refer frequently to death if the Geneva Story Completion test were given to them in English words. The test is set out below.

Story Completion Test

1. A boy (little boy, girl, little girl) went to school; when play-time came, he didn't play with the others but stayed all alone in a corner. Why?

[1] M. Thomas, '*Méthode des histoires à compléter...*', *Archives de Psychologie*, 1937

78

2. A boy was quarrelling with his brother (sister, friend), and their (his) mother came up to them, and . . . What happened then?

3. A boy was having dinner with his mother and father. The father got very angry, because . . . Why?

4. One day the father and mother were annoyed with each other, and they quarrelled, and the reason was . . .?

5. One Sunday the boy (or, they all) went out for the day with his (their) father and mother; when they came home in the evening, the mother was very sad. Why?

6. The boy had a friend he liked very much; one day this friend came to him and said, 'You come with me and I'll tell you a secret, and show you something, but you mustn't tell anyone about it!' What did he show him? What did he tell him?

7a. When the boy went to bed at night-time, what did he think about?

7b. One night he cried when he went to bed; he was very unhappy. Why was that?

8a. Then he went to sleep, and what did he dream about?

8b. He woke up again, in the middle of the night, and was very frightened. Why?

9. Then he went to sleep again, and this time he had a lovely dream. A fairy appeared to him and said, 'I can make anything you wish come true; tell me what you want, and then I will touch you with my magic wand and your wish will come true. You can have three wishes.' What did he wish for?

10. Then the fairy said, 'You are growing into a big boy; do you want to be big and grown-up, or would you like to stay a child for a long time, perhaps for always?' The boy said . . . What did he say?

11. Then the fairy gave him £100,000 to spend. What did he do with it?

In England the test was given to most of the children represented in Table 1 (p. 48). The children interviewed in clinics were assumed to correspond to the children studied in the Swiss research, in respect of emotional disturbance. The children omitted from the English study of Story Completion were (a) those under 5:0, unless their intelligence level was above average, and (b) the home-records children.

One reason for the latter omission was that the necessary

rapport between psychologist and child was established on a basis of previous ignorance of the child's background on the adult's part. Before giving the test the experimenter invariably talked informally with the child, asking about the composition of his family and his own position in it. Other particulars were often spontaneously given; no question which elicited signs of withdrawal was pressed. If a young child had lost one or both parents by death, divorce or separation, or knew only one parent, story 4 was omitted. The administration of the test was individual and oral throughout.

The original French was somewhat reduced in our translation. We did not follow up responses with further questions so freely as had been done in Geneva. Nevertheless it was found that forty-five of the ninety-eight children referred in their 'completions' to death, funerals, killing or ghosts, and when ambiguous references were included, such as 'He got run over' or 'She lost one of her children' the total rose to 60 per cent. This compares with 66 per cent by the Swiss children.

The question immediately arises, is the frequency thus measured a function of the test situation rather than of children's thought about death in general? The former would be probable if either the test situation were unrepresentative of the conditions which stimulate the child's thought and behaviour in daily life, or if one or more of the story openings gave such a strong suggestion of death-response as to make its completion in this form customary.

Considering first this latter point of conventional closure, we may take story 2 as an example. Six out of every ten of our sample completed this with a punishment *motif*. When a modified version of the test was presented in a later research to boys aged 11 to 14, German boys referred to punishment without exception, and of English boys 53 per cent did so.[1] The opening of story 2, then, suggests a punishment response. None of the story openings proved suggestive of a conventional closure relating to death or allied concepts to such a degree as this. The largest proportion of

[1] A. Kaldegg, 'Responses of German and English secondary school boys to a projection test', *British Journal of Psychology*, 39, 1, 1948

such completions, when ambiguous references are included, was not more than one third of the sample for any one story. Stories 5, 7b and 8b together accounted for the majority of the references to death, but such references were given by one or more children in completion of every opening from 4 onwards. Examples are shown in Table S.C.T.1 below.

TABLE S.C.T.1: *Death references in completion of diverse story openings*

Story Opening No.	Name Age	Story Completion
4	Pamela Q* (10:11)	'They wanted to get rid of their children.'
5	Pamela Q	'Because she had lost something . . . or perhaps somebody died?'
5	John D (11:7)	'Because she hadn't enjoyed herself – perhaps they'd lost one of their children, miss?'
5	Patricia K (8:4)	'Because she'd lost one of her children.' (How?) 'The child was paddling in the water, and a great big fish came up and ate her.'
5	Josie I (7:0)	'Because the father – because somebody might have died down there, the father or anybody.'
6	George K (9:3)	(Long silence; then speech hurried and indistinct.) '. . . don't mind saying . . . a boy just say . . . that his mother was dead.'
7a	Lily O (10:5)	'About someone would come in her room and kill her.'
7b	Lily O	'Like someone in her family might have died or gone away in hospital while she was in bed.'

* The initial in each case is not that of the surname, but represents the intelligence ranking from A(high) to Z(low), e.g. D represents I.Q. 129–31 and V represents I.Q. 71–3

8a	Ralph O (9:10)	'He dreamed that somebody had been took off in a lonely lane and when they found him he went to be hanged.'
8b	Albert I (10:1)	'A burglar had got in his window and took all the things away and smashed up the home and killed his mother and father.'
9	Albert I	'His mother and father to come back to life again; and to have his home back, and all the furniture and stuff back.'
10	Eric G (10:9)	'Stay little for a long time; then he would live a bit longer.'
11	Josie I (7:0)	'Save it, and buy something nice – a present for her mother or a bunch of flowers to put on her father's grave.'

Is the frequency of death references in this test situation due to the stimulation of fantasies unrepresentative of the child's usual manner and content of thought? This question may be answered by consideration of the degree to which the children appeared to identify the people in the stories with themselves and their relatives. Here it must at once be noted that the fantasy nature of the suggestion and situation encouraged the child *not* to make a complete identification, to which they often cheerfully responded. Thus Josie I, quoted twice in Table S.C.T.1 above, had both parents living; she had killed her father off only in fantasy. Nevertheless there was frequent evidence of close identification, of which instances are given in Table S.C.T.2 below.

TABLE S.C.T.2: *Identification of subject with child in story*

Story Opening No.	Name	Age	Story Completion
6	Ernest V (9:1)		'Showed shop where he took apples and oranges. Ronnie Morris takes oranges from the shop with me.'
7a	Margaret C (4:8)		'Snow White. I heard her on the wire-

IMAGINING

		less but I haven't seen her. I've seen her dead, there, in a story book, and going to live with the prince. . . . They were lovely pictures.'
7a	Ian S (8:3)	'I am caught in a trap now! He'd better go to sleep. I generally go to sleep. Everybody does, don't they?'
7b	Bill H (7:0)	'Because he was cold. He had no clothes on him much.'
8b	Willie K (6:7)	'Because it was so dark, and he thought it was someone in his house, a ghost or somebody, or a burglar. I suppose he heard a sound, a noise. . . . That's what I'm frightened of . . . because I went to the pictures and I saw a man with eyes as big as that! . . . He killed 'isself . . . I think about bears with him and all.' (Were there bears in the picture?) 'No, but I just think about them, too. I think of them under the bed. Then I run downstairs to my mum . . .'
9	Bill H (7:0)	'He wished he could be a good boy for always . . . that he could grow up as a man and have a motor car, and have good jobs. And . . . to keep his handkerchief and not always have a dirty nose in school.'
10	Bert D (9:8)	(When grown up, wants to be) 'an air pilot. My uncle used to be a pilot, but he got killed in a crash.'
11	Ernest V (9:1)	'Spend it on toys, what I'm going to do, railway set; lot of milk and biscuits to eat.'

The child's identification of self with the 'hero' may be shown, alternatively, by signs of conflict about responding. Thus two nine-year-old boys completed each opening readily until 8b, to which one repeated 'Frightened, frightened' distractedly, before fitting a reply into a fantasy-series about bird's-nesting, while the other, after long silence, said 'Don't know'. Margaret F (7:8) to many openings responded only by soundlessly opening and shutting her mouth, but completed opening 10 with: 'She wanted to grow up. To have a house to herself.'

How do the children seen in clinics compare with the rest? The percentage of these children who referred to death or allied concepts was found to be slightly below the average. The difference was not statistically significant. Responses suggesting psychological distress, such as those of Margaret F, occurred not only in the clinic. Some of the children diagnosed as requiring psychotherapeutic treatment, however, responded in a manner not typical of the general sample; the examples shown in Table S.C.T.3 below were, except in one case, given by children under treatment who were not members of the sample.

TABLE S.C.T.3: *Completions by children diagnosed as psychiatrically disturbed*

Story Opening No.	Name Age	Story Completion
1	Charlie R* (7:0)	'Because the little boy was naughty, and when it was over the little boy never went up, and a master told the little boy to go down and he never took no notice, so a policeman came to school and said to the master, "Anyone been naughty?" . . . said he would put the little boy in prison, no food, nothing, won't see his mother any more.* Then the little boy promised to be good. Then he went out and got lost, went on a charabanc, fell off, broke his head, the doctor couldn't fix his head on.'
7a	Peter V (8:2)	'He thought about Jesus. He say, "Oo, would you come in my house, please?"'

* Charlie's mother was a patient, resident in a mental hospital

8b	Ernest V (9:0)	'Someone in the bed might do something to his eyes, would bash into something, happened to kid up the road, cut her head off and she came to dinner next day.'
5	Edna K (11:1)	'Because the little girl was very ill, and the mother was sad because of another reason. The father got in a smash and he was dead, so she had only her little girl, and now this poor little girl nearly died. The lady run for a doctor and a nurse and a lot more doctors. They cured the little girl but ... she died at convalescent, and the lady she went silly, and that was why she was so unhappy.'

The question then arises: what does death mean to the children in the sample as a whole – not necessarily the deeply disturbed children represented in Table S.C.T.3 – when they make such references. Since no such reference is made in the story openings, the opening themes offer evidence of contexts in which the thought may spontaneously occur to the child. There was clustering of death references around openings 5, 7b and 8b. Here the cues were of sorrow and of fear; first, the sorrow of a mother, then that of a child; then the fear of a child in the night. When the mother's grief is suggested, it tends to be attributed to the loss of a child or (less frequently) of the child's father; that of the child, to the loss of one or both parents. In both these contexts, death is conceived as distressing separation. When fear is the cue, the reference to death may either appear in the context of violent aggression from an external source – external, that is, to the home – or in shadowy or ghostly form, in which case it seems to point to a source within the home. In both versions the fear appears to be excited by aggression, in the former case directly, in the latter, as a consequence of the child's own previous aggressive fantasy against another person. Lily O and Albert I (Table S.C.T.1, p. 81) imagine death as aggression, with subsequent retaliation (Lily) or reparation (Albert). Ghosts appear in this context, as for instance in the responses of Edna L (7:0) shown below. (This child, both of whose parents were living, looked miserable and undernourished.)

TABLE S.C.T.4: *Fantasies of death, ghosts and resurrection*

Story Opening No.	Story Completion by Edna L (7:0)
5	(Mother sad) ''cos the father died.'
7a	(In bed E thought) 'somebody was coming in her house.'
7b	(She cried) ''cos her father died.' (What happened then?) 'She died herself.'
8a	(She dreamed) 'that somebody walked in her house and made her frightened.'
9	(She wished) 'that her father would come alive again.' (And then?) 'A little pony.'

Against the background in which it most commonly appeared spontaneously in the children's fantasy, death is seen as typically a sorrow-bringing thing and a fear-bringing thing, grievous because it involves separation of child and parent, or of parents from each other, and frightening as the consequence of malevolence in action, either one's own or that of other people. When the idea occurred in the context of the mother's sorrow on return from a family outing, it was often suggested that a child had been drowned. This may have been due to the environment of these children, most of whom lived in south-east London not far from the river. A family excursion tended to suggest a trip to estuary or seaside. Psychoanalytic sessions with individual children might have provided data to show that death in this form represented an unconscious thought of return to the womb. Freddie L feared that the burglar who killed him would put his body in a sack and throw it in the river. Such fantasies tempt the depth-psychologist. Since most of these children were interviewed only twice, it was judged that the material did not provide a basis for the construction of interpretations derived from the psychoanalysis of other subjects, adult or child. In a few cases, however, longer-term relationships permitted some testing of associations suggested by the story-responses.

Freud, in his paper on *The Uncanny*,[1] referring to the theme of the sandman who tears out children's eyes, writes: 'This fear of damaging or losing one's eyes is a terrible fear of childhood.' He adds that it is often a substitute for the dread of castration. In our sample the educationally subnormal and extremely disturbed boy, Ernest V, provided the only record of a child frightened for his eyes. This child referred to his father as dead, disclaimed any wish to have him back, and gave responses replete with aggressive fantasy and regressive wishes. In orthodox Freudian analysis, death has to be traced to some other unconscious idea as source, since Freud stated that death itself has no unconscious correlative. Ernest's fantasies of death referred to others, not to himself, and should perhaps be interpreted in terms of fear externalized in aggression. (He was not a member of the sample studied by the writer, but the patient of a colleague; it is not known whether he was diagnosed as suffering from castration anxiety.) Anna Freud[2] interprets fear of death as a cover for castration anxiety in an account of psychoanalytic treatment of a boy. A research carried out at Yale found a relationship between fear of death and castration anxiety.[3] Behaviour attributable to castration anxiety appeared rarely in our research, perhaps mainly because we were not giving the term so wide a connotation as is done by psychoanalysts. It remains possible for the data quoted to be reinterpreted.

The frequent sea and river themes used by the children in completing the stories may have been a consequence of their east London environment, but there was no environmental clue to the persistently recurrent theme of bird's-nesting. Its appearance in the responses of the few rural boys would not have seemed

[1] (1953 edn, vol. 17,) 1919
[2] A. Freud, *The Psychoanalytic Treatment of Children*, 1946
[3] I. Sarnoff and S. M. Corvin, 'Castration anxiety and fear of death', *Journal of Personality*, 27, 1959

remarkable, but frequent fantasies on this theme occurred in the responses of the children resident in London's dockland, where trees and visible bird's-nests are rare, though sea-gulls, sparrows and pigeons are common enough. Kaldegg[1] and Foulds[2] have also noted the frequency of references to bird's-nesting in schoolboys' responses. In several of the completion-series in our sample the bird in the nest with the eggs seemed to symbolize the mother with her young, or her fertility, while the child appeared to be exercising unconscious aggression in an attempt to steal or destroy this fertility. The combination of simplicity and complexity in such fantasies may be illustrated by the latter part of George D's series. George was interviewed at the clinic which served the dockland schools. An early mastoid infection had left him deaf in one ear, and he had been supposed slow or stupid at school, though his I.Q. proved to be high (129). He came from a good home, from which he had been separated for a considerable period at the age of five years on the occasion of the mastoid operation.

TABLE S.C.T.5: *Bird's-nesting and Oscillation*

Story Opening No.	Story Completion by George D (8:3)
6	(The other boy) 'had been cruel to a bird and taken its nest away and by accident dropped the eggs and broken them. But the boy liked animals, and told his mother, who told the other boy's mother.'
7a	(In bed he thought) 'about the trouble he had got into for breaking the bird's nest; his mother told him that to the birds he was like a giant.'
7b	'He had dreamed that a giant had taken him away, and he knew it was God's punishment for breaking the eggs, and he never did such a cruel thing again.'

[1] Kaldegg, *op. cit.*
[2] G. A. Foulds, 'Characteristic projection test responses in a group of defective delinquents', *British Journal of Psychology*, 40, 3, 1950

8b   'For the dream had frightened him so much he cried out for his mother, and then he said he was only dreaming and it was about giants.'

9   (He wished) 'that animals would like him, and that he would never break an egg again, and that he would always be kind to dogs – to weak creatures.'

10   (He wished) 'to stay a child always . . . to play with birds and dogs, and friends as well.'

11   (With £100,000) 'he bought lots of kinds of animals, had a bird-haven, and a beast-haven, and people came to buy eggs from the creature-haven, and one of his hens laid a golden egg . . . pure gold, and he could spend it.' (What did he spend it on?) 'On more hens.'

Kaldegg found that a response about aggressive bird's-nesting tended to be followed by a response about punishment from the father. In George's series, the theft is followed by retaliation from a father-figure (a giant, God), then by his own identification with this figure, and then by his provision of a haven as reparation to his victims, and his own admission to that haven, which we may interpret as God's heaven. He has, however, renounced with his aggressive impulses the wish to be an adult father, to grow up, though not his wish to possess the female and her young.

George's responses appear to illustrate his manner of resolving the Oedipus conflict in this stage which Freud called the latency period. They also illustrate a feature of children's fantasy which is frequently found in series which include death references. This is an oscillation between two figures, in which they alternately die and reappear, or in which a single figure alternates between death and rebirth or resurrection. A sequence of this kind has already been given in Edna's responses (Table S.C.T.4, p. 86). Patricia K told of the child being eaten by a big fish (Table S.C.T.1, p. 81); later, however, 'the mother heard someone crying in the bedroom, and it was a lovely new baby for her, and the same name as the other little girl'. A similar oscillation, either of aggressor and victim or of the death and rebirth of a single victim, occurs in the responses of Lily O and Albert I in the same table. In the cited analysis by Anna Freud the father-figure in the boy's dream repeatedly lives at his son's call and dies at the mother's.

The oscillation found in the children's fantasies was sometimes expressed in terms of primitive talion or tit-for-tat. Thus Freddie G (8:8) was told by his friend the secret 'that he knocked some boy out, and people didn't know who done it, but he [Freddie] went and let it out on him'. The series continues: (7a) [Freddie] 'thought about the boy who told him about knocking out the boy; (7b) he felt unhappy because he hurt himself; (8a) he dreamed about the boy knocking *him* out; (8b) he was frightened because the boy was just about to knock him out, and he woke up with the fright; (9) and wished for a pair of boxing gloves'.

This oscillation of fantasy-aspect seems to resemble the oscillation or shifting of pattern of visually perceived figures, which may occur when the eyes are fixed on a pattern of dots or lines in ambiguous perspective, or on a picture in which figure and ground admit of alternative interpretations. The change occurs independently of the observer's volition. The phases are mutually exclusive.

The visual stimulus is actually identical throughout. In the oscillations of fantasy, two persons or states are seen to be involved, as for instance the father and child in Edna's and George's fantasies, the mother and child or the child's condition relative to the mother in Patricia's. This gives a clue to the derivation of the fantasy process. Oscillation occurs when figures or conditions of a single figure are being identified. It may be that an impulse towards identification of figures or of conditions causes the original pattern to form and starts the movement of oscillation. The child, for example, may desire to take the father's place and, while remaining himself, monopolize the affection of the mother. In fantasy-fulfilment of the wish he then identifies himself with the father; the figure then oscillates between the identified forms. The identification process which originates the oscillation (by this hypothesis) may have a regressive element. The earliest perceptions of the child, it is assumed, lack discrimination of subject and object, of persons as distinct from self. The child is then perceptually immanent in the parent, the parent in the child. In imagining himself as parent the child therefore has a pattern already laid down in his earlier ways of thinking, to which he may *reculer pour mieux sauter*.

There is as yet no technique by which to check the hypothesis of similarity of process of oscillation in visual perception and in fantasy. In this hypothesis, the condition of basic identity is common to both processes. There is, however, an important functional difference between them; in fantasy, successive phases influence each other. In both fantasy and sensory oscillatory processes the completion of a later phase brings adjustment of a balance which the persistence of the earlier phase has upset. In the sensory operation these adjustments may be measured physiologically. In fantasy, it may be expressed in ethical terms: *It serves you right! Tit for tat!* In the sensory process, the original phase may return apparently unchanged; in fantasy, however, the reversion involves revision. Substitution of father by child implies the destruction of the father, which was, in a sense, desired; but when the pattern oscillates, will not the child be similarly destroyed? This is frightening; in fantasy, it occurs; as Edna says, *She died herself* (Table S.C.T.4, p. 86). Fear leads to remorse about the initial destruction; a sense of guilt (*I ought not to have done it*) which is embryonic in so far as the regret is due to the boomerang effect rather than the success of the aggressive impulse. In fantasy that impulse is then negated; reparation is made; the parent is restored to life. Will this save or destroy the child? With a fairy-wish it seems possible that the child may in some form also be resurrected (as a little pony, perhaps) or stay a child always, like George, in heaven where God is the father.

Retaliation occurs at many levels of social behaviour, from the impulsive returning of blow for blow by young animals at play, to the nuclear tests arranged successively by great powers. Social deprecation of retaliatory behaviour tends to obscure the distinction between this and unrestrained violence or sadism. In

THE DISCOVERY OF DEATH

retaliation, an attempt is made to right a balance. It therefore pre-supposes a supporting framework within which both parties should be maintained in equilibrium. The liberty, equality and fraternity of individuals are implied in the process of retaliation. It is not a function of the subservient; only those of approximately equal status may gain morally by voluntary renunciation of it. It is an ethical procedure, though not an expression of the ethic which is generally rated most highly in Western civilizations.

The process of oscillation which retaliation represents in the ethical field involves reciprocal functions of members without change in the total pattern of interaction. Alternation of role of victim and avenger is designed to preserve equilibrium; but how prevent a ding-dong struggle, a perpetual vendetta? When succeeding phases leave cumulative deposits of emotion, none exactly reproduces an earlier phase; simple antagonisms which initially work out in blow for blow become complicated activities wherein victory and loss for one become victory and loss for both. Meanwhile the members of the groups, or the common group, to which the antagonists belong, if not deeply implicated personally, see the alternating phases as a single phase of conflict, to which its own alternative, peace, might succeed. The imposition of this view upon the confused antagonists may effect a transition to a new synthesis with super-ordinate oscillation: mutual hate and aggression may become mutual love and co-operation. The slaughter and blood-guilt of the house of Atreus culminates in communal sacrifice and the worship of gods more rational and serene than the Furies.

George's, Edna's and Josie's fathers had not actually died. In the families of some of our subjects there had been actual, recent death. What form did the fantasies of these children take? The question is part of a larger one: how do children mourn the loss of a loved object? Do they carry on the work of mourning, as Freud called it, in the same way as adults?[1] Here we shall only attempt to answer that part of the question to which the responses

[1] Martha Wolfenstein answers this in the negative, with full discussion, in M. Wolfenstein and G. Kliman (eds.), *Children and the Death of a President*, 1965

of our subjects and the observations of other students of childhood provide clues.

In Griffiths's study of imagination in childhood[1] it was reported that a little girl was preoccupied with aggressive impulses (death wishes) against her sister, Dorothy. Her father was dead. A friend called Dorothy also died, and the sister became ill. The child then ceased to express her antagonism towards the sister. Adults generally repress the thought, or at least suppress the expression, of death wishes against others, unless humorously expressed. 'As to the death of another,' Freud wrote, 'the civilized man will carefully avoid speaking of such a possibility in the hearing of the person concerned. Children alone disregard this restriction; unabashed they threaten one another with the eventuality of death, and even go so far as to talk of it before one whom they love. . . . The civilized adult can hardly even entertain the thought of another's death without seeming to himself hard or evil-hearted.'[2] The child, therefore, in the repression described by Griffiths, was maturing. We found as Griffiths did, that when the actual death of a member of the family was in question, the child would not refer to it in fantasy. It was noted, however, that though this persisted when an actual death had occurred, there was then no reluctance on the part of the child to refer to the event in reality. The event did, however, affect the character of their fantasy, as will be shown.

The psychiatrist Lindemann has stated that almost all American adults suffering severe bereavement are impaired in their functioning for a period often lasting about six weeks.[3] (It is not suggested that the phenomenon is peculiar to Americans.) The line between pathological and non-pathological mourning behaviour may be difficult to draw. It appears to be a pathological symptom if the mourner takes emergency measures to avoid the painful implications of the mourning process. One of the most

[1] R. Griffiths, *A Study of Imagination in Early Childhood*, 1935, pp. 141 ff.

[2] S. Freud, *Thoughts for the Times on War and Death*, J. M. Tanner (ed.), 1915 (1953 edn, vol. 14)

[3] E. Lindemann, 'Psycho-social factors as stressor agents', *Stress and Psychiatric Disorder*, 1960, p. 14

striking of these measures is selective forgetting. The image of the deceased disappears from consciousness, or returns only in dreams, and will only be recalled with great reluctance during waking hours. This form of pathological behaviour is diametrically opposite to the behaviour observed in bereaved children when in contact with a stranger. The loss appears to be kept in the forefront of consciousness and is readily referred to in serious conversation with a sympathetic adult, but fantasies of the death of the deceased relative are inhibited. There are certain forms of behaviour of bereaved children which appear not abnormal in childhood, but would suggest pathological tendencies in the adult. These will be illustrated later with reference to children's fantasies.

In the paper entitled *Mourning and Melancholia*[1] Freud discussed mourning both as normal and as pathological process. (The term 'depression' is commonly used by English-speaking psychiatrists today in place of 'melancholia'.) He characterized mourning as the reaction to the loss of a loved one. The pathological form of mourning he traced to the mixture of hate with this love, that is, the ambivalence of the relationship. The distinctive features of the pathological state were a lowering of self-regarding feelings, with self-reproach, sometimes culminating in a delusional expectation of punishment; insomnia; self-punishment, such as refusal of food or, in the extreme, suicide. Freud distinguished between two presentations of melancholia, which likewise provide major categories in the current diagnosis of the depressions: one in which the illness, if it does not issue in self-destruction, may be worked through to a remission, as normal mourning is, and one in which there is alternation either with a more normal state or with mania, the latter being marked by excess of energy-expenditure and apparent cheerfulness. In the normal mourning process, memories and hopes involving the lost object are hypercathected (i.e. charged with extreme emotion) prior to being, as it were, emptied and detached from the emotional life. Freud considered that nothing normally prevents this activity proceeding through the preconscious to consciousness, but that in pathological mourning, ambivalence gives rise to

[1] 1917 (1953 edn, vol. 14)

repression, so that the way to consciousness is blocked. The hate which, at an earlier stage, undermined the erotic relationship, had to be hidden from the self; fixation on the object was too strong for the whole relationship to be given up. Identification of self and object therefore persisted after withdrawal of love. After the death of the object, the erotic cathexis, transformed into primal narcissism, functions dissociatively. The hatred felt towards the object, repressed, is now expended upon that part of the self identified with the object.

In our total sample there occurred one known case of the recent death of a mother (Marlene – see p. 50, example A.2), two of a father, and two of siblings. One of the latter will be quoted first.

Ralph O (9:10) was a village boy, interviewed under happy circumstances in the summer-house of a private garden where he and some friends had come to play. Asked about his family, he said he had two elder sisters and a new baby brother; he added, 'I was a twin, and when he was one-and-a-half he died.' His first memory was: 'When I was a twin, my mother kept rocking me about in the cradle, and the more I cried, the more she used to do it.' His completions of story openings 8a and 9 were as follows: 'He dreamed that somebody had been took off in a lonely lane, and when they found him he went to be hanged' (said in a low, hurried voice). [He wished] 'that his . . . that he'd have a happy life, and he wouldn't do anything wrong; and he'd be free.'

The local scoutmaster reported that at the camp fire Ralph would sometimes burst into tears and have to be led away and comforted, though no one knew why he cried. Among his school-fellows he was not regarded as a 'sissie'. There was no doubt, however, of the persistent importance to this boy of the death of his twin eight years earlier, or of his fear of punishment, in the form of imprisonment, and of wrongdoing by fate rather than by his own will. His first memory, which may be later fantasy, tells of unsatisfied longing for more feeding or handling by his mother. A psychoanalyst, Arlow,[1] states that twinship is basically a highly ambivalent relationship fraught with special psychological hazards; in the initial phase there is the wish to possess the breast

[1] J. A. Arlow, 'Fantasy systems in twins', *Psychoanalytic Quarterly*, 29, 1960

and the mother without regard for the sibling. An earlier authority wrote, 'I have myself seen jealousy in a baby and know what it means. He was not old enough to talk, but whenever he saw his foster-brother at the breast, he would grow pale with envy.' [P.R.21.][1] Ralph's record suggests that his infantile tie with his twin, deeply ambivalent, and the twin's subsequent death, resulted in the development of a sense of guilt side by side with that of the concept of death, and by their interaction came a terror of retaliatory punishment. Was his repressed first wish 'That his twin might come alive again'?

Donald H (6:7), unlike Ralph, looked an unhappy child. He was pale, and dark under the eyes. His manner, though friendly, was unremittingly serious; he fidgeted constantly with his fingers. His teacher reported that he was teased by his (London) schoolfellows as a 'sissie', and that a new baby was expected. Preliminary conversation was as follows:
Q: 'Have you any brothers or sisters?' D: 'No ... Mummie had some little babies and they died, every one of them.' Q: 'Before you were born or afterwards?' D: 'After me.' Q: 'Can you remember them?' D: 'Yes, Leslie, when I was about four.'

His story completions, which I shall not interpret, included the following:

TABLE S.C.T. 6

Story Opening No.	Story Completion by Donald H (6:7)
6	(The secret) 'A big hole with something inside it.'
7a	(In bed he thought about) 'the hole with something inside it.'
7b	(He cried) 'because ... there was ... gone out of the hole.'
8a	(He dreamed) 'the thing went out of the hole. When he woke up, he looked in the hole, and there it was.'

[1] Augustine of Hippo, *Confessions*, I, 7 (A.D. 398) (1962 edn, p. 28)

9   'He wished to get up. He wished there was
       nobody there.
       He wished that a burglar wouldn't take
       him.'
10   'Wanted to grow up, go to work.'
11   (He would buy) 'a ring . . . put it on his finger.'

Many researches have been devoted to the problem of relationship between experience of bereavement during childhood and
psychiatric disturbance in adult life. Of death of siblings, one of
the earlier studies was by Rosenzweig,[1] who found that a significantly large proportion of male schizophrenic patients, compared with members of control groups, had experienced death of
siblings, mostly younger than the patient and occurring before the
patient's sixth year. Later studies make the picture less clear. A
diagnosis of schizophrenia may be given in America to patients
who in Europe would be classified as depressive.[2] Studies of
parental bereavement in childhood have in some cases shown high
association with subsequent mental disorder, but later research
suggests that, in England, such association is significant only for
in-patients (i.e. severe) depressives bereaved of the mother before
age 15.[3]

Turning to the cases in our sample in which the child had
recently suffered the loss of the father, we find in Bernard N (8:2)
a fear of imprisonment like that expressed by Ralph O (p. 95
above). Bernard, interviewed in his London school, was of

[1] S. Rosenzweig, 'Sibling death as a psychological experience with special
reference to schizophrenia', *Psychoanalytic Review*, 30, 1943
[2] S. Rosenzweig and D. Bray, 'Sibling deaths in the anamnesis of schizophrenic patients', *Archives of Neurological Psychiatry*, 49, 1943
[3] A. Munro and A. B. Griffiths, 'Further data on childhood parent-loss in
psychiatric normals', *Acta Psychiatrica Scandinavica*, 44, 4, 1968, and 'Some
psychiatric non-sequelae of childhood bereavement', *British Journal of Psychiatry*,
115, 1969, supply references, and cover English and Scottish normal and psychiatric patient samples. O. Bratfös, 'Parental deprivation in childhood and type
of future mental disease', *Acta Psychiatrica Scandinavica*, 43, 4, 1967, reviews a
large Norwegian sample, mainly rural, suffering various kinds of deprivation

healthy, attractive appearance. Relevant to our purpose are preliminary questions and parts of the Terman-Merrill test as well as
the Story Completion test. They are tabulated together below.

TABLE S.C.T.7 *etc.*: *Responses of Bernard N (8:2)*

Q: 'What's your name?' B: 'Bernard.' Q: 'And your other name?'
B: 'Don't know.' Q: 'What's your mummie's name?' B: 'Mrs [N].'
Q: 'And your dad?' B: 'Haven't got a dad.' Q: 'Any brothers or
sisters?' B: 'Yes.' Q: 'How many in your family?' B: 'Eight; there
would have been nine if my dad was alive. . . . He died up Kennington
Park. He was so glad he had the baker's job, and he was ill of a night,
and he fell down, and a policeman [came and told the mother he had
died.] My mum was crying . . .'

Terman-Merrill test

(a) Q: 'What is silly about this: a man called one day at the post
office and asked if there was a letter waiting for him. "What is
your name?" asked the postmaster. "Why", said the man, "you
will find my name on the envelope." ' B: 'He didn't tell him his
name . . . he wouldn't tell him his name, because he didn't want
to be put away and put in the police station.'
(b) Q: 'What's the thing for you to do when you have broken
something which belongs to someone else?' B: 'Get put away in
a home. . . . Where all the other naughty boys go.'
(c) Q: 'What is silly about this: In an old graveyard they have
discovered a small skull which they believe to be that of Nelson
when he was about ten years old.' B: 'Because he was fighting
when he was ten years old. Because he shouldn't go to fight.
Because he shouldn't have joined the army.'
(d) *Definitions.* (i) Obedience. B: 'When you don't disobey God.'
(ii) Dead. B: 'When your father's dead.'

Story Completion test

7a (He thought) 'that there was going to be a war; that he may get
put in prison.'

7b (He was sad) 'because somebody may have hit him or pinched him.'

8b (At night he was frightened) 'because there may have been someone in the house.'

9 (He wished for) 'a magic wand. To change all things into different things. Changed an animal into a man, a real man.'

10 (He wished) 'to stay little; because he didn't like it when he was grown up. He tried to make himself smaller.'

The Opies[1] tell of the traditional negativism of the child asked for his name ('What's your name? Same's me dad's! What's your dad's? Same as mine!'). The schoolchildren interviewed for this research did not respond in this way to us. It is possible that Bernard was uncertain whether his name remained the same after his father's death; more probably his reluctance to give it may be explained by his response to problem (a); he is afraid of being 'put in the police station'. The father's death was announced to the family by a policeman, probably with concern and sympathy. The child, however, connects policemen with punishment. Like Edna (Table S.C.T.4, p. 86), Bernard in fantasy fears that someone may be in the house at night; he imagines a metamorphosis between animal and human, he wants to bring magically into being 'a real man'. Like Eric G (Table S.C.T.1, p. 82) he wants to stay little. Eric said if he did so he would live a bit longer. The boy of Bernard's fantasy goes further; he tries to shrink. In schizophrenia there is frequently a delusion or expressed fear of bodily shrinkage or disappearance.

Bernard knows that in reality he was in no way responsible for his father's death, yet he is obsessionally preoccupied with guilt and social punishment. In the normal fantasies of a little boy his father may be destroyed, and replaced by himself. Now for Bernard, at his father's sudden death, fantasy invades reality. In the fantasy there was retaliation, reparation, oscillation of the two figures. Where will the invasion stop? The child tries to keep them apart. The death of a father must not be the subject of a

[1] I. and P. Opie, *The Lore and Language of Schoolchildren*, 1959, p. 42

story, it must be firmly real. *Dead* means when your father's dead.

What are the psychological processes behind the child's fear and sense of guilt? We may distinguish two processes, both at work here. One is the fact, commonly observed, of regression to earlier modes of behaviour under conditions of emotional stress. Second is what Freud found characteristic of the mentality of the young child, and described as a narcissistic overestimation of subjective mental processes, or a belief in the omnipotence of his own thinking. The baby's needs and desires are met by his mother, and so he is conditioned to associate his desire with others' acts in accordance with that desire.

Two arguments may be advanced against the theory of infantile development of belief in his own efficacy. Parents may suggest that the child is born with a highly effective mechanism for communicating his needs, and is therefore more likely to infer a connection between his actual crying and the adult response than between the wish that impelled the cry and the action taken. Or it may be pointed out that the infant's desires are not invariably fulfilled, so that conditioning to the association between desire and fulfilment would not follow. The latter argument would carry weight if conditioning depended on invariance of the fact or manner of reward, but experiment with animals shows that this is not so; the probability of association within a limited time interval is sufficient. Now, unless the probability were positive that the desires and needs of the baby would be fulfilled within a certain time after the need arose, he would be unlikely to survive. Thus there is built into human psychology, largely owing to long infantile dependence, a tendency to believe that what is wished and vocally demanded will come about. As for the former argument, the importance of vocalization, it is to be noted that the *word*, the *spell*, the *charm* have great importance within the system of narcissistic, magical thinking, along with the magical efficacy often attributed to prayer and the mystery attached to names. Such vocalization, however, appears to be a secondary activity within the system, not its essential foundation.

Narcissistic belief in one's own powers, and also its reduction and denial, would both have survival value within this scheme, the former by assisting the control of physio-psychological reaction to delay in the satisfaction of needs and desires, the latter by promoting the organism's ability to control the physical environment. They subsist in the mentality of the individual in proportions which vary with age, personality and culture. Before he learns to speak the infant finds out that wishes divorced from action, indeed from appropriate action, do not bring about their own consummation. The learning of language often appears to be accompanied by a similar belief to that of the cradle infant, namely, that a vocalized desire involves its fulfilment. Thus one of our subjects, aged 2:2, finding the gate to the road latched above his reach, clearly did not suppose that either his wishing or crying would open it, but on achieving what was for him a new communicative level with the words 'Gake [sic] shut', was evidently not only disappointed but puzzled that it was not opened for him. Words and cries, like wishes, prove to have less power than earlier impulse suggests; this also has to be learned.

Belief in the power of thought, wish and unsupported word is only gradually abandoned. In early years it is accompanied by the attribution to others of a similar power, without recognition of distributed sovereignties because self and others have not initially been clearly distinguished. The infantile non-discrimination of self and object arises in the situation of giving-receiving which is embryonic loving; it persists in the situation of withholding-hurting which is embryonic hating. Later, when discrimination begins, these activities appear as necessarily mutual; if I hate, I am hated; if I love, I am loved. Frustrations aroused by social training and in the sharing of love arouse hate which is felt as dangerous to both sides. Psychoanalysis has made this story familiar and vivid. The child at this stage denies, masters or represses the disapproved impulses as being no part of his *real self* or *ego*, identifies the self with the disapproving parent, and by this means hopes to retain the parent's love, reinforce his own, and strengthen his ability to master reality. The serious illness or the death of a loved-hated object – parent or sibling – acts as a blow against this developing structure. While the reduction of valuation of his own wishes is incomplete and unstable, the event casts doubt upon the element of reciprocal love in the relationship; it seems that the misfortune may be the effect of his ill-wishing, and the child fears the recoil upon himself. The tendency to regression under stress increases the likelihood of reactivation of infantile belief in the power of his own thoughts and wishes at an age when he would normally have outgrown it, with this consequence of irrational anxiety. Such, we believe, was Bernard's situation.

The death of a parent is further distressing because the love-aspect of the relationship has frequently been reinforced by attributing parental discipline to the demands of a super-parent, God or society, between whom and the child the parent is seen to act as a rather endearingly inefficient buffer. The sense of guilt is therefore made more alarming by the sense of exposure to the direct action of a remote and severe authority from which the parent had sought to protect him. *Obedience* now means to Bernard *when you don't disobey God.*

Our records included one case of a father's death in which we formerly found no trace of anxiety or guilt. Further study of this record, however, in the light of the hypothesized relationship between mourning, depression and mania in adults suggests that the psychological state expressed by the child represents a condition contributory to mania in the adult. The following record was made at the interview:

TABLE S.C.T.8: *Responses of Irene M* (7:8)

Notes. Neat, pale, tall, slim, fair child. In intelligence tests, accepts success, considering herself, 'good at that sort of thing'; also accepts failure on grounds that she 'doesn't properly learn about that'. Wants to exhibit her personality, under a quiet manner.

Definition of dead: 'Somebody dies, and they have a funeral, like my daddy did.' Q: 'Any brothers or sisters?' I: 'None . . . but I've got an uncle living with me. Only since my daddy's dead.' Q: 'Your father's brother?' I: 'Well, I don't properly know.' (Smile.) Later she referred to her 'brother', who, she says, 'is not so much of a scholar as I am. He's twelve. He's not my brother, he's my uncle. He won't soon be living with me, because my granny's gone to a convalescent home . . .' (i.e. the grandmother would soon be well enough to have her young son home again).

Story Completion test

---

1 'Well, p'r'aps she had some knitting or something to play with, and never wanted no one to play with her. I'm quite fond of playing on my own . . . I've got a nurse's set. I bought it at Woolworth's.'

2 'Well, if I was her mother I'd say, Now then, you shouldn't quarrel or I'll smack you or tell Daddy about you.'

3 'Well, p'r'aps he went and choked hisself, and the children laughed at him.'

4 'Well, p'r'aps one had some money and the father didn't, 'n they started quarrelling because the little old man wanted some money.'

5 'Well, she might 've lost one of her children, or one of them might 've got hurt.'

6 'Well, she might've had something in her pocket that she never wanted nobody to see.'

7a 'Well, I expect she thought about her mother and father – or the fairies.'

7b 'Well, she might 've . . . her mother might 've gone away, or died, or something like that.'

8a 'Well, I expect she dreamed about all the little fairies was all crowding round her, and one of them made her fairy queen.'

8b 'Well, I suppose she seen her own shadow, and she thought it was someone in the door, and she was frightened of that.'

9 'Well, I expect that she . . . she wished if her mother got lost that she would come back again, and that she should become fairy queen and her brother would become king.'

10 'I'd like to grow up . . . and have a little baby . . . I expect that [is what the little girl would answer].'

11 'A new house, and new furniture in it, and I expect she bought a bracelet or a ring and some new clothes and shoes.'

Q: 'What do you want to be, when you grow up?' I: 'A nurse, to nurse babies.'

The first thing noted in this record is the child's self-love and high self-estimation, observed and recorded before the Story Completion test was administered. It is to be noted also that although she imagines the death of her mother, with subsequent reparation, there is no fantasy-expression of the death of the father who has actually died. Her completion of opening 2 was most unusual, in that she identified herself not with one of the children, but with the mother. This confirms the implication of the previous response, in which she suggested that not playing with children but behaving as an adult (knitting, nursing) was her suitable role. The feature of Irene's responses most likely to strike the reader, however, is the quite sadistic contempt for the father. No sense of guilt or fear of punishment appears in Irene's reactions. Her father's death seems only to have enhanced her assurance of superiority over the father-image. Since we are ignorant of the mother's relations with her family, the analysis of Irene's behaviour necessarily leaves many questions open. During his lifetime one may assume that the little daughter would have liked the father to treat her as a woman, which he would not do. Freud in his paper on *Mourning and Melancholia* wrote that mania, the state which may alternate with depression after bereavement, is marked by behaviour like that of a person for whom a long struggle is suddenly 'crowned with success'. Irene's struggle with what seemed like her father's contempt is now over, and she crowns herself queen in fantasy. It is possible that the relationship between the children preceded the father's death, causing Irene conflict at that time owing to identification with her mother and preoccupation with the conjugal relationship. Her contempt for the dead father and her self-satisfaction are so extreme that they do not seem attributable to a recent chance visit of the young uncle. She has succeeded to her mother in that she now has a mate while her mother has none; her mother, killed off, is resurrected in fantasy only on these terms.

Yet there are signs that Irene is on the defensive. The opening of each completion with the word 'Well' gives an impression of deliberation, with unconscious assumption of an adult role, unusual in a child so young. Her own shadow which frightens her, seen on the door at night, is surely the *doppelgänger* which Rank has explained psychoanalytically and Freud attributed to repression.[1] Other children express fear of a burglar, or someone coming into the house, or a ghost; these are representatives of externalized anxiety; Irene, the supreme narcissist of the sample, fears her own shadow. Rank interpreted the double as, first, an insurance against the destruction of the ego, and later a harbinger of death rather than an assurance of immortality. His time-sequence referred, without definition of aeons or age, to the development both of the human race and the present-day individual. By this interpretation, Irene's shadow symbolizes her own death and testifies to her repressed fear of the consequences of her own impulses.

In these children who have suffered bereavement of a parent or sibling we find complex and extreme forms of reaction to the thought of death. The chances of sampling produced them for our study. None of these four – Ralph, Donald, Bernard, Irene – were seen at child guidance centre or clinic, nor had been referred by school or home for psychiatric advice. Their reactions and fantasies are the special forms occurring under stress, of the reactions and fantasies common to children in the course of their emotional and intellectual development.

[1] O. Rank, 'The *Doppelgänger*', *Imago*, 3, 1914, quoted by S. Freud in *The Uncanny, op. cit.*

CHAPTER 6

ACTING

It is clear that children kill in fantasy. They also kill in reality. The development of the concept of death has practical implications.

Anna Freud has written:

It is a common misunderstanding of the child's nature which leads people to suppose that children will be saddened by the sight of destruction and aggression. Children between the ages of one and two years when put together in a playpen will bite each other, pull each other's hair and steal each other's toys without regard for the other child's unhappiness. They are passing through a stage of development where destruction and aggression play one of the leading parts. If we observe young children at play, we notice that they will destroy their toys, pull off the arms and legs of their dolls or soldiers, puncture their balls, smash whatever is breakable, and will only mind the result because complete destruction of the toy blocks further play. The more their strength and independence are growing the more they will have to be watched so as not to create too much damage, not to hurt each other or those weaker than themselves.[1]

An earlier close observer of infants noted that 'if babies are innocent, it is not for lack of will to do harm, but for lack of strength. . . . Mothers and nurses say they can work such things out of the system by one means or another.'[2]

The saint was evidently doubtful of the success claimed by mothers and nurses. Observations of the behaviour of young children above nursery age show frequent incidence of aggression towards those weaker than themselves. When the victim is an

[1] A. Freud and D. Burlingham, *War and Children*, 1943
[2] Augustine of Hippo, *Confessions*, I, 7 (1962 edn)

animal, the child's violence may contribute to his concept of death. The following examples are quoted first from Susan Isaacs's records and then from our own:

[P.R.22.] Some of the children chased a cat which came into the garden. In digging, Frank (5:3) found a worm, and he and Dan (3:8½) cut it into pieces with the spade, and stamped on it. Paul (3:10½) remarked, 'It's dead now.'

[P.R.23.] Christopher and Dan (3:11) found some worms. Paul (4:0) wanted to kill them as soon as he saw them, and Frank (5:5) squashed some snails which Paul found on a wall.

[P.R.24.] Harold (5:3) found another dead rat in the garden. He and Frank (5:6) stamped on it. [Eleven days later] when the children were changing the water of the goldfish Frank . . . said to the others, 'Shall we stamp on it?' They ran out into the garden with it. (Mrs I) followed after them, but not quite quickly enough. Before she could stop them, they had thrown the fish out into the sand and stamped on it. They stood round and looked at it, rather excited, and obviously wishing they hadn't done it, and Frank said, 'Now, let's put it into water, and then it'll come alive again.' They put it back into the water, but soon saw that it was dead, and later on they buried it in the sand. All the children, including the instigator, Frank, were obviously full of regret at having done this, and a wish that they had the fish back again. (N.B. This was the only incident of its kind in the school.)

[P.R.25.] Priscilla (6:6) wanted to pull a worm into halves, and said she would marry the boy who did. . . . Dan (4:9) eventually did pull the worm in halves. Frank (6:4) then pulled the rest of it apart; they were very excited about this.

[H.R.23.] Timothy (3:11), with Judith (7:6), found, after rain, a washed-up worm. J: 'Don't tread on it, Tim: it may not be dead.' T: 'I like it to be dead' (treading on it).

[H.R.24.] Richard (3:0) accidentally killed a kitten by dropping it, together with his teddy bear, into a bin containing a residue of egg-preservative. This kitten was very small, adopted too early from the litter because its mother had been run over, but Richard was at first nervous of it, and would run round it saying, 'He won't hurt me, he won't hurt me', keeping his toes out of its reach. He had recently overcome his timidity to the extent of holding and fondling the kitten.

[H.R.25.] Richard (4:7): 'I killed the black cat. I cut it in half in the coal shed, with a chopper.' M: 'Oh, why did you do that?' R: 'I thought we didn't want it any more.' M: 'Could I see the body?' R: 'No, it isn't there now. I stucked it together again, and it walked away.' (M's note: We have no cat; neighbours have a black cat in which R has been interested.)

[H.R.26.] R (5:1): There was a drowsy bee crawling about us when we were having tea in the garden; M brushed it off R; we all watched it; finally R said he would tread on it. M: 'Don't; it won't hurt you if you leave it alone.' But a little later R did tread on it, and seemed pleased with himself.

[H.R.27.] R (5:3) (to M, not heard distinctly): 'Jean and I . . . go out for a walk . . . find ants, to tread on them.' (Jean is a friend aged about 4:3.)

[H.R.28.] R (5:4) wanted M to kill an earwig which she found in an apple, but she did not want to do so. He then wanted to kill it himself. M gave it to him in a piece of paper. He took it out on the stone step, and a knife; M did not watch this. He then returned cheerfully to the kitchen, saying, 'It moved, very slowly, the first time after it was dead. Why did it do that, Mother?' He then returned, cut it into little bits, and came back with the knife.

[H.R.29.] Ben (8:6), Richard (5:4), David (5:4) at tea with M. D: 'I love wasps; because we kill them.' B: 'Oh, do you? I don't. One stung me once, on the nose.' R (with beaming smile, like D's): 'Yes, I love killing things, too.' B: 'I hate killing things' (continuing with a long statement of non-aggressive sentiment, and a reference to nature).

[H.R.30.] Ben (9:1) and Richard (5:11) in the garden with their father. R: 'Here's a nice thin worm.' B (angrily): 'Why did you kill him? . . . You mustn't do that; it hurts them, doesn't it?' (to F). F: 'Yes . . .' R: 'It doesn't matter, with *worms* . . . I like to watch them.' F: 'Well then, *watch* them.' R: 'That one's gone suddenly long.'

[H.R.31a.] Ben (8:5) preparing to go to the Zoological Gardens with his grandmother. M: 'Have you a clean handkerchief in your pocket?'

B: 'Yes, and I've got my pen-knife, in case I want to kill anyone.' (He
then amended this, saying he might want to kill an animal and bring
its skeleton home.)

Those who observe with scientific intent the behaviour of
children often seem to protest too much that the individual infant
is not actually the little monster he appears to be. For instance,
Jung, reporting a conversation between a father and daughter
(aged four) during the birth of a younger sibling ([P.R.26.] F:
What would you say, if you got a little brother tonight? Anna:
I would kill him) appends, *kill* is a perfectly harmless expression
on the lips of a child, only meaning, to get rid of, as pointed out
a number of times by Freud.[1] Isaacs, after the record of Priscilla
(6:6) quoted above, adds, 'It should be noted how few instances
of actual cruelty are recorded against Priscilla.' [H.R.31b.] When
Richard (5:3), finding a dead mouse in the garden, asked 'Can I
tread on it?', prodded it with a stick, and seemed disappointed
that a small animal which was at his mercy could not be an object
for a display of power on his part, it was also noted that he did
not seem to wish to cause it *pain*. Sully[2] reported similarly; he
refers to 'that odd mixture of sociability and love of power'
marking the child's relationship with animals.

The adult's tendency to exonerate the child may appear sentimental. *Kill* may be, as Jung says, a harmless expression, but
babies may need to be protected from children not much older
than themselves who may actually injure them. Should Richard's
mother hand him earwigs to cut up? Should he be discouraged
from killing earwigs but permitted to kill wasps? If he kills wasps,
should he be censured for enjoying that activity? Dr Isaacs appears
so anxious to show that all children resemble parents in having
impulses of both cruelty and tenderness that she is led to disregard
differences between children's and parents' behaviour, and perhaps also differences between children themselves, in this respect.

The tendency to exonerate the child is so general, among

---

[1] C. G. Jung, *The Development of Personality*, 1954
[2] J. Sully, *Studies of Childhood*, 1895, p. 240

observers whom we have reason to hold both trustworthy and sophisticated, that it must be given some weight. The observer is in a position to judge from the child's accompanying behaviour (facial expression, gestures etc.) how the recorded activity should be interpreted. It is rarely if ever possible to place all such data on the written record; interpretation is inevitable. The concern of the parent or teacher, however, is usually not so much with the validity of the psychologist's interpretation of observed aggressive actions of the young child as with its prognostic implications. Does it signify that sadism or other anti-social activities will be characteristic of the individual child's personality in later life?

To his analysis of a five-year-old boy Freud[1] added a postscript many years later, stating that the child had developed a stable personality. It may be similarly appended here of Timothy and of Richard, more than twenty years after the observations recorded above, that in the course of their careers in different families, schools, national military service, professions and often different continents, neither has been the subject of a diagnosis of maladjustment or neurosis, or accused of bullying, cruelty, sadism or masochism. Although treading on worms and cutting up earwigs are not practices which the adult would choose to encourage in the child, such behaviour does not appear to be psychologically abnormal or prognostic of disordered personality.

The home records show fairly consistent behavioural differences between children. One type, of which Clifford Sully seems an extreme example, abhor killing, while another, which Richard and Timothy may exemplify, openly enjoy killing small animals, until about their seventh year, when enjoyment in playing with them seems to become stronger than the desire to kill them. The fact that Richard, David and Timothy were all younger siblings with no sib younger than themselves suggests that the impulse to act out mastery against smaller living things occurs most frequently in such circumstances. This was also the position of the boy Carrots[2] in Renaud's autobiographical sketch. Clifford Sully,

---

[1] S. Freud, *Analysis of a Phobia in a Five-year-old Boy*, 1909 (1953 edn, vol. 10)
[2] J. Renaud, *Poil de Carotte*, 1895

however, was also a younger child with no younger sib, which casts doubt on the generalization.

The observer who may tend to exonerate the aggressive child may be moved not only by appreciation of the complexity of his immediate motivation but also by experience of variation of his behaviour. The child's aggressive impulses and actions contribute to his concept of death, but impulses of avoidance or prevention of death may be observed as early as aggressive actions, sometimes in the same child.

The studies of Rasmussen and of Sully provide examples of children's reactions to death at earlier ages than any in our own records. The boy whom Sully notes as being uneasy after killing a fly (p. 51, A.3 above) was only 2:2 years old. Ben was a year older when he asked the meaning of the word *dead*. Shortly after, it was recorded:

[H.R.32.] Ben (3:3) picked some buttercups and then immediately threw them away. M suggested it was a pity not to keep them longer, but he said, 'No, 'cos they'll go dead.'

This spontaneous behaviour suggests a distaste for contact with objects associated with death, quite independent of any process of decomposition of animal flesh, or even the withering of the plant. The idea of dying, rather than the consequence, appears to have aroused the avoidance impulse in the child.

The desire to prevent death also appears to arise at a very early age. Isaacs observed: The children had found various insects and put them into a bowl of water.

[P.R.27.] Tommy (3:3) protested, 'These things don't live in water' [and the next day he] insisted on taking a worm out of the water when the others put it in, saying, 'They don't live in water – they don't *live* in water.'

[P.R.28.] Of Clifford Sully (3:6) it was recorded that 'like other children', he was at this time much troubled about the killing of animals for food; 'again and again he would ask with something of fierce impatience in his voice: "Why do people kill them?" ... He contended that people who eat meat must like animals to be killed. Finally, to clinch the matter, he turned on his mother and asked, "Do *you* like them to be killed?" '

[P.R.29.] Another of Dr Isaacs's children, Dan (3:6), was deeply concerned on behalf of a small dead rat found in the garden by the children. 'They said, "It's dead", and ran about holding it.' Mrs I took it away for fear of infection. Dan said, 'You won't hurt it, will you?' She took it to the other end of the garden, and hid it. Dan asked her, 'Where have you put it – you've not hurt it, have you?'

The last of these records demonstrates the limited comprehension of *dead* under four years of age even in a child of high intelligence. The behaviour of the children in general suggests an unconscious identification of the self with the small animal. It is not supposed that such identification is a simple thing, fully accounting for the observed behaviour.

The conflict aroused in the child between impulse and conscience, in the context of aggression towards smaller creatures, is the subject of a passage in Charles Darwin's autobiography, of particular interest as the contribution of so supremely skilled a naturalist. He was himself the fifth of six children, with one brother older than himself:

[P.R.30.] 'I can say in my own favour that I was as a boy humane, but I owed this entirely to the instruction and example of my sisters. I doubt indeed whether humanity is a natural or innate quality. I was very fond of collecting eggs, but I never took more than a single egg out of a bird's nest, except on one single occasion, when I took all, not for their value, but from a sort of bravado. I had a strong taste for angling. . . . When . . . told that I could kill the worms with salt and water . . . from that day I never spitted a living worm, though at the expense probably of some loss of success. Once as a very little boy . . . I acted cruelly, for I beat a puppy, I believe, simply from enjoying the sense of power; but the beating could not have been severe, for the puppy did not howl. . . . This act lay heavily on my conscience . . . probably all the heavier from my love of dogs being then, and for a long time afterwards, a passion.[1]

This passage, pre-Freudian and obviously sincere, is full of

[1] *The Life and Letters of Charles Darwin*, F. Darwin (ed.), 1888, vol. 1, ch. 2, pp. 29–30

points of interest: there was a desire to deprive the mother-bird of all its eggs, which conscience forbade; conscience was once defied over this prohibition, and also once when a puppy, passionately loved, was beaten, by a younger of two brothers. In his doubt whether *humanity* is innate, Darwin makes no distinction between the sexes, though his reference to learning it from his sisters suggests a belief that girls tend to be more humane than boys. Wordsworth, who, like Darwin, lost his mother at the age of eight, also suggests this:

> Oh! pleasant, pleasant were the days,
> The time, when, in our childish plays,
> My sister Emmeline and I
> Together chased the butterfly!
> A very hunter did I rush
> Upon the prey: with leaps and springs
> I followed on from brake to bush;
> But she, God love her, feared to brush
> The dust from off its wings.

If the boy, in a particular social environment, tends to learn *humanity* from girls or women, the question remains open whether the girl is innately more predisposed to learn this lesson herself, or is influenced by a more consistently persuasive social environment, or whether both factors are present and interactive. Shakespeare, in *Macbeth*, suggests no difference between the sexes in cruel impulse, but the woman found she could not carry out the murder herself ('Had he not resembled my father as he slept, I had done't'), and in *King John*, when the king arranges for the murder of his child nephew, his mother, the child's grandmother, is present, not objecting, and dismisses John with her blessing. In describing the cruel behaviour of a little boy in *Coriolanus* Shakespeare presents it through the eyes of two women who are delighted by the child's inhumanity. They attribute it, admittedly, to inheritance from the father, whose violently aggressive character their society has taught them to approve, and which one of them has fostered. The child's mother is of a gentler character; Shakespeare seems to have observed individual but not general sex differences in the characteristic which, nowadays, we hardly dare to call humanity.

VALERIA: How does your little son?

VIRGILIA: I thank your ladyship; well, good madam.

VOLUMNIA: He had rather see the swords, and hear a drum, than look upon his schoolmaster.

VALERIA: O' my word, the father's son; I'll swear, 'tis a very pretty boy. O' my troth, I looked upon him o' Wednesday half an hour together; he has such a confirmed countenance. I saw him run after a gilded butterfly; and when he caught it, he let it go again; and after it again; and over and over he comes, and up again; catched it again; or whether his fall enraged him or how 'twas, he did so set his teeth, and tear it: O, I warrant, how he mammocked it!

VOLUMNIA: One of his father's moods.

Among Dr Isaacs's children Priscilla, like Lady Macbeth, incites the male to violence which she does not herself perform. In our home records Judith suggests Timothy should not kill, but on another occasion she herself, half in fun, longs for the death of a little boy:

[H.R.33.] Judith (6:11), returning with M from escorting to a bus an aged aunt: 'I think it is time aunt F died now; it would be better for her. May I go to her funeral when she does die? I should like to. Will you go?' M: 'No.' J: 'Well, if Granny or Uncle S died, would you go?' M: 'I might.' J: 'Then can I go too?' M: 'Children aren't taken to funerals; they are such sad things. . . . You might one day watch a funeral in [the local] cemetery of someone that doesn't belong to us.' J, emphatically and with glee: 'I should love to go to Thomas O's funeral; he is an awful little boy, and can't spell, and takes hours to write anything; I simply hate him!'

Violence is found more characteristic of the male sex in man, and in many animals differences in aggressiveness are found to be associated with sex. But in human beings the biological and cultural factors in aggressive behaviour are so difficult to untangle that no confident assertion can be made that the male is innately more aggressive than the female. Infants of both sexes may attack others physically; both require training and physical restraint against aggression in the nursery. A child's aggressive behaviour may result in the grievous harm or even death of the victim. A fatal consequence may not be accidental. But murder by a child of normal intelligence, though not unknown, is extremely rare. One such event, by a little girl, not neglected or impoverished, has recently been recorded in England. Without information about the intimate circumstances of this particular case, general observation may suggest the pressures giving rise to such behaviour. The cultural process which restrains aggression may also impose frustrations intensifying aggressiveness. If aggression is restrained against a specific object without emotional relief or social redirection, the frustration which aroused that aggression may redirect it against substitutes. This child had a younger brother. In many cultures a daughter is little valued compared with a son, and a loved first-born girl may suffer bitterly when a boy follows. Where this is the traditional and complete cultural pattern, girls generally accept the social norm even with grace. In our own culture traces of the same tradition survive, but variably; a little girl who suffers may not be socially conditioned to acquiesce, but driven to victimize those she identifies with her younger sibling as source of her distress.

Fortunately the impulse of children to kill something smaller than themselves is usually directed towards animals, and restrained by a tendency to identify themselves with the animal, or wish to play with it. When Dr Isaacs organized the dissection of a dead mouse, the record shows these competing impulses at work in children under seven, and our own records of spontaneous activity at the same age testify to what Sully described as the odd mixture of sociability and love of power characteristic of the young child's relationship with animals. For example:

[P.R.31.] At the beginning of the dissection Priscilla (6:10) again had some qualms, and wanted to be assured that they were 'not hurting them'. She also said, 'You wouldn't do this to us, would you?' While dissecting, Priscilla and Dan (5:1) carried on a play of 'mother' and 'doctor', with the dead mice as children. They pretended to telephone to each other about it, saying, 'Your child is better now. . . .' P telephoned to D: 'Your child is cut in two.' D replied, 'Well, the best thing to do is to put the two halves together again.'

[H.R.34.] Richard (6:1). While gardening, M and R found a woodlouse. R, delighted, carried it off to the porch on a trowel; watched it for about a quarter of an hour, hedging it off from escaping, and then said he wanted to keep it in a box. M said that would be rather cruel to it; it would not like to be away from the ground. This did not deter R, who procured a tin with a lid. He put the insect in this, and then was fetched to go to bed; as he went upstairs he said, 'I do like being cruel to animals.'

[H.R.35.] Richard (6:4) during a stay in the country enjoyed chasing chickens and even geese, which were by no means timid. He became very fond of the household dog, and when M wrote to the country family later, R wrote to the dog. It was about the same size as himself, and very lively.

The humanized dramatic play carried on by Priscilla and Dan comes as a normal interlude between the early stage of ignorance or confused conception of death (A–B categories) and the later stage of rational biological conceptualization (D–E categories). The idea is acted out in funeral games, often involving animals, and interest is shown in the rituals associated with human death – an interest often discouraged by adults, as it was by Judith's mother.

The spontaneous impulse at this stage seems to be towards participation, in reality or in play, in those social activities which, among primitive peoples, have their charter in mythology. The child would rather bury ceremonially than dissect. Jung, in a note later to his early account of psychic conflict in a child, raises the question of children's preference for fantastic or mythological explanations of birth and death at a certain age, even when they know or have access to a 'scientific explanation'. Dr Isaacs's records show such preference frequently demonstrated in children's actions.

Mythology plays a great part in psychoanalytic explanations of behaviour, though perhaps not in the sense Jung intended when

ACTING

contrasting scientific and mythological explanations. Observation of the behaviour of children suggests to a psychologist that a wider field of myth should be drawn upon for such explanations. The father is not the only figure competing with the child for love, nor the mother the only person on whose affection and care the child depends; nor is the father the object most available for a child's aggressive attack. Anxiety about aggression towards the younger brother is traditional in the mythology of Western civilization through the story of Cain and Abel.[1] The younger brother killed the sacrificial lamb; the elder killed the younger, and was authoritatively condemned, not to a similar fate but to perpetual exile from the social group. Cain was the typical murderer of whom Christendom learned from Judaism before Oedipus was brought from Greece to take his place.

Outside the Hebrew tradition, fratricide was not so authoritatively branded. When Solomon succeeded to the throne of David, he had to have a reason before he had his brothers killed,[2] whereas the society which followed on earlier Greek rule in Byzantium acquiesced in fratricide at the highest levels; Eastern emperors would bear no brother near the throne. Gibbon[3] records how when Mahomet II ascended that throne in the fifteenth century at the age of twenty-one, he 'removed the cause of sedition, by the death, the inevitable death, of his infant brothers'.

Our records suggest that elder children tend to fear the strength of impulses to destroy the smaller living object, but may under excessive provocation succumb to it. Younger siblings seem to have more need to assure themselves of their individuality and potency by acting towards small living things with the mastery which they have suffered but not been able to exert themselves within the family. But because he is the smaller, the younger

[1] Genesis iv
[2] I Kings i, 50–53; ii, 12–24 and 36–46
[3] *Decline and Fall of the Roman Empire*, 1776, ch. 68. See also Shakespeare, *Henry IV*, Part Two, V, ii:
> 'Brothers, you mix your sadness with some fear.
> This is the English, not the Turkish court.'

child seems later to restrain or even reverse his aggressive impulses by identification with the victim, and the desire to play with one smaller than himself.

Aggressive activities normally involve some anxiety. Before considering the question of children's anxiety about death I will break off to discuss what they are taught about it.

CHAPTER 7

BEING TAUGHT

CHILDREN'S concepts of death tend to reflect those of the society in which they are reared. They learn much more than they are intentionally taught. In this chapter I am mainly concerned with what they are taught, and more particularly with the traditional content of what is taught. This may be considered under two heads, formal and informal. The formal includes specific instruction, at home or at school; the informal covers casual verbal reference and customary and ritual behaviour. The education may be called religious, if all that is told to children within this universe of discourse is included, whether its temper is atheist, agnostic, freethinking, humanist, animist, necromantic or based on the traditions of any form of the religions which have world-wide following. All these inculcate an attitude to dying and the dead which is an essential part of their doctrine and practice.

Studies of child psychology and development are concerned with everything a child is taught, anywhere, but each separate study is limited by the scope of its observations in space and time. Gesell was conscious of theoretical width and actual limitations when he wrote, in an article on child psychology:

> The [current] rationalistic temper is dissolving the rigidities of dogmatic theology and of dogmatic ethics which so powerfully influenced the psychological attitude to children from the time of St Augustine to that of Jonathan Edwards – and of Charles Dickens. Pre-scientific interpretations of the mind of the child imputed to him . . . an almost demoniacal self-will born with his original sin.[1]

In studying what the child is taught about death, it is parti-

[1] A. Gesell, 'Child psychology', E. Seligman (ed), *Encyclopedia of Social Sciences*, 1930

cularly necessary to see that teaching as part of the general historical process to which Gesell refers.

The way the child conceives of death depends largely upon his age and maturity level as well as on what he is taught. Our own study showed that age and intelligence level on the one hand and culture on the other were relatively independent factors in determining the category of definition of the word *dead*. The definitions given by children from homes of Catholic and Protestant parents fell into categories by mental age irrespective of confessional background. The work of Elkind in the United States likewise shows that formal differences such as those represented by our A–E categories cut across differences in denominational environment.[1]

Researches in America, Australia and England among adolescents and young adults suggest that the majority have been taught as children about heaven and hell as incentive to good and deterrent to bad behaviour.[2] Do they continue to believe it? Brown[3] studied the degree of conviction with which Australian university students held or denied belief in a Judeo-Christian background; 21 per cent did not call themselves Christians. The rest were divided into four denominational groups: Roman Catholic, Church of England, Methodist, and other Protestant denominations. One of the propositions presented was: 'There is a hell in which the wicked will be everlastingly punished.' The percentage in each group who expressed positive certainty about this was:

Roman Catholic	92 per cent
Methodist	16 „ „

[1] D. Elkind, 'The child's conception of his religious denomination', *Journal of Genetic Psychology*, 99, 1961, pp. 209–25

[2] R. G. Kuhlen and M. Arnold, 'Age differences in religious beliefs and problems during adolescence', *Journal of Genetic Psychology*, 64, 1944; F. H. Hilliard, 'The influence of religious education upon the development of children's moral ideas', *British Journal of Educational Psychology*, 29, 1959; P. Poppleton and G. W. Pilkington, 'The measurement of religious attitudes in a university population', *British Journal of Social and Clinical Psychology*, 2, 1963

[3] L. H. Brown, 'A study of religious belief', *British Journal of Psychology*, 53, 3, 1962

Church of England	10 per cent
Other Protestant	47 „ „
Non-Christians	6 „ „

Young people who believe in an after-life in heaven or hell have been taught this by their parents or by parental consent in almost every case. Among schoolchildren it is found that with increasing age the number believing this steadily declines, yet the belief persists in each succeeding generation of children. It would seem as though modern parents use such beliefs in the way Polybius in the second century B.C. said they were used by the government of ancient Rome:

Seeing that the multitude are full of lawless desires . . . the only resource is to keep them in check by mysterious terrors. . . . Wherefore to my mind, the ancients were not acting without purpose or at random when they brought in among the vulgar those opinions about the gods and the belief in the punishments in Hades; much rather do I think that men nowadays are acting rashly and foolishly in rejecting them.[1]

Plato was eminent among the ancients who disseminated belief in the punishments of Hades. In his work is found for the first time the geographical separation of hell, purgatory and paradise, and the horribly concrete notions of graduated bodily punishment.[2] This teaching was designed as a political instrument, to save the philosopher-guardians from needing to coerce the people physically; hell and heaven were alternatives to police, prisons, torture chambers and concentration camps on earth. The influence of Plato and his administrative device may be gauged by the fact that Freud could state, some 2,300 years later: 'Civil governments still believe that they cannot maintain order among the living if they do not uphold the prospect of a better life after death.'[3] The offer of 'pie in the sky' was, however, supported by the simultaneous prospect of post-mortem torment (according to Plato) for the unjust, and according to the early Church for 'the

[1] Polybius VI, 56 (1959 edn)
[2] H. Arendt, *Between Past and Future*, 1961, pp. 111, 130
[3] S. Freud, *The Uncanny*, 1919 (1953 edn), vol. 17

fearful and unbelieving and the abominable and murderers and whoremongers and sorcerers and idolaters and all liars'.[1]

It is highly doubtful whether the superstitions prevalent in Rome at the time of Polybius had actually been disseminated by 'the ancients' or their followers. What Bertrand Russell has termed 'the religiosity of the Hellenistic age' arose, as he says, from below, like the Methodism of the eighteenth century in England, not by imposition from above.[2] The rulers of the Roman Empire were extremely, indeed excessively, tolerant, hesitating to tamper with any religious practice, even if it required human sacrifice, so that in every country of the ancient world there flourished cults older than the Olympian mythology which the Romans officially adopted, and eastern religions not unsophisticated also flourished. Myths of after-life and retribution had been given superb literary form by the Jews of Alexandria before the Christian era, and a question put to Jesus about the after-life was drawn from one of these books, and answered with reference to the same source.[3] It seems that the inclusion in Christian doctrine of the Platonic myth of the Last Judgment and Hell occurred at a time when, with the downfall of Rome and the assumption of secular power by the Church, that body faced the problem which had faced Plato in planning his Utopia, namely, how to maintain authority with a minimum of physical coercion. As late as the ninth century A.D. a brilliant Irish-born cleric, John Scotus, 'considered the notion of a material Gehenna to be a remnant of pagan superstition that real Christians should get rid of',[4] but, according to the historian of the Roman Church, 'no one, after him, has ever dared to take up . . . a doctrine so little suited to . . . the Latin tradition'.[5]

[1] Revelation xx, 1–10; xxi, 8
[2] B. Russell, *A History of Western Philosophy*, 1940, pp. 272–3
[3] See *The Apocrypha of the Old Testament in English*, R. H. Charles (ed.), 1913, especially the Wisdom of Solomon and the Book of Enoch, and *ibid.*, vol. 2, referring to the incident recorded in Matthew xxii, 23–33; Mark xii, 18–27 and Luke xx, 27–36
[4] E. Gilson, *History of Christian Philosophy in the Middle Ages*, 1955, pp. 127–8
[5] *ibid.*, p. 274

About a thousand years before John Scot the Irishman, Epicurus tried to save men from the fear of *post-mortem* torment by rational exposition of the impossibility of sentience after death. Bertrand Russell considered that the fear of death is so deeply rooted in instinct that the gospel of Epicurus could not at any time make a wide popular appeal. Conceptualization is a biological development so late that it appears theoretically unsound to postulate that a concept may be the cue for an instinctive reaction. Nevertheless Russell's view carries weight if interpreted as referring to a deep, general aversion to ego-annihilation. The Epicurean-Lucretian argument which seems to offer relief from distressful anticipation, in fact leads mankind to the confrontation of a deeper and more rational distress, whereas not only Elysium but also Tartarus offer a perpetuation of the ego.

Evidence of the persistent beliefs of children in heaven and hell alongside the persistent decline in such belief during adolescence suggests that in the transmission of culture between the more and the less sophisticated members of a population an attempt is made to solve problems of moral control along the lines proposed by Plato. In both home and community, the religion called in to support a moral code may not represent a personal conviction. In the community, organized destruction of the myth has, in the past half-century, tended to accompany excessive use of the forms of physical coercion which Plato aimed to avoid.

In the *Republic* Socrates, speaking of the retribution to be meted out to the just and the unjust in the after-life, explicitly exempted from punishment those who died young. The early Church, when adopting the Platonic version of the many available myths of after-life, made no such concession, except in so far as the consequences of sin fell heaviest on the church member, and full membership began at baptism as an initiation into *adult* life. The Augustinian doctrine by which original sin condemned the unbaptized infant to eternal damnation after death, induced parents to seek, and the Church, at first reluctantly, to concede, the baptism of infants.

In folk-lore there was peril for the infant in the period between birth and baptism; the peril of the soul, expounded by Augustine, was applied to the baby's person too. 'I have heard old people say of sickly infants,' wrote a folk-lorist, 'Ah, there will be a change when he has been taken to church; children never thrive till they have been christened!'[1] In England the practice of baptizing infants has declined much less than that of attendance at regular church services. It has been estimated that two out of every three children born in the United Kingdom are the subject during childhood of a religious educational undertaking by parents and godparents, the majority of whom rarely attend other religious services. Whether the motivation of parents who seek baptism for their children is social-conventional, magical or religious, the fact is likely to influence what the child is taught, and the way his questions are answered. In the ceremony most commonly used in England the child's sponsors are exhorted that it is their duty to see 'that this infant is taught, so soon as he shall be able to learn, what a solemn vow, promise and profession he hath made by you . . . and to provide, that he may learn the Creed, the Lord's Prayer, and the Ten Commandments, in the vulgar tongue, and all other things which a Christian ought to know and believe to his soul's health'.[2]

Many parents and godparents may hopefully transfer to the national educational system the responsibility for carrying out this undertaking, but at the very least the manner in which they answer questions is likely to be influenced, even if unconsciously, by their participation in the baptismal rite. They know 'Thou shalt not kill' is one of the Ten Commandments. The Christian creeds refer to death and resurrection. The majority of children in the United Kingdom are brought up in homes where an undertaking has been given, however light-heartedly, to teach them in traditional manner about death and concepts allied to it. In studying children's development this fact, and the correspond-

[1] W. Henderson, *Folklore of the Northern Counties*, 1879, pp. 14, 15
[2] 'The Ministration of Baptism of Infants', *The Book of Common Prayer of the Church of England*

ing conditions in other countries and cultures, is not to be disregarded.

It is a comforting, anxiety-reducing doctrine that the sacrament of baptism confers upon the recipient a grace remitting sin. Calvinists, many of whom for conscience's sake left England for America (Calvinism having been rejected by the English finally in 1642), or Holland or France for South Africa, carried with them a doctrine of original sin based, like St Augustine's, on child psychology, but leading to rather different, less comforting conclusions.

Among the thousands of children committed to my care, I cannot say with truth that I have seen one whose native character I had any reason to believe to be virtuous.

It is the duty of the Christian parent to lead his child, as soon as possible, to a knowledge of . . . the wickedness of his heart, and the necessity of a new heart to prepare him for heaven.

So wrote two reverend American gentlemen in the nineteenth century.[1] Unitarians, including the Hollis Professor of Divinity at Harvard, held that infants had also amiable qualities which indicated that their depravity was not evidence of a nature entirely sinful. But children, being morally corrupt, must not be falsely led to believe that having been baptized, they needed no conversion.

The antidote to this Calvinistic child psychology came also from Geneva, in the work of J.-J. Rousseau, whose teaching of the nobility of primitive man and the innate goodness of the child have inspired liberal movements in education to our own day. He himself, as he confessed, was frequently troubled by the fear of hell, but he was able to dismiss it; he could not believe himself damned.[2]

[1] H. Shelton Smith, *Changing Conceptions of Original Sin*, 1955, pp. 68-9, 79 ff., 146

[2] J.-J. Rousseau, *Confessions*, I, 6. 'The fear of hell frequently troubled me. I asked myself, "In what state am I? If I were to die this moment, should I be damned?" According to my Jansenists, there was no doubt about the matter; but according to my own consciousness, I thought not.'

> A little child,
> That lightly draws its breath
> And feels its life in every limb,
> What should it know of death?[1]

Calvinist clergy might have answered with a sermon on the parent's duty; Wordsworth, like Rousseau, taught the essential innocence of childhood and the nobility of natural man, and answered the poetic question by describing a child's inability to exclude the dead from the living membership of her family. What is here most striking to the psychologist today is the attitude of an adult who seeks not to teach the child but to learn what and how the child himself is thinking.

Among a considerable proportion of the English-speaking world a period of general acceptance of church guidance in the education of children was followed by a period of free-thinking, agnostic humanism or indifference. The institution of national compulsory primary education came, in England, during an intervening period. Illiteracy was reduced and reading matter cheapened. Change in what and how the child was taught about death may be illustrated by changes in the reading matter provided for children.

The Pilgrim's Progress was from the mid seventeenth century onwards the best-seller *par excellence* in this field, in England and America, for children and adults. As late as 1932 a publisher-savant[2] wrote:

> I confess to reading [Bunyan's] *Holy War* rapturously – as an adventure story – when I was a boy. Both [this book and *The Pilgrim's Progress*] have been translated into almost every known language – into very many not known in Europe in Bunyan's day . . . [and the latter] has even been put . . . into words of one syllable. In each and every form it is a children's book.

When it was written it competed with work such as that of the

[1] *Poems*: 'We are Seven'. (Wordsworth noted that this stanza was written by Coleridge)
[2] F. J. Harvey Darton, *Children's Books in England*, 1958

Puritan minister Janeway, who wrote *A Token for Children: being an Exact Account of the Conversion, Holy and Exemplary Lives, and Joyful Deaths of several young Children*. In 1702 Dr Thomas White, D.D., prefaced an account of tortures gladly borne by young saints with the advice to children to read 'no Ballads or foolish Books, but the Bible [and] . . . treatises of Death, and Hell, and Judgment . . .'.[1]

Janeway and White were the forerunners of a long line of writers for children who were either clergymen or wives or daughters of clergy: Fénelon, Isaac Watts, Wyss (*Swiss Family Robinson*), Mrs Sherwood (*The Fairchild Family*), Mrs Gatty, Mrs Ewing (*Jackanapes, the Story of a Short Life*), Kingsley (*The Water Babies*), Farrar (*Eric, or Little by Little*), George MacDonald (*The Princess and Curdy*) and Dodgson, *alias* Lewis Carroll. The output of the earlier part of this period shows children not being shielded from the thought of death, as the Katz parents wished to shield their boys, and Dr Isaacs found adults generally wished to do, but rather having it thrust upon them. When the Fairchild children quarrelled and fought their father told them of the first murderer (Cain) and then, after supper, took them for a walk through a gloomy wood to see a gibbet, on which the body of a man hung in chains; it had not yet fallen to pieces, although it had hung there for some years. The dress was still entire, but the face of the corpse was so shocking that the children could not look at it.[2]

In later editions of the book this passage was omitted. As the temper of the times changed, references to death in children's books thus became less frank about physical changes associated with dissolution and less frequent in comparison with other interests. But deathbed scenes remained common, for example in the works of Charlotte Yonge; and Lewis Carroll, in the 1876 edition of *Alice* added a postscript as an Easter greeting, in which

[1] F. J. Harvey Darton, 'Children's books', *Cambridge History of Literature*, vol. II, 16
[2] Darton, *Children's Books in England*, pp. 176–7, quoting Mrs Sherwood, *op. cit.*

he asked child readers, 'Surely your gladness need not be the less for the thought that you will one day see a brighter dawn than this?'

In earlier works it was not generally the biological processes of dissolution which were brought to the child's attention, though the stages of decline preceding decease were often described in detail; the attention was rather drawn to the life after death and the conditions for securing an enjoyable immortality. Such a direction of attention may provide a form of defence against anxiety. Death is put out of focus when the gaze is fixed on the life beyond it. The consequence may be an imaginative perception of heaven and hell of a vividness beyond men's reach today, except through reading Dante, looking at Michelangelo's *Last Judgement* or Piero della Francesca's men and angels in the *Nativity*, or hearing Handel's setting of Job's mysterious words. When the conditions of life after death are conceptually linked with the attitude and behaviour of the individual during his terrestrial existence, dying appears as a transitory incident of minor importance; a river the pilgrim must ford to reach his goal in another country.

Bunyan's theme of pilgrimage – that is, of personality as process rather than static condition – provided a prophylactic against anxiety and a stimulus to activity, expressed simply and clearly especially in the second part of the *Progress*, written for mothers and children:

> Hobgoblin nor foul Fiend
> Can daunt his spirit;
> He knows he at the end
> Shall Life inherit.
> Then Fancies flee away,
> He'll fear not what men say,
> He'll labour night and day
> To be a pilgrim.

For a period up to and around 1900 there appeared a tendency for adults to enjoy watching the child play with the idea of death. They were taught to recite poetry in which the theme of death was chosen, perhaps partly because the alternative theme of sex was considered unsuitable. Gosse[1] recounts of his own childhood:

[P.R.32.] At this party . . . it was proposed that *our young friends* should give their elders the treat of repeating any pretty pieces that they knew by heart. Accordingly a little girl repeated 'Casabianca' and another little girl, 'We are Seven'. I was then asked . . . . Without a moment's hesitation, I stood forth, and in a loud voice I began one of my favourite passages from Blair's *Grave*:
> 'If death were nothing, and nought after death –
> If when men died at once they ceased to be,
> Returning to the barren Womb of Nothing
> Whence first they sprung, then might the debauchee . . .'
'Thank you, dear, that will do nicely!' interrupted the lady with the curls.

The English schoolchild's repertory at this period included Byron's lines on 'The Destruction of Sennacherib' ('The Assyrian came down like a wolf on the fold'), Macaulay's 'Horatius' ('And how can man die better Than facing fearful odds'), 'The Burial of Sir John Moore at Corunna', and a poem about the battle of Blenheim featuring a skull found on the spot by little Wilhelmine, whose inclusion in the *dramatis personae*, along with her infant brother, apparently recommended the item as particularly suitable for the young.[2] The relegation of the treatment of death to poetry, mainly about battles long ago, aided the process of repression by the adult and suggested it to the child. Many such 'pretty pieces' found their way by parody into the collections of childish ribaldry, most notably 'Casabianca'.[3]

Rhymed mockery of death invaded at this period the adult

[1] E. Gosse, *Father and Son*, 1906 (1925 edn, p. 254)

[2] The latter poems, by C. Wolfe and R. Southey respectively, were included in F. W. Palgrave's *Golden Treasury* (1st edn 1861), circulated to schoolchildren and constantly republished for sixty years

[3] From *Poems* by Felicia Hemans ('The boy stood on the burning deck/ Whence all but he had fled.' His father had told him to wait there, and rather than disobey he perished in the flames)

literary world. Belloc's *Cautionary Tales* and Graham's *Ruthless Rhymes* appeared in the first decade of the twentieth century. Consciously they represented a reaction against the sentimental treatment of death in such works as *Uncle Tom's Cabin* and *The Old Curiosity Shop*. They now appear as a manifestation of the unconscious repression which impels the hysteric to swing from tears to laughter in the refusal to face reality. The literary swing from saccharine tenderness to fantastic toughness showed most clearly in the treatment of death of, or caused by, children.

Little Eva of *Uncle Tom's Cabin*, little Nell of *The Old Curiosity Shop*, Augustus and Harriet of *Struwwelpeter*, as well as the subjects of many of Belloc's and Graham's verses, all died in childhood. Behind the sentimental fiction, the kind German physician's playful if grim warnings, and the Edwardian jocosity, lay the fact of an extremely high child mortality rate. To have watched the death of their children, or of their siblings when they were children themselves, was the common lot of parents. The mother's death in childbirth was also frequent, with little distinction of social class. Of the authors I have cited, Rousseau's mother died at his birth, Dante, Pascal, Voltaire, Wordsworth, Darwin, George Macdonald and Gosse each lost his mother before his ninth year. Gibbon's mother died when he was ten; he was the eldest of five brothers and a sister, all of whom died in infancy. An early biographer illustrates contemporary opinion about the loss of those who would if surviving share a man's patrimony: 'their decease must have contributed to render the circumstances of our author more easy, and he seems fully sensible of the indulgences he enjoyed from Providence'.[1]

Under such conditions the child tends to learn of death by immediate experience within his circle of parents, siblings, aunts and cousins. The application to humanity cannot be avoided. The suggestion of a simple positive association between death and old age is ruled out. Janeway prefaced his book for children by asking parents, 'Are the souls of your children of no Value? . . . They

[1] Anonymous Introduction to 1808 edition of *Decline and Fall of the Roman Empire*

are not too little to die, they are not too little to go to Hell.'[1] When books written for children in earlier days stressed the application of death to themselves, it was not only in accordance with the religious spirit of the period but also with the facts of mortality.

As the religious temper changed and the infant mortality rate diminished the layman took over the production of literature for children. Moralizing was gradually eliminated and death removed from the centre of the scene. In the fairy tales gathered from folk-lore and presented as juvenile literature during the nineteenth century (which children in earlier times had heard by direct oral tradition from parents or servants) there is certainly much about killing and dying. In such a context, however, this has for the child the remoteness of fantasy, and fulfils the functions of fantasy. But even the folk tales were transmitted more prettily by Andersen or Lang than by Grimm, whose name seemed appropriate even to those who preferred his style and matter.

Lay personnel have also largely taken over the field of religious education. In England this became a statutory task of the nation's schools under the 1944 Education Act. Recent inquiry suggests that the majority of parents of young children wish it to remain so, though in a society where religious tolerance is traditionally and constitutionally respected the combination of religious freedom and compulsory education demands social skill and care in application to the schoolchild.

The theme of this chapter has been what the child is taught, and how he has been taught, in relation to the concept of death, within the culture of Western civilization during recent centuries. Other chapters contribute a commentary on the teaching, through examples of the behaviour of the children so taught; but some examples directly related to the content of the teaching may be given here. Indeed, such examples are necessary because the child so often reacts in a way the teacher clearly did not expect. Charlotte Brontë was probably using recollections of her own childhood in reporting the response of rebellious Jane Eyre, aged ten, to the question whether she knew that after death the wicked

[1] Darton, *Children's Books in England*, ch. 4

go to hell, and what she should do to avoid it. She replied, 'I must keep in good health, and not die.' [P.R.33a.] Our own records provide an example of a younger child's reaction to traditional teaching, equally independent:

[H.R.36.] Richard (6:6) at lunch with M. R: 'Miss S [his teacher] says there is a God. But I don't believe there is.' M: 'Don't you, Richard?' R: 'No. Because nobody's ever seen Him. So how can you know He's there?' M: 'Did you tell Miss S?' R: 'No. But I told the other children.' (Interval in recording owing to the necessity for serving food.) R: 'Miss S says there must be a God. Because He made the world. But I don't think the world was *made*. I think it just *came*. . . . Perhaps a pilot would know. Because He's up in the air.' M: 'I don't think He's up in the air.' R: 'Up in heaven – only we've never seen Him on the ground, God.'

In discussing a large-scale research and educational programme on religious education under way in New York State, the authors of a survey of child development in the U.S.A. wrote:

Children who have been brought up under the influences of traditional religious institutions seem to have not only confused but also absurd and meaningless ideas about God, heaven and hell, as has been shown by numerous surveys. . . . [For instance] a child was found to be puzzled by the way He (God) made everything from nothing. . . . It seems questionable if an attempt should be made to teach young children the standard theological concepts of Christianity . . .[1]

When the standard theological concepts of Christianity are conceived as those quoted of the American Calvinist divines of the eighteenth and nineteenth centuries, it does indeed seem questionable, but not for the reasons suggested. It has been argued by philosophers that a proposition which is not verifiable is in a sense meaningless; propositions about God, heaven and hell must be put in this category, and on this view, children's ideas will necessarily be meaningless on such subjects. Through the ages, however, such propositions have been discussed by adults considered intelligent by the criteria of their time, who have also frequently

[1] F. K. and R. V. Merry, *The First Two Decades of Life*, 1958

accused each other of harbouring confused and absurd notions. The puzzles of children about theological issues, like their animistic thinking, may be more akin to those of adults than has been generally recognized. A child brought by traditional teaching to wonder about 'creation out of nothing' is spontaneously occupied with a problem that has exercised a succession of thinkers from Aristotle, Epicurus and Philo to Augustine, Erigena, Aquinas, Hume and Spinoza.[1] By means of this wonder, the child might be led to feel at home in the mansions of philosophy, and then be led on to problems of astronomy. Nor does the child's thinking on such issues lack an independence which may itself be encouraged as a kind of limbering-up for scientific speculation. It seems to us that Miss S's teaching of traditional religious concepts to Richard had their value, presenting him with perennial problems, which is one of the functions of education.

When the children of agnostic parents learn orthodox beliefs from attendants or teachers, they may become deeply concerned to save their parents from the dangers they believe to follow upon unorthodox views. Thus Pasternak relates that:

[P.R.33b.] [in] early childhood . . . I was filled . . . with an anguished pity for my parents who would die before me and whom it was my duty to deliver from the pains of hell by some shining deed, unheard of and unique.[2]

His parents were Jewish, his nurse Russian Orthodox Christian.

[P.R.34.] Rasmussen's younger daughter, Sonia, accepted the religion she learned in her Norwegian Protestant school and wished to persuade her agnostic parents to do so. Aged 7:1, she used the argument of Pascal: 'Daddy might just as well say his prayers, for if He [God] is there, then it's a good thing for him to do it, and if He isn't there, then of course it wouldn't do any harm.'[3]

Wordsworth, in religion a child of his time in England, when

[1] See H. A. Wolfson, *Religious Philosophy*, 1961, pp. 249–50
[2] B. Pasternak, *An Essay in Autobiography*, 1959
[3] V. Rasmussen, *Diary of a Child's Life*, 1919, p. 80

he could no longer find in nature the intense joy he had experienced in childhood, found philosophic consolation in the Platonic theory of prenatal life and the idea of the soul's immortality; then he had to defend himself against 'good, pious persons' who concluded 'that I meant to inculcate a belief in a prior state of existence'.[1] His defence led him, fortunately, to describe his childhood experience factually.

[P.R.35.] Nothing was more difficult for me in childhood than to admit the notion of death as a state applicable to my own being. . . . It was not so much from feelings of animal vivacity that my difficulty came as from a sense of the indomitableness of the Spirit within me. I used to brood over the stories of Enoch and Elijah, and almost to persuade myself, that, whatever might become of others, I should be translated, in something of the same way, to heaven. With a feeling congenial to this, I was often unable to think of external things as having external existence, and I communed with all that I saw as something not apart from, but inherent in, my own immaterial nature. Many times while going to school have I grasped at a wall or tree to recall myself from this abyss of idealism to the reality. At that time I was afraid of such processes . . .

The boy had been taught that Enoch 'walked with God: and he was not for God took him'; that Elijah 'went up by a whirlwind into heaven, and Elisha saw it'. Having learned these myths, he found within himself the impulse that had created them. Freud has said that below the conscious level, thinking does not admit the notion of our own mortality. A poet is perhaps one who more easily becomes creatively conscious of what is normally unconscious. For him, and for the child, the myth provides a bridge between the unconscious way of thinking, which knows only of living, and the conscious conception of death.

In New England, opposition to Calvinist doctrine and psychology was formerly expressed perhaps most forcibly by Unitarians, a body more powerful and probably more numerous than in

[1] W. Wordsworth, Notes preceding 'Ode on Intimations of Immortality from Recollections of Early Childhood' in 1857 and subsequent editions. *Poetical Works*, E. de Selincourt and H. Darbishire (eds.), 1947, vol. 4. See also vol. 8, p. 202

England, its place of origin; and the rationalistic temper to which Gesell referred as influencing twentieth-century child psychology may be traced back to John Stuart Mill in England and to the circle which Henry Adams described as Mount Vernon Street, the centre of Boston Unitarianism, in the 1840s of his childhood.[1] Its attitude was:

Social perfection was sure, because human nature worked for Good, and three instruments were all she asked – Suffrage, Common Schools and Press. . . . Education was divine, and man needed only a correct knowledge of facts to reach perfection. . . . The Unitarian clergy . . . proclaimed as their merit that they insisted on no doctrine, but taught, or tried to teach, the means of leading a virtuous, useful, unselfish life, which they held to be sufficient for salvation. For them, difficulties might be ignored; doubts were a waste of thought; nothing exacted solution.

The consequence, for the boy and his brothers and sisters, was to make religion seem unreal; the mild discipline of the Unitarian church was thrown off at the first possible moment, and for ever.

That the most powerful emotion of man, next to the sexual, should disappear, might be a personal defect . . . but that the most intelligent society, led by the most intellectual clergy, in the most moral conditions . . . should have persuaded itself that all the problems which had convulsed human thought from earliest recorded time were not worth the discussing, seemed . . . the most curious social phenomenon he had to account for in a long life.

Thus an unusually perceptive observer noted what is still one of the most striking phenomena of the modern scene. As Adams pointed out, religion is not only an intellectual exercise, but is found in anthropological studies to provide the channel for social participation in the complex powerful emotions aroused by the crises of each individual life; initiation to adult status, marriage, birth and death. In the atrophy of religious emotion he believed that he and his siblings were representative of many of their contemporaries in America and Europe. And in persuading them-

[1] H. B. Adams, *The Education of Henry Adams*, 1918, pp. 33, 34

selves that all the problems which had convulsed human thought from earliest recorded time were not worth the discussing, the intelligent group of which he wrote were certainly not alone; the exceptional fact was that the sufferer should himself have recognized the strangeness of the social phenomenon.

Flugel[1] remarked in 1939 that while many books on the psychology of sex had appeared in recent years, including some that dealt with the impact of sexual ideas on the mind of the child and the practical problems to which this impact gives rise, there was no corresponding literature on the psychology of death. Eighteen years later the persistence of the gap was remarked by Alexander[2] in an article entitled 'Is death a matter of indifference?' A considerable literature has since grown up on the effect of childhood bereavement on mental health in later life, and twenty years after Flugel's observations, Dr Feifel edited a notable collection of papers on 'The Meaning of Death' which included references to childhood. The subject is touched on in studies of religious behaviour[3] but observations generally refer to students at high school or university,[4] or to young children receiving psychoanalytic treatment. The assassination of President Kennedy resulted in a number of researches into young people's reactions.[5] Such studies tended to be based either on psychotherapeutic sessions with disturbed individuals or on standard measures of personality and anxiety. To the question of anxiety and distress in children's reactions to the idea or fact of death we will now turn.

[1] J. C. Flugel, Introduction to S. Anthony, *The Child's Discovery of Death*, 1940

[2] I. E. Alexander *et al.*, 'Is death a matter of indifference?', *American Journal of Psychology*, 43, 1957

[3] M. Argyle, *Religious Behaviour*, 1958

[4] References earlier in this chapter, also R. L. Williams and S. Cole, 'Religiosity, generalized anxiety and apprehension concerning death', *Journal of Social Psychology*, 15, 1968

[5] M. Wolfenstein and G. Kliman (eds.), *Children and the Death of a President*, 1965. See also S. I. Harrison *et al.*, 'Children's reactions to bereavement: adult confusions and misperceptions', *Archives of General Psychiatry*, 17, 5, 1967

CHAPTER 8

ANXIETY AND STRESS

THE prospect of eternal pain or pleasure, however remote, tends to arouse emotion. Even those who being 'not Socratics but sceptics, concerned to adjust not to the dying animal that will be sloughed off to free some eternal spirit, but to the dying animal that becomes putrid meat and nothing else',[1] do not sound entirely unmoved. Some anxiety about death appears normal and inevitable for man. In the individual life, how and when does it begin? To be more specific, *Is death a source of anxiety to children? If so, under what conditions does such anxiety occur? What behavioural form does it take? How may it be socially harnessed and allayed?*

A beginning has been made to answering the first question in the analysis of the responses to the Story Completion test discussed in Chapter 4 above. The evidence is provided not by frequency of reference but by the context in which reference to death is made. It was typically seen as a sorrow-bringing thing separating parent from child, and a fear-bringing thing as the effect of aggressive hostility; it may set up a process of talion-oscillation involving fear of punishment for aggressive impulses. The fear of punishment appeared strongly in the responses of some of the children who had actually suffered bereavement.

The fear of punishment was explained in terms of the psychological process which Freud called in lay language the *omnipotence of thought*, and Piaget calls *efficacy*; the infant's tendency to think that his own wishes have power to influence events without physical intervention. Having not only loved but also hated the departed parent or sibling, the child may fear that he has murdered

[1] E. Hyman, 'Psychoanalysis and the climate of tragedy', H. Feifel (ed.), *Freud and the Twentieth Century*, 1957. The use of the word 'meat' is remarkable

137

him by his aggressive thoughts or death-wishes, and then become anxious about social or personal repercussion in the form of imprisonment, ghosts, or his own death. Our research suggests that the death concept is not formed until the child's powers of effective action have greatly reduced the tendency to *efficacy-thinking*. Such anxiety is therefore unlikely to arise in reaction to bereavement occurring before the development of the concept; it tends to arise, however, on a basis of regression, which itself is a normal temporary reaction to experiences demanding personal readjustment, such as the death of a member of the family, after the child has an elementary concept of death.

Behaviour manifesting an unusual degree of anxiety was recorded in the responses of Bernard N (whose father had recently died), of Ralph O (whose twin had died in infancy), and of Donald H (whose siblings had died, and whose mother was pregnant). Anxiety not abnormal in degree has been recorded by other observers of the behaviour of children who had no experience of mortality in their own family, as in the unease of the child (aged 2:2) when he killed a fly (reported by Sully), and the conversation of Ben (3:3) recorded on p. 111. On the other hand, Marlene (2:11) showed no anxiety at her mother's sudden death in her presence; Ursula (3:4) asked without apparent anxiety why a dead animal did not move; Francis (4:5) was fascinated but apparently not at all distressed by a pictorial representation of the death of Moses (p. 52 above). It seems unusual for anxiety about death to appear before the formation of a fairly clear concept, but records also show that it does so occasionally.

A single longer record serves to illustrate the development of the concept of death in a young child who had not suffered a loss in her own family, but who expressed anxiety in the course of an unusually rapid learning process. The record is contained in a letter written to me by the mother of the child (whom we will call Jane), from their home in southern England, in November 1940:

[H.R.37.] Jane (3:9) 'is a first and only child; healthy; started to speak at one year . . . very intelligent and affectionate, but physically a little clumsy. Has had the same people mind her since birth, myself, my husband and her nurse. . . . She has received no religious instruction of any kind on my orders, and has so far never met death in connection with any human being of her acquaintance, nor its description in any books. The war and bombs have not been mentioned in her presence, and she thinks all air raid noises are guns and hasn't asked why they are fired. A few days [ago she] began asking me questions about death. She had two hours previously asked me how babies were born and she had seemed quite satisfied with my explanation and the analogy with our cat having had kittens. The death conversation on the other hand was a failure – owing to my inadequacy – and I have been rather worried about it since. The conversation began by Jane asking if people came back again in the spring like flowers. (A week or so before she had been very upset by her favourite flowers dying down and we had consoled her by saying they would return in the spring.) As I have no orthodox religious beliefs I said, I now realize foolishly, that they did not return the same, but different, possibly as babies. This answer obviously worried her – she hates change and people getting old – for she said "I don't want Nan to be different, I don't want her to change and grow old." Then, "Will Nan die? Shall I die too, does everyone die?" On my saying yes, she broke into really heartbreaking tears and kept on saying, "But I don't want to die, I don't want to die." This rather upset me and I stupidly tried to console her by hedging – a fatal thing with a child as I know if I had not been wrought up myself. I tried to make things better by saying everyone and everything died, when they were old and tired and therefore glad to do so. She then asked how people died (as if it hurt), whether when they were dead they opened their eyes again (she has seen a dead bird once), whether they spoke, ate and wore clothes. Suddenly in the middle of all these questions and tears she said "Now I will go on with my tea", and the matter was temporarily forgotten.

'Not for long. The next day she heard a nurse out of doors say a child she knew had nearly died. Shortly after she came and told me with an anxious look. It upset the little I had told her about only old people dying, I feared (not that she has an idea of age – as far as she is concerned she may be "old" by next birthday). I replied he was quite well now and running about (which he is) and said when people were ill you put them to bed and the doctors came and they got well. She seemed really pleased and told her nurse what I had said.

'The following day November 11th the matter cropped up again over the armistice poppies. She came in to me flourishing her purchase, saying cheerfully "You see *it* won't die!" Since then no more. . . . It is a great relief to me to tell it. . . . It took me all unawares as although I expected the questions about birth etc. those about death I hadn't thought of yet, and my own ideas are very hazy.'

As is inevitable in such records, there is much about this case that we do not know, despite the honesty and ability of the observer and her attempt to provide relevant detail. The beliefs of the nurse are not recorded. She may have held that there is a special providence in the fall of a sparrow. The dead bird may have excited in the child questions which the nursemaid could not answer in accordance both with her own beliefs and with the regulations laid down by the mother. The point with which we are mainly concerned here, however, is simply that distress appears in the behaviour of a child in her fourth year, in relation to the concept of death. This case has been quoted at some length for the purpose of giving individual background for an answer to the query *Is death a source of anxiety to children?* because here it was possible to exclude both the experience of loss of a member of the immediate family and the association of death with religious teaching. Records of the expression of such anxiety have also been quoted in earlier chapters, from Rasmussen, whose daughter in her seventh year insisted that her mother should share her coffin, and from Sully, of the distress of Clifford, aged under four years, about the killing of animals. The answer appears to be definitely in the affirmative; the thought of death may be a source of anxiety to children at a very early age, without their limited knowledge leading them to any essential delusion about its nature.

What is anxiety? The word has somewhat different significance for the psychologist and the psychiatrist. By a psychologist's definition, anxiety is 'a hypothetical state accompanying or resulting from the anticipation of noxious stimulation such as pain, restriction of functional freedom, diminution of status, or failure to attain a goal'. *Functional freedom* may be restricted by prison walls, the harness put on dogs in conditioning experiments, or by social or geographical distance which prevents the expression of love; *diminution of status* may be by physical or social descent; *goals* are sought for consummatory pleasure. *Anticipation* implies a relation between a percept which is taken for a signal and an event which the percept is taken to signalize; anxiety is conditional upon uncertainty within this signalling relationship, either in respect of the duration of the time-interval, or the actual occurrence of the later event, or its quality.

During the interval between signal and event, physiological phenomena typical of anxiety may be introspectively or objectively observed. These symptoms vary greatly between individuals, and in the same individual between types of precipitating situations. They generally involve increased physiological arousal[1] – more rapid breathing, pulse and heart-beat, 'butterflies in the stomach', variation of galvanic skin resistance, dry mouth, irrelevant motor activity, insomnia, muscular tension.

The word *fear* is sometimes used as a synonym for anxiety. If they are to be distinguished, one may keep *fear* for reactions to a source of danger known to be present in the immediate environment, like a lion in the path, or ice cracking around the skater. Reaction to fear may be either flight, concealment, extreme passivity or attack. Anxiety may also be distinguished from fear by length of interval between signal and event signalized, or by lack of opportunity to carry through a response physiologically initiated, or by vacillation, or (when a long interval is anticipated) by the character of the physiological reaction. Selye was the first to describe the *general adaptation syndrome* which may develop under the *stress* of long-term anxiety.

Freud in his early work described anxiety as a result and symptom of disturbance of sexual function, due to the repressive blocking of energy of id impulses. Later he rejected this view,

[1] On the literature of arousal and of stress, reference may be made to R. S. Lazarus, *Psychological Stress and the Coping Process*, 1966; M. H. Appley and R. Trumbull (eds.), *Psychological Stress*, 1967; in addition to the works of H. Selye

teaching that anxiety may be aroused by perception of internal or external danger when the consequent fear is repressed. In both formulations the anxiety is assumed to arouse the ego to defend itself, either from the danger of inadequately controlled id impulses or from direct external danger. Mowrer has suggested that anxiety may also arise from repressed superego impulses; that is, from the danger to the ego of repression of the voice of conscience.[1]

The concept of anxiety has been influenced by work on the physiological effects of stress, but the concept nevertheless retains unitary character, since it is observed that the kind of situation which arouses a physiological stress-response in a particular individual must be related to significant events in that person's life. The concept, however, is somewhat nebulous, and may require further definition, or conceptual subdivision, if it is to continue to provide a base for scientific investigations.

Marett believed that fears, though not all of one type, were of one parentage biologically speaking, namely, the fear of death.[2] Rank held that all anxieties are caused by the original experience of the birth process, and that physiological and psychological reactions associated with fear recapitulate the birth reaction.[3] The central position of the Oedipus complex in Freudian psychology makes it inevitable that neurotic anxiety should be analytically resolved into a repressed fear of castration. A commentator states, however, that 'for Freud, no single event is the creator, nor any single form of anxiety – separation or castration or death – characteristic of anxiety as such'.[4]

A description more easily grasped, though equally general, is the identification of anxiety with Hull's concept of *drive*, defined as *motivation to activity*. This identification was partly due to the necessity, when transferring learning theories from rats to men, of recognizing that man is not generally motivated directly by

[1] O. H. Mowrer, *Learning Theory and Personality Dynamics*, 1950
[2] R. R. Marett, *Faith, Hope and Charity in Primitive Religion*, 1932, p. 41
[3] O. Rank, *The Trauma of Birth*, 1929
[4] F. J. Hacker, in Feifel (ed.), *op. cit.*, p. 133

impulses to satisfy biological needs to eat, mate, or escape electric shock, but by anticipation of the distress which he has learned (either through personal experience or social suggestion) will follow the frustration of such desires. Mowrer, in 1939, suggested that anxiety is to be regarded as a motivating agent essentially similar in manner of operation to hunger, thirst, sex 'and the many other forms of discomfort that harass living organisms'.[1]

Of this concept of anxiety it may be said, as Dr Magda Arnold has said of the concept of stress, that if every instance of normal functioning involves anxiety, the concept has lost all meaning. Frustration is not anticipated in *all* normal functioning. 'The organismic reaction in stress is the *extra*-ordinary, intensified activity that is required to counteract disturbance and restore normal functioning.'[2] Correspondingly we may describe anxiety as organismic reaction to the *anticipation* of disturbance of normal function. Anxious behaviour may then be expected to resemble stress behaviour, when the condition requiring such reaction has not yet occurred, but is foreseen, consciously or unconsciously. But the physiological reaction to anxiety may be, and has on occasion been experimentally found to be, as great or greater than that which occurs on exposure to the actual event.

The anticipatory reaction, anxiety, is largely determined by the *appraisal* of the stressor, the concept of the future event. The appraisal is cognitive; control is operated through manner of knowing. If there is some happy illusion about a future or current stressful event, it may lose its power to stress; or an event falsely conceived as fatal may actually cause death in anticipation, or cause death to be accepted rather than life. Such current experimental findings may lead to the argument that it is an advantage to men to have illusions about death in general, if anticipation of immortality or reincarnation is an illusion which reduces anxiety. The argument of Pascal and of Kierkegaard was less simple. To Kierkegaard, anxiety was the inevitable effect of refusal to accept

[1] O. H. Mowrer, 'A stimulus-response analysis of anxiety and its role as a reinforcing agent', *Psychology Review*, 45, 1939
[2] M. Arnold, 'Stress and emotion', in Appley and Trumbull (eds.), *op. cit.*, p. 124

the lack of rational foundation for decision about questions of life and death, which lack is in the nature of things inevitable. This refusal led men to erect systems of religion, metaphysics, political utopias and abstract philosophies which rationalized their own limitations of their liberty. *Rationally* there could be no decision; man was free to lead his life and to die in accordance with a freely chosen, *necessarily non-rational*, view. He argued further that such questions should engage the whole man as personal, urgent and anguished:

> Socrates did not know with certainty whether he was immortal. . . . But his life expresses the fact that there is an immortality and that he himself was immortal. The question of immortality, he says, concerns me so infinitely, that I stake everything on that *if*.[1]

Montaigne presents fundamentally the same argument without the anguish, thus illustrating how men's reactions to stressful ideas may be emotionally related to the differing circumstances of their upbringing (for Kierkegaard's childhood was depressing in the extreme, Montaigne's not):

> If we have not known how to live, it is wrong to teach us how to die, and to give the end a different shape from the whole. . . . They may boast as much as they please, that 'a philosopher's whole life is a contemplation of death'. It seems to me, however, that it is indeed the end but not the aim of life; it is its conclusion, its extreme point, yet not its object. Life should contain its own aim, its own purposes; its proper study is to regulate itself, guide itself, and endure itself. Among the many duties included under the general and principal head of knowing how to live, is this article of knowing how to die; and it would be one of the lightest if our fears did not weigh it down.[2]

Let us return to the children, and the manifestations of anxiety in their behaviour, as defined in these various ways. Jane was certainly engaged in *a quest personal, urgent and anguished*. When the problem became too stressful to be endured – 'in the middle of all these questions and tears' – she diverted her attention from

[1] S. Kierkegaard, *Journals* (1958 edn)
[2] M. de Montaigne, *Essais*, III, 12 (1958 edn)

144

the whole inquiry. 'Now I will go on with my tea.' This be haviour suggests the operation of repression. She had been *upset* by flowers dying down in autumn; the word suggests that the reaction was observed as emotional by its physical expression. Then, like Ben of our home records, she asked whether people returned in the spring, and was *worried* to hear they did not. Again this suggests, in a child of under four years, reactions physically observable. A concept of death was being gradually constructed, accompanied by behavioural expressions of anxiety.

Among human beings, Jane first associated the idea of dying with her nursemaid, the mother-substitute. In our home records likewise it was frequently found that the earliest reaction of the child to the realization of the death of human beings was concern at the thought of *separation* from the mother or the person who gave the child most constant care. Thus Jeremy, four days before he told his nursemaid that he would die but not without his toy rabbit, had begged her to stay with him always. [H.R.38.] 'To which [the record continues] the nursemaid replied . . . surely he wouldn't want her when she was ninety, and very old? G, Jeremy's elder sister, then broke in: "Why, Mummy will be dead then! You won't live to be older than that, will you, Mummy?" This was said quite cheerfully and with no sign of the slightest apprehension.'

The cheerfulness, however, was the elder child's, not Jeremy's. He was coping with the anticipation of deprivation of love and care which to him seemed inevitable if the nursemaid were no longer with him. The anxiety of small children at separation from the mother is classified, in our first definition above, under the head of *restriction of functional freedom*, the function being in this case that of *libido* or love, given and received.

The quality of this anxiety, its psychiatric import and its biological basis have been illuminated by the work of René Spitz and John Bowlby with infants, and of Liddell and others with animals. From the research-findings in these fields it is possible to appreciate what the concept of death means to the young child, when he sees in it the threat of separation from the mother or mother-substitute. Bowlby finds that separation-anxiety is at its maximum in the human infant between the ages of 6–7 months and 2½ years.[1] It appears, therefore, that the period when separation occasions maximum anxiety precedes the period when the concept of death normally begins to develop. The ability to form concepts, and the more effective communication systems which accompany the process – the learning of language – tend to reduce the strength of the psychosocial tie with the mother or her substitute, and with it the force of separation-anxiety.

All infants in our culture experience periods, however brief, of absence of the mother or substitute attendant. This is an elementary source of grief and frustration. The earliest conception of death may then tend to stimulate anxiety about separation, although the process of concept-formation in general tends to reduce it.

The depth of the biological stress of mother-infant separation has been demonstrated in Liddell's researches with sheep and goats. Experimental neuroses had been induced in adult animals; even when remarkably persistent, these did not affect the life-span. After twenty years' work, the research team 'seemed to be facing a blank wall. Then a heavy door swung slowly on its hinges and we found ourselves in a new room, the animal nursery. It was due to René Spitz's observations on hospitalism in infants deprived of adequate mothering that our focus of interest shifted to the new-born sheep and goats, and the protective functioning of the mother in shielding her young from the impact of psycho-social stress.'[2] Infant animals, some accompanying and some separated from their dams, were submitted to stressful situations. It was found that the former did not suffer during or after the test, whereas the latter developed an experimental neurosis, at first resembling in symptoms that of the adult animal, with diffuse agitation, but then distinctive in passivity and refusal of all

[1] J. Bowlby, 'Separation anxiety', *International Journal of Psychoanalysis and Psychiatry*, 41 and 42, 1961

[2] H. S. Liddell, 'Experimental neuroses in animals', J. M. Tanner (ed.), *Stress and Psychiatric Disorder*, 1960, pp. 59–64

visible response. Stress-conditioning of lambs and kids *in isolation* typically resulted in their death within the year. Still more striking was the observation that separation from the mother for an hour following birth, even without stress-experimentation, also commonly resulted in the death of the lamb or kid at an early age. 'We must broaden our conception of conditioning,' Dr Liddell writes, 'to include mutual conditioning between mother and new-born by which the mother's presence becomes a conditioned *security signal* to her offspring.' When the young animal is alone, almost any event may arouse anxiety, which if experienced in the mother's company would be perceived with equanimity.

The results of the animal experiments are clearly not applicable without modification to the human situation. The time-scale, for instance, is essentially different. By the time the human infant's anxiety at separation is maximal (by Bowlby's findings), the young animal, if reared in normal contact with its dam, has developed the stress-reactions of the adult of its species. What appears to be common to both beast and man, however, is a need for the presence of a mother-functional figure during infancy, as safeguard against the anxiety which may be induced by unfamiliar events experienced in isolation. Apprehension by the child of a concept involving departure, disappearance or cessation of human contact is therefore liable to be primarily referred to the relationship felt to be most important to the child, and the thought of separation from the mother figure is liable to arouse deep anxiety.

It was therefore normal for Jane to refer the idea of death, in the first deeply anxious instance, to the nursemaid who had cared for her since birth; Jeremy's reaction was the same. In so far as anxiety about death tends to draw emotional content initially from the separation-anxiety that man shares with other mammals, it appears to be readily displaceable on to substitutes for the mother; that is, on to persons who have fulfilled the intimate maternal function towards the child over a considerable previous period. For the human condition this may be a safeguard of psychiatric importance.

In this respect, then, Jane was an ordinary child. The rapidity with which she reached the next stage of conceptual development was, however, unusual, for she immediately proceeded to ask, 'Shall I die too; does everybody die?' It was the affirmative answer to these questions which aroused the most violent reaction, the 'heart-breaking tears'. The thought sequence is normal, but it is usually spread over a much longer period.

In the development of Jane's anxiety about death there is no record of a stage through which many children pass. The importance of the mouth in the perceptual activity of the infant is patent to every observer. Psychoanalysis has developed the theory of the oral phase of mental development. The end of the fully oral phase may be assigned to about the age of 2:0 when locomotive and prehensile skills have been acquired. The full oral phase is therefore over before the concept of death begins to develop in most children. Nevertheless in many children, immature death-concepts take the form of oral fantasy. Thus Clifford Sully (3:2) imagined that a dead bird in a tree was there because a 'snake ate it up, and then spit it out again'.[1] [P.R.36.] Patricia K told the story of the child who was lost by her mother because 'a great big fish swallowed her up'. Fairy tales are full of such oral fantasy about death of a kind which is no death: Red Riding Hood's grandmother is eaten by the wolf, but later recovered from the beast's belly; Hansel and Gretel eat part of the witch's house, she welcomes them inside but plans to cook and eat them. Freud has said that cannibalism is the sexual aim in the oral phase, and Melanie Klein has developed the theme. Oral death is not conceived as final. Swallowing forms part of a fantasied life-cycle, of which the next phase is birth or spitting out or vomiting up again, or the kind of Caesarian operation performed on the wolf who had eaten the grandmother. Death as a final process plays no part, having no conceptual identity.

That Jane (so far as we know) did not go through a stage of oral conceptualization of death suggests no abnormality, for there is much variation in the behaviour of normal children in this re-

[1] J. Sully, *Studies of Childhood*, 1895, p. 150

spect. Another fantasy of man's destiny which also seems anxiety-free and variably present is the idea that as the child grows bigger the parent grows smaller, until their size and function are reversed. Thus Richard (3:11) remarked as M undressed him for his bath, that when he was a man, she would be a little boy or girl, and he (R) would bath her and put her to bed. [H.R.39.]

Sully gives several examples similar to this.[1] Ernest Jones referred to this belief in child-parent role-reversal in an essay entitled, 'The Significance of the Grandfather',[2] considering it one of the sources of the belief in reincarnation, connected with incestuous wishes, and subserving a hostile attitude towards the parents. I am doubtful whether Dr Jones's interpretations of the psychological processes underlying this fantasy are valid for all its manifestations. In the case of Richard and of the children quoted by Sully, the imagined functions of the child in the reversed situation are those of a female, not a male, parent or grandparent. As for reincarnation, Richard was remarkable for his resistance to this idea, when suggested to him by his elder brother, to whom it was familiar and acceptable.

The child's separation anxiety takes on a rational or rationalized form as he grows older. Sonia Rasmussen seemed to be suffering from some anxiety about loss of parents as providers when she proposed the happy solution: 'Supposing I hadn't any Mummy and supposing I hadn't any Daddy, I daresay there'd be some lady or other who would give me sixpence.'[3] [P.R.37.] Although anxiety may be controlled, it is not necessarily extinguished by a defensive operation undertaken at any one time. Two years later, in a conversation with their mother begun by the elder sister saying 'How people do love their fathers and mothers! You mustn't die before I'm grown up!' Sonia said, 'I shall be with you, of course. You mustn't die before I die.'[4] [P.R.38.] Her defence against the anxiety of death as separation from the mother was a

[1] ibid., ch. 4
[2] E. Jones, Papers on Psycho-Analysis, 1938
[3] V. Rasmussen, Diary of a Child's Life, 1919, p. 52
[4] ibid., under date 7.8.19

denial of that separation by the determination that they would be buried together.

This idea of burial together is, of course, a very common fantasy, and indeed a common practice. In our home records we have two on this theme:

[H.R.40.] Judith (7:2), when her mother's mother was seriously ill, became frightened for her own mother, and then began to think about her own death: 'Next year I shall be eight, but I might die before my birthday; I might die before Christmas and get no presents; I might die next month – or next week – or this next minute, but I don't feel like it. I want to wait and die when you and Daddie die. It would be nice to die all together!'

[H.R.41.] Ben (7:2), in his mother's bed for a minute or two before breakfast, talking about measles, said happily: 'I'd like to die.' M: 'Why?' B: 'Because I'd like to be in the same grave as you.'

A psychoanalyst has said that in the unconscious a grave is hardly ever a symbol of death;[1] and Plato wrote that the mother-hood of earth is relevant not only to marriage and birth but to death also.[2] Bovet[3] quotes Pierre Loti as saying, 'My mother is the only person in the world about whom I have not experienced the feeling that death will separate us for ever.' [P.R.39.] An American medical student responded as follows to a questionnaire about reactions to bereavement:

[P.R.40.] When I was a little kid I was terribly afraid of death, as soon as I got to know about it. I used to hope I'd be an exception to the general rule. Even in after life I never got used to the idea, although I've cut up lots of stiffs. But do you know, when I saw my mother tucked away down there in that grave, I had no fear of death, none at all. I'd just as soon have cuddled up down there beside her as not, and since that time I haven't had the least fear of death. I remember noticing

[1] M. Grotjahn, 'The representation of death in the art of antiquity and in the unconscious of modern men', C. B. Wilbur and W. Muensterberger (eds.), *Psychoanalysis and Culture*, 1951, pp. 410–24
[2] W. F. J. Knight, *Cumaean Gates*, 1936
[3] P. Bovet, *The Child's Religion*, (1928 edn), p. 31

at the time that the grave wasn't so very deep, and it sort of brought her home to me. Yet when the coffin was being lowered into the grave, I wanted to holler, 'Stop!'[1]

In all these instances, anxiety is clearly about death as separation from the love-object, and the defence has taken the form of a belief or hope of union in death; indeed unconsciously of a closer union in death than was possible in life. The theme of union in death is familiar in literature; Antigone and Haemon, Romeo and Juliet, and the true lovers of countless ballads are united in the tomb. It may be that in the evolution of man, the concept of Earth as mother goddess was cause and consequence of the practice of burial.

To return to factual observation: Jane had seen a dead bird before she began to question her mother about death. The importance of animals in children's development has already been noted. Freud said that parents are represented in dreams or the unconscious by large animals, sibs by small ones. We have found that small animals may also represent himself in the child's imagination. The representation of parents by animals in dream or waking fantasy often appears to be a screen for ambivalent or hostile impulses towards parents, which may then arouse a sense of guilt, or anxiety about retaliation. The modern child, however, has been found to express hostility openly enough without any screening:

[H.R.42.] Clarissa (4:7) and her mother had been talking about vets and killing cats. C described how a cat was killed, and then said: 'You'll die before I will . . . I'm younger than you, so you'll die first, won't you?' M: 'Yes.' C, chanting happily as she went to her bath: 'You'll die before me, you'll die before me.' M went to the bathroom and kissed the child, who was looking very happy. C: 'You *like me*, don't you?' M: 'Yes, of course I do.' C: 'T's sister doesn't like me, really. All the other children in that form like me except J.' (Note by M: T is Clarissa's school friend. The sister, in the form above, is older than both of them.

[1] H. Becker, 'The sorrow of bereavement', *Journal of Abnormal and Social Psychology*, 27, 1932

J, as a member of that class, has shown some hostility to her juniors, and C had made plans to kill her with bow and arrows.)

[H.R.43.] Ben (6:4) had been forbidden by his mother to play with his ball until they reached an open space free from traffic. He became surly and then said: 'I wish you had never been alive! And then other times I don't feel like that at all! Are you like that with your mother?' M: 'Yes.' B then immediately became merry and obedient.

In these instances, and in others quoted earlier, death has been conceived not primarily as separation but as end-result-of-aggression. The association of death and aggression does not invariably appear to set up in young children a sense of guilt or anxiety. The little boy aged 2:2 who killed a fly was seen to be uneasy about it, but children of our records who appeared to enjoy aggressive activities against small animals were not found to harbour anxiety in connection with the death-concept at that developmental stage, nor did they subsequently require psychiatric attention.

The introduction of self into the menaced circle, however, alters the tension associated with the concept. In children who only reach this stage gradually, a transition stage may be observed. It was so with Richard. During his fifth year a shoot was arranged by the local council, to reduce the population of grey squirrels in a wood near his home. He was much concerned about this (for he could hear the shots), until he was told that the little animals were not native English squirrels. Somewhat later (aged 5:0), seeing a troop of soldiers, he became alarmed, but was relieved to think that 'We won't die, because English don't shoot Englishes!' [H.R.44.] He was clearly anxious to avoid identification with victims of aggression. Clifford Sully (4:4) was more generally antipathetic to aggression; he broke off his toy soldiers' guns 'when I thought they were just naughty men who liked to kill people!'[1] [P.R.41.]

The tendency of children to become anxious through identification of themselves with small-animal victims has already been

[1] Sully, op. cit., p. 476

noted in the reactions among Dr Isaacs's schoolchildren to dissection. The child gradually learns that men, under given conditions, kill some living things with social approval. He may proceed to plan his own inclusion in a class against which aggression is not approved, or which is, as he supposes, immune from death.

To help the young child in his anxiety about death the parent frequently suggests that old age supervenes. Jane's mother tried this, also Rasmussen to Ruth aged 4:7 and Ben's mother to him aged 3:3. The adoption by the child of this form of defence may have results unexpected by the parents, and some of considerable importance in later life. Deducing that children, as such, do not die, the child may wish not to grow up. Arrest of social maturation may appear as a symptom in certain forms of psychiatric disorder, and be traceable to this association. Another possible consequence of a child's acceptance of this form of defence, which may be a happy one but may become obsessional, is the arousal or intensification of interest in number and time – a subject to which I shall return in a later chapter.

Let us first illustrate the former points from individual records. The belief that children as such do not die comes to light occasionally from the response to some item in a test of general intelligence. One such item requires the examiner to ask the child: 'What is foolish [silly, daft] about this: In an old graveyard in Spain, they have discovered a small skull which they believe to be that of Christopher Columbus when he was about ten years old?' To this one of our subjects, Mary U, answered: 'When you're ten years old, I don't see how you could die, unless someone kills you.' Another child responded: 'Columbus couldn't have died when he was ten, because a boy couldn't have been an enemy.' Schilder and Wechsler[1] report responses of similar import from American children who were asked, during clinical examination, 'Can a child die?' 'No,' one boy replied, 'boys don't die unless they get run over.' [P.R.42.]

[1] P. Schilder and D. Wechsler, 'The attitudes of children towards death', *Journal of Abnormal and Social Psychology*, 45, 1934

The class of *children*, then, like Richard's class of *Englishes*, was supposed immune from death. Such a belief could scarcely have been entertained by the young in the time, say, of Gibbon, or today in countries with a high infant mortality rate, such as India. Even here and now it affords very brief comfort to the normally intelligent child. Mary U, quoted above, was aged 11:1, but of subnormal intelligence. To Stephen's statement, aged 4:10, that his brother, being two-and-a-half, would not die for a hundred years, another child retorted, 'Everybody'll be dead when they're a hundred!'

Stephen 'turned to putting shoes on, *apparently quite unmoved*, as though the whole matter had slipped from his thoughts'. This observed transition from excited talk to apparent oblivion offers a parallel to Jane's behaviour ('Suddenly . . . she said "Now I will get on with my tea", and the matter was temporarily forgotten.') These are outward signs of the process of repression. Four months later, it became clear that Stephen had not forgotten the earlier event. At tea with his mother and younger brother, a conversation took place which she recorded as follows:

[H.R.45.] S (5:2): 'Where's your Mummie?' (He had asked this the day before, without any comment on the answer.) M: 'In heaven. She died some time ago. I think she was about seventy.' S: 'She must have been eighty or ninety.' M: 'No, only seventy.' S: 'Well, *men* live till they're ninety-nine.' (M made no comment, and the subject changed without further reaction from S. The next day, also at tea-time, the subject was brought up again.) S: 'Who was my Mummie when I was one [year old]?' M: 'I was. I've always been your Mummie.' S: 'When are you going to die?' M: 'Oh, I don't know. When I'm about seventy or eighty or ninety.' S: 'Oh!' (Pause.) 'When I'm grown up, I shan't shave, and then I shall have a beard, shan't I?' (He went on to tell a story about how he saw an old man with a long beard, and he was blowing his nose on it. He was obviously very pleased with the story. The conversation then drifted off. From a conversation on the previous day, M gathered that he thought that men grew beards when they became very old.)

From his small schoolfellow's generalization that everybody

will be dead when they are a hundred Stephen seems to have originally drawn the conclusion that this is the normal term of human life. His grandmother's death at an earlier age indicated that the rule was inapplicable to women. Its validity for men is restated. It seems, however, advisable for men to ensure the acquisition of the accompaniments of masculinity and age. A beard being one of these, Stephen proposes to abstain from shaving when the opportunity occurs. The question has clearly also stimulated an interest in numbers, to which we shall refer again later in observations on this child. Unlike the decision to grow a beard, this persisted into adult life.

Rasmussen writes that both his daughters were extremely afraid of death from their fifth year. Here also we find the association of death with age:

[P.R.43.] Ruth (4:7): 'Will you die, father?' F: 'Yes, but not before I grow old.' R: 'Will you grow old?' F: 'Yes.' R: 'Shall I grow old, too?' F: 'Yes.' (Three months later.) R: 'Every day I'm afraid of dying . . . I wish I might never grow old, for then I'd never die, would I?'[1]

A similar wish was expressed by Eric G, as recorded in responses to the Story Completion test (p. 82 above). Desmond I (9:6), a village boy, said that the story hero 'wanted to stop a boy, so that [sic] as he grows older, there is less life in him'. Sully records a similar sentiment in a little girl (3:6), who asked to have a large stone placed on her head to prevent her growing old and then dying.[2] [P.R.44.] In responses to story-opening 10 it was found that thirty-one out of eighty-eight children gave a preference for staying a child a long time rather than growing up quickly. Among those who did so there were more boys than girls, and more clinic-interviewed cases than others, but neither difference was considered statistically significant; there may, however, be a sex-clinic interaction difference which is significant.[3]

[1] V. Rasmussen, *Child Psychology*, 1921, p. 38

[2] Sully, *op. cit.*, p. 121

[3] G. A. Foulds recorded 16 per cent of 'normal' boys of 9½ years giving a stay-little preference: 'Characteristic projection test responses in a group of defective delinquents', *British Journal of Psychology*, 40, 3, 1950

The Story Completion test does not give the child an opportunity to make a flat denial of personal mortality, such as we find on record in a number of cases from both home and clinical observations. Clifford Sully (3:10) 'when driving in the country with his mother on a lovely May day ... in his happiest mood ... suddenly exclaimed "I shall never die!" '[1] [P.R.45.] Ruth Rasmussen (5:0) announced, 'I won't ever die!'[2] [P.R.46.] Edward G, examined at a clinic (Schilder and Wechsler), said, 'I shall not die – when you are old you die. I shall never die.' [P.R.47.] Afterwards this boy said that he would also get old and die. All these children already had a concept of death; indeed, Ruth had expressed continued and deep anxiety about it. Nor in the case of any one of them was the assertion of personal immortality long maintained. Clifford during his fifth year 'plied his mother with questions about death and burial'. Both he and Ruth showed anxiety about death during the months following their assertion of immortality.

The temporary, blissful, unreasoning conviction of personal survival appears to be due to an invasion of consciousness by a state of mind normally unconscious. The Sully boy's reaction recalls Wordsworth's description of his own childhood experiences: 'I communed with all that I saw as something not apart from, but inherent in, my own nature. . . . Nothing was more difficult for me . . . than to admit the notion of death as a state applicable to my own being.' There is a sense of immanence and permanent living union of self and world which negates the possibility of individual decease.

The negation of personal mortality was not permanently maintained, so that in studying the episode as a function of the child's development one turns to the interpretation by which Ferenczi,[3] following a suggestion of Freud, showed that negation of a

---

[1] Sully, *op. cit.* (1903 edn), p. 463

[2] Rasmussen, *op. cit.*, p. 41

[3] S. Ferenczi, 'The problem of the acceptance of unpleasant ideas', *Further Contributions to Psychoanalysis*, 1926. See also S. Freud, *Negation*, 1925 (1953 edn), vol. 19

perceived but distasteful fact may have a positive aspect; that is, it may promote the building of a pragmatic relationship between individual and environment.

Negation of reality is a transition phase between ignoring and accepting reality; the alien and therefore hostile outer world becomes capable of entering consciousness, in spite of pain, when it is supplied with the minus prefix of negation, i.e. when it is denied.

This observation has always seemed to me an insight of genius, interpreting behaviour with impressive validity. More distressing than the instances of such spontaneous, temporary negation were the occasions when the mother found it necessary to make the negation on the child's behalf. This may involve a parent in one of the most difficult situations he has to face, and if not flexibly handled may result in later psychiatric disturbance for the child. Dr Morgenstern reports one such case:

[P.R.48.] The first notion of death may release intense affective reactions in the child. A little girl of four years old wept for twenty-four hours when she learned that all living beings die. Her mother was unable to calm her by any other means than the solemn promise that she, the little girl, would never die. This same little girl, at the age of fifteen, had a long-lasting and extremely severe hysterical cough. Psychoanalysis of the case showed that this was in effect an act of self-punishment for unconscious death-wishes against her mother, her sister and her brothers. She saw herself as stricken with tuberculosis and dying . . .[1]

This record repeats, in more extreme form, the experience of Jane's mother and, in the earlier stage, of Jane herself. In a record of our own the mother also finds herself having to give the child some assurance, amounting to a modified negation, to tide him over a difficult moment:

[H.R.46.] Richard (5:1) lately at bath-time has begun to whimper and be miserable about dying. Yesterday as he swam up and down in his bath he played with the possibility of never dying, living to a thousand, etc. Today, R: 'I might be alone when I die. Will you be with me? . . .

[1] S. Morgenstern, 'La pensée magique chez l'enfant', Revue Française de Psycho-analyse, 7, 1, 1937

But I don't want to be dead, ever; I don't want to die.' Some days previously, when he had seemed afraid of not knowing *how* to die, M had told him he need not worry, because she would die first, so he would know how it was done. This had seemed to reassure him. However, M now told him that she would be with him when he died, and then added: 'But you won't die for a long time, Richard. You won't die till after you understand about it.' At this a smile gradually broke over his serious, unhappy face, and he said, 'That's all right. I've been worried, and now I can get happy.' He jumped about on the bath-mat, and sang. A few minutes later, R: 'I wish I could dream in the day-time.' M: 'What would you like to dream about?' R: 'About going shopping and buying things.'

In a similar episode in the Katz family, the mother found herself compelled to deny his mortality to the anxious child:

[P.R.49.] Theodor (5:2): 'Do animals come to an end, too?' M: 'Yes, animals come to an end, too. Everything that lives comes to an end.' T: 'I don't want to come to an end. I should like to live longer than anybody on earth.' M: 'You need never die; you can live for ever.'

In his discussion of this record, Professor David Katz wrote: 'We have tried as far as possible to keep away from the children any conception of death, especially in connection with human beings. Of what use would it have been to disturb them with thoughts about death, which must necessarily be extremely mysterious and terrible to them, if they hear of it and yet have no consolation of any kind to support them. . . . But once again an unsolicited helper must have interfered in our plans. . . . When his mother gives him a truthful answer, Theodor for the first time reveals fear of death. . . . In view of his distress, M decides to console the child in the final sentence.'[1]

One admires and is grateful for the scientific integrity which permitted Dr Rosa Katz to record that she had told the boy something that wasn't true. In these records, several facts are notable: the three children are all concerned to deny a fact that they have apprehended, and the mothers, with more or less reluctance, assist the child's denial. The French mother was the

[1] D. and R. Katz, *Conversations with Children*, 1936

most reluctant. Her child developed later a neurosis in which death-associations played a part. It would seem that all the mothers acted against their rational judgement in helping the denial, but by consenting to be parties to the negation of reality the parent was actually helping the child to accept reality later.

The parent's reluctance to deny reality on the child's behalf is supported by three considerations: the desire to satisfy his own conscience; the desire to do so particularly in relation to the child, as the child's model; and the fundamental wish to maintain a code for social communication corresponding to pragmatic reality and natural law, or in other words, to teach the child by example to tell the truth about matters of serious concern. The arguments in favour of supporting reality-acceptance are strong. Nevertheless in this context there is danger in doing so. The knowledge that the denial is itself an easing of acceptance may make the parent's task easier. He may anticipate a charge of un-reliability, of lying, when the child's own need for denial is past. If openly accused, he may answer, 'You could not take it, *then*.'

When adults attempt to keep from the child such facts about death as his personal experience would otherwise present to him, he may suspect deception, and develop anxieties in consequence more morbid and persistent than those which the perception of the reality would have aroused. This appears in a case reported by Erikson.[1] [P.R.50.] Sam's grandmother died at Sam's home, during his fourth year. Although he may have seen the coffin, his mother told him that the grandmother had gone away. Sam had an epileptiform attack that night, and was taken into hospital for observation. One month after being discharged, he found a dead mole, and became morbidly agitated. He asked about death, and in the night had convulsions. Two months later he had a third attack, after he had accidentally crushed a butterfly in his hand. The diagnosis of Sam's case was that a psychic stimulus, the idea of death, had helped to make manifest a latent potentiality for epileptic seizures. The 'really dominant pathogenic psychic stimulus' was held to be the boy's fear that his mother might die,

---

[1] E. Erikson, *Childhood and Society*, 1950

because he had thrown something at her and hit her a few days before his grandmother's death. From the abbreviated account of this interesting case one may add a surmise that Sam feared also, perhaps in retaliation, his own death, and painfully identified himself with the small dead animals, so that their death acted as violent stimulus to his fear for himself.

When Jane's mother found herself unable to resolve the child's difficulties, she shared the child's distress. When she turned to textbooks on child development for help on this problem she did not find it. Instinctive infantile fears of loud noises or of being dropped were held to be the basis upon which, by conditioning, other fears were built up. A standard American text,[1] quoting researches by Gesell and others, reported that children of six years showed fears of the supernatural, such as ghosts and witches, and of the elements, such as thunder, rain, wind and fire; some also showed fear that the mother might die, or of being late for school. By seven years, children 'were showing deeper, more worrisome fears such as fear of war, spies, burglars, people hiding under the bed'. Parents, the writers said, often find it difficult to answer questions about death, and 'their hesitancy sometimes implies to children that there is something to fear about death. . . . Children who are often ill sometimes feel the anxiety of their parents that they may die, and hence tend to carry *a vague uneasiness which healthy children do not experience*' (my italics). Such pronouncements, far from helping parents of children such as Jane or Theodor or Ruth, are likely to deepen their distress. Indeed, although the sampling techniques employed were doubtless sophisticated and the researches planned on what was considered a sound methodological basis, generalizations were unscientifically drawn from culturally biased observations. How is the conclusion reached that the fear of the seven-year-old about people under the bed is 'deeper and more worrisome' than the fear of the six-year-old that his mother may die? The illogicality of the exposition and the patent insensibility to the phenomenon

[1] M. E. Breckenridge and E. L. Vincent, *Child Development*, 1960, pp. 136, 138

of man's fear of death, which anthropology and history have demonstrated to be one of the most common and powerful of human motivations, can be attributed only to conventional (i.e. culturally induced) repression of this fear by the writers themselves and those whose researches they report.

If the parent turned to the psychoanalyst or psychiatrist for help, he was still unlikely to find it, though the tide may be beginning to turn in the medical as well as the academic psychological field. Dr C. W. Wahl[1] wrote twelve years ago:

The phenomenon of the fear of death or anxiety about it (*thanatophobia* as it is called), while certainly no clinical rarity, has almost no description in the psychiatric or psychoanalytic literature . . . and when it is noted . . . it is usually described solely as a derivative and secondary phenomenon, often as a more easily endurable form of 'castration fear'. There is good clinical evidence that this kind of displacement occurs. . . . But it is also important to consider if this formulation also subserves in part a defensive need on the part of the psychiatrists themselves.

It is the child who holds the secrets . . . to this ancient riddle of death, and of our methods of handling and coping with this fearful eventuality. . . . It is only recently, however, that we have been able to learn from this source. Freud . . . expected [fear of death] to appear, if at all, subsequent to the oedipal period, and . . . as a symbolic product of the fear of castration attendant upon the improper resolution of the Oedipus complex. Present day experience does not altogether support these views. Thanatophobia is frequently encountered in children. . . . Its appearance seems to be contiguous to the development of concept formation and the formation of guilt, both of which greatly antedate the Oedipus complex.

At one period of the development of Freudian theory, Ruth Mack Brunswick suggested and Freud accepted the theory, that the little girl, desiring sexual intercourse with her father, reacts neurotically to the administration of enemas by the mother. In one instance at least, a little girl's neurosis involving anxiety about death was interpreted on these lines:

[1] C. W. Wahl, 'The fear of death', H. Feifel (ed.), *The Meaning of Death*, 1959, pp. 19, 21

[P.R.51.] A little girl (7:6), daughter of devoted parents of average intelligence and modest economic standing, was brought to the analyst because of dog-phobia, developing two months after she had had measles, and had been given enemas. The phobia was cured after two months by allowing satisfaction for anal impulses, etc. The interesting point is that the neurosis shortly returned again, and one of its symptoms was inability to count, and apparent loss of all knowledge of numerical relations. . . . This, it appeared, came from fear of death – how soon the schoolmistress, the doctor, her mother, would die. She told the analyst that she had a compulsive feeling to think about death and graveyards. When they spoke at school about All Souls Day (*La Fête des Morts*) she was deeply upset, and could eat nothing.[1]

It seems to me probable that the enemas had nothing to do with the etiology of the neurosis and distress, but that the dog-phobia arose from a fear of retaliation for aggressive wishes against a parent or sibling fantasied as animals, the amnesia for numbers from the association of death with age, and the distress at reference to *La Fête des Morts* from its implication of the inevitability of death for the self.

Like the nakedness of the fabled emperor, the fear of death, though patent to unsophisticated observation, has until recently been invisible to psychologists and psychoanalysts, with the notable exceptions, in the older generation, of Professors J. C. Flugel and Gardner Murphy. The child's concept of death and anxiety about it have been constantly described in terms of *nothing-but*. Rank considered it 'one of Freud's greatest merits that he has called our attention to the child's negative idea of death'. Freud's statement that to the child death meant little more than departure or disappearance has been frequently quoted. One American psychologist has said that death means to the child simply hospitalization! We have certainly found that during the early stages of language and concept learning, children's notions of death may be limited; generalization is unsound, for these limited concepts have a great variety of content. There is no

[1] E. Sterba, '*Analyse d'un cas de phobie des chiens*', *Revue Française de Psychoanalyse*, 7, 4, 1934

warrant for supposing that inadequacy of the concept ensures its emotional insulation. The supposed departure of the mother may cause suffering and despair as keen as any loss in adult life, and if the researches of Bowlby, Spitz, Liddell and their successors are to be given due weight, we must suppose that the anticipation of an impending event involving such distress will tend to arouse anxiety in the child. Some repression of such anxiety is clearly common and normal in childhood. Distress as deep or deeper than that associated with separation may occur with the realization that one's own death is inevitable. Some temporary denial of reality may have positive value, in relieving anxiety and permitting subsequent acceptance. And, as we have observed in the case of Stephen, some of man's most valuable interests and achievements, individual and social, may have their origin in the desire to avoid mortality.

Denial of personal mortality is only one among several ways in which the child gradually becomes able to assimilate emotionally and intellectually the realities of his physical and social environment. Another 'mechanism' used by child and adult is the harnessing of repressed desires by which the hated object becomes loved and, if not sought, played with, tempted. In fiction this attitude in the child has been brilliantly expressed by Morante.[1] The lonely boy, whose mother had died at his birth, makes up his own Code of Absolute Truth, 'but none of the laws of the code mentioned the thing I most hated: death. . . . In my own natural happiness I chased all my thoughts away from death. . . . But at the same time, the more I hated death the more I exaltedly enjoyed giving proofs of my own temerity: no game was enough fun if it lacked the fascination of risk.'

The age to which Freud assigned sexual latency is the period of *daring* and accepting *dares* – to put one's hand in fire, climb the tree or crag, walk along the top of the wall, lie under the train, run last across the street. The tendency of people to seek out or play with danger was noted by some research workers in 1958 as something of a puzzle for psychologists, not entirely

[1] E. Morante, *Arturo's Island*, 1957 (1959 edn, pp. 32, 33)

consistent with prevalent theories of homeostasis or reinforcement.[1] It is, however, not so inconsistent with the development of theories of man's need for perceptual stimulation, based on studies carried out at McGill University. In the current view, the organism is seen as seeking varied sufficient levels of stimulation rather than the re-establishment of a static optimum condition. The character of *dare* behaviour during the pre-adolescent post-infant period brings it fittingly into the scheme which includes the concerted mockery of death described by the Opies, and the bravado which armed Joyce Cary's childhood against ghosts.

[P.R.52.] The country people avoided the mill in the dark, and though Harry and I stoutly denied the existence of ghosts, we would not go alone at night through the [mill] yards . . . my imagination created for me grey faceless shapes, like little rags of cloud, trooping from window to window [of the ruined mill] . . . and staring after us out of their no faces, with eyes like bats. They were faceless because my will was so resolute not to believe in ghosts. They had eyes because, in spite of my will, I felt watched. . . . In spite of these terrors and though there was a direct path to the mill-pool through the buildings, we used nearly always to go by the yards. Partly this was bravado, because we were ashamed to be frightened, partly it was the attraction of the enterprise . . .

We did not believe in ghosts, but we were frightened of them; and I at least, as a child, was frightened of the dark. Also, I was nervous of heights. Therefore every dark cave or haunted wood, and every high building or mast, seemed to say to me: 'I dare you,' and I was ashamed not to dare.[2]

The daring feats of adults make good publicity, but the spontaneous enterprise of the young is by its very nature forbidden, and so not usually to be observed directly by the adult. It is forbidden for the sake of the child; unfortunately in the crowded conditions of modern city life it may find no outlet but in deeds forbidden also for the sake of other people and the sanctity of the

[1] S. L. Witryol and J. E. Calkins, 'Marginal social values of rural school children', *Journal of Genetic Psychology*, 92, 1958
[2] Joyce Cary, *A House of Children*, 1941

law. Boys break into premises, or drive before they are old enough to hold a licence. When interviewing young delinquents I have not seldom conjectured that a persistence of the childish inability to resist a dare, rather than any anti-social motive, has brought them into conflict with the law. The illegality itself, in adolescence, may add spice to the enterprise.

Even in the younger children of the above quotation and of our records, there seems a pressure to mix reality and fantasy in the enjoyment of the feared. The children who ventured into the deserted mill

. . . therefore made much of rat-hunting, and Harry would say: 'It's important to kill the rats – they eat up every year millions of pounds' worth of stuff. Besides, they carry plague and all kinds of disease'; and both Kathy and I would warmly support him. 'People *pay* rat-catchers to kill them.' All of us knew that the rats were water-rats and perfectly harmless, but we did not say so as there would have been no good motive for our exciting journey through the old mill . . .

[H.R.47.] Richard (6:11) asked for Grimm's *Fairy Tales* to read during rest time, saying he liked it very much. Ben (10:1) said he did not like it. B: 'Richard's afraid of witches, and I'm afraid of ghosts.' R: 'I'm afraid of witches and ghosts and burglars and *everything*!' B: 'Oh, burglars are *real*, you needn't be afraid of *them*! You needn't be afraid of anything that's in reality. You'd just run down and dial 999' [i.e. the police]. (Note by M: 'Our telephone is not on the dial system.')

In the *dare stage*, children devise a mixture of reality and fantasy in facing their fears and the challenges of life. Panic must be prevented, distress mastered by living through terrors not entirely fanciful, or dangers not fanciful at all but invited.

Even anxiety about separation and about the retaliatory nature of aggression may have the function of bringing into the imagination at the same time the possible accompanying alleviations, such as Sonia Rasmussen's sixpence. When bereavement comes, after earliest infancy, it is not for the first time; even the young child has had this experience before, in imagination.

Some examples have been given of the immediate psychological effect of bereavement on the child individually observed at home or at school. What is the probable long-term effect? Psychiatrists have been concerned to find whether childhood bereavement is likely to augment the risk of mental disorder. Valid comparison demands information about the numbers of bereaved from a similar background who do and do not become psychiatric patients in later life. An early study by Dr Felix Brown[1] which suggested a high incidence of later depressive illness among those bereaved in childhood has been followed by numerous subsequent researches, and recently a large-scale investigation of psychiatric and other patients has been carried out in Edinburgh and Leeds.[2] It was found that 15 per cent of the 'normals' had lost a parent by age 16. The proportion of psychiatric patients who had lost a father by this age was not significantly higher in any diagnostic category; and only among the most severely depressive patients, and then only with reference to maternal bereavement, was there any difference between the mentally disordered and the psychiatrically normal patients. A study of 4,000 cases, many rural, by Dr Bratfös[3] in Norway included childhood loss of a parent for causes other than death, and found separation by death not especially predictive of mental disorder.

Brief résumé of such researches necessarily omits some significant detail. The diagnosis of severe depression may be given in Europe to some patients who would be classed as schizophrenic in America. There is evidence[4] that among adult depressives, women bereaved of the father in adolescence, and men or women bereaved of their mother in childhood are more likely to attempt suicide. When a total group is confronted with death, as Ameri-

[1] F. Brown, 'Childhood bereavement and subsequent psychiatric disorder', *British Journal of Psychiatry*, 112, 1966

[2] A. Munro and A. B. Griffiths, (a) 'Further data on childhood parent-loss in psychiatric normals', *Acta Psychiatrica Scandinavica*, 44, 4, 1968, (b) 'Some psychiatric non-sequelae of childhood bereavement', *British Journal of Psychiatry*, 115, 1969

[3] O. Bratfös, 'Parental deprivation in childhood and type of future mental disease', *Acta Psychiatrica Scandinavica*, 43, 4, 1967

[4] O. W. Hill, 'The association of childhood bereavement with suicidal attempt in depressive illness', *British Journal of Psychiatry*, 115, 1969

cans were on the assassination of President Kennedy, adults may be confused and insensitive in their handling of children. This observation was made by a team of psychiatrists[1] with reference to the nursing staff in the children's ward of a psychiatric hospital. The nurses, themselves upset, expected the reactions of the children to resemble their own. The anxious adult is affronted by the child's immunity from distress. He (she) judges the immunity to be anti-social, without seeking its source, which might involve him in painful self-analysis.

The observation made in the hospital ward may apply beyond its walls.

[1] S. I. Harrison *et al.*, 'Children's reactions to bereavement: adult confusions and misperceptions', *Archives of General Psychiatry*, 17, 5, 1967

CHAPTER 9

DEATH AND TIME

DEATH and time are closely related in man's thought, by the evidence of mythology and literature. Yet the *time* of different cultures varies greatly, while death keeps a similar essential aspect for adults everywhere. Time is more difficult to conceive than death; its physical manifestations are more elusive. It has been said that through the realization of death man is enabled to perceive time.[1] Sober study of the association of the two concepts in the development of the child, and in history, suggests that the truth of this proposition is limited. The concept of death and the concept of time seem to be continuously interactive; there is two-way traffic.

Newton's tutor, Isaac Barrow, defined time as *the continuance of any thing in its own being*.[2] St Augustine said that to the question 'What is time?' there can be no quick and easy answer, though in conversation no word is more familiarly used or more easily recognized.

What, then, is time? I know well enough what it is, provided that nobody asks me; but if I am asked what it is and try to explain, I am baffled. All the same I can confidently say that I know if nothing passed, there would be no past time; if nothing were going to happen, there would be no future time; and if nothing *were*, there would be no present time. . . . The extent to which something once was, but no longer is, is the measure of its death; and the extent to which something once was not, but now is, is the measure of its beginning.[3]

[1] M. Heidegger, *Sein und Zeit*. For those unable to understand the German exposition, H. J. Blackham anglicizes Heidegger's thought in *Six Existentialist Thinkers*, 1952-1961

[2] G. Whitrow, *The Natural Philosophy of Time*, 1961, p. 130

[3] Augustine of Hippo, *Confessions*, XI, 14 (1962 edn)

The child, in his early thinking about time, tends to confuse time and being. Faced with statements or questions about events when he himself was non-existent, he may become confused, and either deny the fact explicitly or become involved in contradictions. As an example of denial, we have already recorded how Ben, aged 3:4, rejected the suggestion that before his mother conceived him he was nowhere, and stated that he was under her feet. Examples of the antinomies of thought into which children may be led by inability to conceive of time separately from their existence have been recorded by Wallon.[1]

[P.R.53.] (C . . . vin infers that he was born before anything existed.) Q: 'But there were houses before you were born?' C: 'Yes.' Q: 'Who built the houses?' C: 'People.' Q: 'Who were these people – they were not your dad and mum?' C: 'They were men.' ('messieurs.') Q: 'Were they born before you?' C: 'No.'

As Wallon says, the child seems to see himself as the subject of all that exists; to explain the preconditions of his own existence there was but a collective *being*, anonymous, consisting of persons undefined and, so to speak, imageless. Things exist only to the extent that they can be perceived by us; it is the solipsist position. The subtle and obscure manner in which solipsism is from time to time presented by philosophers may give the false impression that it is the conclusion of a profound process of analytical thought. In fact, it is very primitive. It is far from being unfamiliar to the child.

Wallon's examples of the child's solipsism in relation to time illustrate it most clearly with reference to the period before the small subject's birth, as with C . . . vin. In our own records we find an illustration of his argument with reference to the other end of life:

[H.R.48.] Richard's mother had referred to 'the Christmas before last'. To this R (4:9) objected: 'But there isn't a last Christmas. They go on and on. Till I'm dead.'

[1] *Les Origines de la pensée chez l'enfant*, 1945, vol. 1, pp. 180 ff., vol. 2, pp. 209 ff. and 404

Through some preoccupation with thoughts of death, common at his age, the child had clearly mistaken the meaning of the word *last* in the context. Where *previous* was intended, he had inferred *final*. Adult parallels to his thought need not be sought only among psychotics and philosophers. Shakespeare put the same idea into the mouth of the childishly romantic Hotspur when he fell mortally wounded:

> But thought's the slave of life, and life time's fool,
> And time, that takes survey of all the world,
> Must have a stop.[1]

A common solution of the problem, in Western cultures, of the relation of time to own-being or ego is diametrically opposite to that of the child C . . . vin. Instead of time being cut off before the ego's existence, the ego is extended into a post-mortem future. In a cross-cultural study of time concepts as related to ego extension, it was reported:

The Western ego may extend infinitely into the future – at any rate it is importantly involved in future events; Hindu egos extend infinitely into both past and future – with a definite understanding of the beginning in the past and the eventual end of the individual soul; Chinese egos start their extensions not from remote time but from the present, flowing into both past and future, with individuality becoming more and more tenuous; and for the Coast Salish, ego extension is hardly temporal at all but carries the individual inevitably into relation with the world about him.[2]

The behaviour resulting from the post-mortem ego-extension of modern Western man has been discussed by Bridgman as irrational:

Every individual hears his fellows talk about death, his own included. He comes to think about death in impersonal terms, that is, in terms of his own experience. The resulting concept is an incongruous hodge-podge, because if there is one thing my own death is not it is a form of

[1] *Henry IV*, Part One, 5, iv
[2] M. W. Smith, 'Different cultural concepts of past, present and future: a study of ego extension', *Psychiatry*, 15, 1952, pp. 395–400

experience. . . . The result is that the programs for action which most people draw up in anticipation of death simply do not make sense.[1]

Here the reference is clearly to death as post-mortem condition, not to the process of dying. Bridgman's reason for considering as irrational the behaviour of most people in Western cultures is rhetorically set out in a series of questions:

> Why should any man *want* to dictate the disposal of his property when it can make no difference whatever to him? Why is a deathbed promise regarded as so sacred? . . . Why do men work for what they think will be the favourable verdict of history? What possible difference can it make what history thinks? Why do we commend the Christian martyr? If he was not working for the distant establishment of the Christian religion was he not failing to appreciate that this could not possibly touch him? . . . was he not showing a rather unrealistic lack of adaptability in the presence of superior physical force? . . . Why does the suicide so often try to leave some sort of note explaining his action? . . . Why is one so anxious to provide for his family after he is dead; why are life insurance companies such a well recognized and influential institution? . . . Why is it that threats to one's family after one's death are the most effective weapon of the GPU? . . . The majority of people simply do not appreciate what it means to be dead. Forms of thought and motives are projected . . . simply by a process of verbal inertia.[2]

It is possible, though not, I think, sufficient, to answer Bridgman in terms of evolutionary theory: there are insects which make elaborate provision for the welfare of offspring that are not hatched until after the parent's death; mammals are often found to be prepared to fight to the death to safeguard their young; man's concern for the future of his family or group beyond the term of his own life may be attributed to similar, innate impulses evolved in the species as a consequence of their survival value. If, however, the exercise of reason is seen as the human characteristic of supreme survival value, then every inherited form of behaviour must argue its case in the court of rationality. Indeed Bridgman

[1] P. W. Bridgman, *The Way Things Are*, 1959, pp. 234 ff.
[2] *The Intelligent Individual and Society*, 1938, p. 170

did not overlook the social value of the altruistic attitudes of man; on the contrary, he asserts that men's 'illogical (*post-mortem*) programs constitute a most powerful social cement, and that if society were suddenly deprived of them it would probably pass through an initial period of high instability'.[1] Nevertheless he is clearly of the opinion that a social cement thus compounded is *ipso facto* undesirable, so that an initial period of instability would not be too high a price to pay for its liquidation.

Disregarding evolutionary theory, the layman might counter Bridgman's question differently, contending that his own behaviour was not illogical, on the following grounds: his (X's) wish for Y's welfare or grief has time-reference primarily to Y's existence, not to his own. When X thinks of a friend's past, present or future misery he, X, is *currently* unhappy; likewise if he thinks of an enemy's success in former years, or currently, or forty years on, he, X, suffers annoyance or anger, or if his enemy is troubled, then X may enjoy *Schadenfreude*. There is nothing illogical in X's concern about Y's condition irrespective of X's own decease. Moreover, Y may be not an individual but a group, with a potential span of existence incommensurate with that of X. Now, as for Y's past condition, X can do nothing to change it, or its effect upon himself, but he may be able to influence Y's future state, and in order to ensure his own greater current happiness he will rationally attempt this. The situation may be complicated by the anticipation that X's own future condition may affect that of Y; this, however, is simply a special case within the more general one. Within this more complex case one may distinguish states of X in which (a) he expects to be able to witness Y's condition and (b) he does not. For instance, X may simultaneously insure against loss to Y from the consequences of X's own (a) disablement or (b) death. In the former event he would be a witness of Y's distress, in the latter not so. The common operative factor is that his current anxiety on behalf of Y is allayed by his action.

The social psychologist may offer another response to Bridg-

[1] Bridgman, *The Way Things Are*, p. 135

man's question. Through time the self builds up a personality around a nucleus which William James called the *pure ego*,[1] by means of unconscious imitations, identifications, and the playing of a series of social roles. These develop through affective relationships between the individual and another person (e.g. a parent) or group (e.g. the family, gang, firm, community, nation). This is a two-way process. The parent functions as such only through the active existence of the child; the group persists as such only through the active identification of its members with its characteristic being. In the total process, something of the temporal character of the group is unconsciously assimilated and appropriated by the individual self, and the personal character of the individual contributes to the character of the normally longer-lasting entity, the group. Customs and laws which recognize and sanction this temporal relationship of individual ego and community provide the foundation of stable societies, rather than an expendable cement of their superstructure. The process originates in social impulse or affect; philosophically and psychoanalytically it is called Eros. Of such impulse, reason is properly a servant, not a judge. Reason may properly guide and control its effects, but not rightly censure as irrational the originating process.

This matter of a sense of immortality arising within the relation between individual and community is central to our theme, and will come up again. It is developed in the *Symposium*. Allied to it is a similar sense in relation to land inhabited by the individual or the community. Modern conditioning of citizens to *nationalist* patriotic reactions tends to obscure the degree to which such an impulse may arise spontaneously. The writer therefore ventures to record an instance from personal encounter with a stranger: a farmer's daughter, middle-aged, unmarried, who had recently nursed her father until his death; she expressed grief that he had no belief in a future life, but had only cared that his successor should make sure that his farm land 'did not lose heart'.

To return to the child. The accepted significance of words denoting temporal relationships is generally learned by children

[1] W. James, *Principles of Psychology*, 1890

in Western cultures during the years 2:0–7:0.[1] 'Telling the time' by the clock may be begun during the fourth year. The 'time' thus 'told' may appear at first to be simply a practical signal for recurrent events:

[H.R.49.] Richard (4:9), after enumerating all the things 'that we wouldn't be able to have if we had no money', including lunch, came to 'clocks', paused a moment, and added, 'but then we wouldn't want any clocks, if we hadn't any lunch'.
[H.R.50.] In a discussion on whether various objects were furniture or tools, it was decided that a clock was a time-telling piece of furniture. Richard (5:6) remarked a little later: 'I know a thing that tell you's [sic] the time of winter – that the leaves are all off the trees.'

In a study of the development of the sense of time in the child, Ames found that time in relation to the ends of things tends to be understood by young children before time in relation to beginnings. It has been stated as a general rule that man tends to live in anticipation rather than in retrospect.[2] But the application of this rule should be limited to the responsible adult. The very old, who would be unlikely to survive unaided under stringent conditions, may be observed to live increasingly in the past, even interpreting events of the day in terms of other persons and places of their youth, while the child, and those freed by personality and society from the obligations of material provision, tend to concern themselves with both past and future, origins and ends. The conception of time which is developed in myth, religion and science appears to be as much associated with the backward look towards personal and cosmic origins as with the forward gaze towards death and the future. St Augustine's study of time is concerned more with problems of creation than with resurrection, and the study of thought about time from Montaigne to T. S. Eliot which we owe to Georges Poulet[3] shows at least a balance

[1] L. B. Ames, 'The development of the sense of time in the young child', *Journal of Genetic Psychology*, 68, 1946
[2] E. Cassirer, *An Essay on Man* (quoting W. Stern), 1944
[3] G. Poulet, *Studies in Human Time*, 1956

between the backward and the forward look, with the scale tipped rather towards memory than anticipation.

Learning to conceive of space and time in accordance with modern Western culture involves children in a step which some find difficult, between an early stage when reference is to recurrent divisions of time – winter, summer; day, night; lunch-time, bed-time – to a later continuous linear concept. The recurrent sequences without clear linearity which represent time to the young child resemble the mythopoeic time described by archaeologists. This, we are told, is an eternal time without definite structure. The immortal Pharaoh may be at once among the stars and in his tomb. Its recurrent rhythms are cosmically determined, yet subject to a certain caprice, so that they influence and are influenced by man's activities. By repetition of actions symbolically associated with the cosmic rhythms of days and seasons man seeks to ensure their continuance. Phenomena which do not embody this ideal are non-significant, frivolous. The significant is the recurrent otherwise unchanging condition of things; the unique transitory event demands only transitory consideration. There is no sense of history in such a way of thinking.

Many children aged under ten years cannot tell why the skull of a ten-year-old child should not be that of a man famous in times long past.[1] The child's difficulty in conceiving the irreversibility of change in time was similarly shown by Richard in his seventh year. Among a series of pictures of kings of England, R was shown one of a king of the same name as himself, pictured as an adult. R: 'I'm six. Was [Richard Coeur-de-Lion] six?' [H.R.51.] Without a concept of age and death related to a linear concept of time, the study of history can hardly begin.

The child Jane, in her early anxiety about death, displaced her affection from living things on to the artificial poppy, saying, 'You see, it won't die!' The ancient Egyptians who, we are told, had very little sense of history, similarly were led by anxiety about death to value supremely tangible, permanent monuments which could be made by man. 'The Great Pyramid of Gizeh is . . .

[1] L. Terman and M. Merrill, *Measuring Intelligence*, 1932

a document in the history of the human mind. . . . For himself and for his sovereign the pharaoh's engineer was achieving the conquest of immortality by sheer command of material forces!'[1]

The modern Western concept of time has been traced to the early religious developments of the Hebrew peoples.[2] To their priests and prophets, time came to represent not mainly a rhythm to be ritually maintained in accord with the behaviour of cosmic powers such as the sun, nor as a tide which beats in vain against stone and cunning artifact, but as a medium in which a transcendent God would be enabled to demonstrate His will and glory through His chosen people. The events by which they reached and conquered their country were continually recounted in their ritual as demonstrating the operation of divine power. Thus it was upon happenings in an historic past, not upon unchanging recurrences of nature, that they put their trust for an uncharted future in which their active relationship with the supreme Power would be the determining factor. To do evil was, then, not only to perform human sacrifice but to worship the sun and moon and to *observe times*.[3]

A cyclic view of time is not necessarily irreconcilable with a linear view. No linear-time theorist denies the cycle of the seasons; already by the time of the writing of the Old Testament books of Kings and Chronicles the Babylonians had developed a sophisticated mathematical astronomy, but their theories of the return of golden years did not deny to time a stretch in which to undertake the operation. There are, however, differences in the degree in which recurrence or one-way linearity are used in religious-mythological explanations of the relations of birth, life, death and time. The Hindu and the Buddhist stress recurrence; the Christian stresses the single way to a goal.

Instances are recorded of anxiety arising from the attempt to conceive infinity of linear time. Stekel,[4] an early disciple of Freud,

[1] J. H. Breasted, *The Dawn of Conscience*, quoted in H. and H. A. Frankfort, et al., *Before Philosophy*, 1949

[2] S. G. F. Brandon, *Time and Mankind*, 1951

[3] II Chronicles xxxiii, 6

[4] W. Stekel, *Conditions of Nervous Anxiety*, 1923, ch. 27

wrote: 'I have often heard very wise and critical people say that they dare not meditate on the question of infinity or on time and space, otherwise something in the head threatened to go wrong.' This he discussed under the heading: *Dread of the dead.* When one of our subjects, Stephen, was 4:10 his mother reported, 'I think he's rather frightened of [the idea of death], as I used to be at the concept of Space.' [H.R.52.] The father of another subject recorded a conscious horror of immense stellar distances, though he was not acquainted with Pascal's note: '*Le silence éternel de ces espaces infinis m'effraye*'. The idea either of endlessness or of ending are equally unacceptable:

[H.R.53.] Ben (3:6) had been told that his mother would die when she was old, perhaps when over seventy. He began worrying about the end or endlessness of numbers, and was told that there was an imaginary end called infinity. The following morning, babbling in his bed before rising, he was heard to say, '*finity!*' and then, after a pause, 'Finity-one, finity-two . . .' and so on.

The child was attempting to bring under control the ending of things, although his concepts of death, time and number were as yet embryonic. The refusal to admit or conceive of an ending is not peculiar to childhood. Early discussions on the Carnot-Clausius principle of entropy produced similar reactions in mature scientists. Haeckel (1834–1919) objected to the principle on the ground that if it were true, we should have a beginning corresponding to the ending of the world which the principle assumed, both of which ideas he considered untenable.[1] The cyclic concept of time continues to exercise imaginative interest, as witnessed by J. B. Priestley's *Time Plays*, and many tales of similar theme.

The period when the Hebrews of the Old Testament found no place in their religion for ideas of personal immortality was also the period of the great prophets. They did not foretell a determinate future; as Cassirer[2] observes, they were not augurs. 'The

[1] Whitrow, *op. cit.*, p. 6
[2] Cassirer, *op. cit.*, p. 53 ff.

future of which they spoke was not an empirical fact but an ethical and religious task.' It was a promise, not a prediction, and referred to a mutual undertaking, begun in trust and the negation of anxiety, to end in the physical and spiritual relief of the poor, light to the blind and freedom to prisoners. There was no denial of man's mortality, butthe cry that *all flesh is grass* is followed by the injunction *Fear not; I will help thee*.[1] In a totally different idiom, Wittgenstein makes the same statement as Isaiah:

The temporal immortality of the human soul, that is to say, its eternal survival after death, is not only in no way guaranteed, but this assumption in the first place will not do for us what we always tried to make it do. Is a riddle solved by the fact that I survive for ever?... The solution of the riddle of life in space and time lies outside space and time.[2]

Among the Hebrews in the second century B.C. under the pressure of persecution a belief in resurrection and *post-mortem* ethical judgement prevailed; the legends of Enoch and Elijah lent support to an ascension theology, and Greek learning contributed to modify the earlier rejection of doctrines of personal immortality. The sophisticated belief in life after death, however, was different from early mythopoeic attitudes. Cassirer notes that Plato, St Paul and the authors of the Book of Enoch[3] all agree in assuming the need for argument about it. The very idea of such argument is alien to the temper of mythopoeic thought, in which an after-life is taken for granted, with little concern for inconsistencies.

The Hebraic view of time was disseminated throughout the ancient world by the Christian Church; not, that is, the single-minded view of the major prophets, but the later view in which the fate of the individual took a more central place. The Babylonian concept of eternally recurrent time had been superseded among the Jews by a time-concept which recognized human

[1] Isaiah xl, 6; xli, 13–14
[2] L. Wittgenstein, *Tractatus Logico-Philosophicus*, 6.4312, 1922
[3] Apocrypha, the Book of Enoch. R. H. Charles notes the influence of this book on the writers of the synoptic gospels

events as unique yet significant. The rise of Christianity, with its central doctrine of the Crucifixion as a unique event uniquely significant in time, was the cardinal factor causing men to think of time as a linear progression without cyclical repetition.[1] The first philosophical theory of time inspired by the Christian revelation was that of St Augustine 400 years later; another 200 years went by before a Scythian churchman in Italy introduced the practice of dating events from the birth of Christ. Previously, events were dated by reference to some occasion lost in the mists of antiquity, such as the creation of the world or the founding of Rome. The measuring of historical time from a recorded occurrence was a scientific advance. The objective superiority of the practice was not, of course, the reason for its adoption. In fact the actual date of the birth of Jesus was apparently not fixed correctly. The event was chosen because it was seen as the temporal origin of man's hope of eternal life. In this context numerical exactitude did not seem of the first importance; 'high heav'n rejects the lore/Of nicely calculated less and more'.

In consequence of the custom of dating from the birth of Christ, the life of Jesus is necessarily presented to children in Western cultures as a central, unique historical event. This may raise for them at a very early age problems such as that which the medieval Church solved by the legend of the Harrowing of Hell.[2] In our records we find that Ben (3:10), having heard that Jesus 'told people how to be good', asked next day, 'Who looked after London before Jesus Christ?' [H.R.54.] (Note appended to the record: *looked after* = told to be good; *London* = people.) A linear concept of historical time is implicit in the question.

St Augustine tentatively concluded that time is subjective.[3] Has time for the modern physicist an objective reference, by means of which he escapes the subjectivity and the socio-religious connotation? This is no simple question. Take the physical problem of the way time is to be scaled. A physicist tells us:

[1] Whitrow, *op. cit.*, p. 30n.
[2] Dante, *L'Inferno*, 4, 46–63
[3] *Confessions*, XI, 27. See also B. Russell, *A History of Western Philosophy*, 1940, ch. 4, IV

If we adopt a purely relative measure of time in terms of specific sequence of particular phenomena, we may be able to *order* phenomena temporally, but not necessarily measure the intervals against the order. The Moon's revolutions are not strictly uniform, nor the rotation of the Earth. Atomic clocks imply the hypothesis that all atoms of a given element behave in the same way, irrespective of place and epoch. The ultimate scale of time is a theoretical concomitant of our concept of universal laws of nature.[1]

It was, however, from theology that science originally drew the concept of universal natural law. Needham[2] considers it doubtful whether science could have reached its present state of development without passing through a theological stage; moreover, the theology required is not a vague general manner of thinking but that theology from which Western science actually derived. The measurement of time went far in Babylon, but became inextricably involved there with astrology and an irrational determinism, such as the Hebrew prophets avoided. 'When we read in the Psalms that the heavens declare the glory of God and the firmament sheweth his handiwork, we hear a voice which mocks the beliefs of Egyptians and Babylonians',[3] for to them the heavens were themselves gods, rather than the testimony of transcendent divine laws.

Thus Needham, following Comte, speaks of a theological stage, yet of theories of time he says, 'It is strange how close to scientific thought theological thought has often been.'[4] Surely Bernard's view is correct, that Comte's three stages coexist in the individual, and the theological provides the impulse to scientific inquiry above the shallowest levels. The physicist's concept of time has been determined culturally as well as objectively; it is a special sociological variant. Newtonian time, we are told, differs from that of Einstein, and the former certainly, the latter probably at least temporarily differs from any time-concept suitable as a

[1] Whitrow, *op. cit.*, p. 41
[2] J. Needham, *Human Law and the Laws of Nature in China and the West*, 1951, p. 42
[3] Frankfort, *op. cit.*, p. 237
[4] J. Needham, *Time, the Refreshing River*, 1943, p. 238

basis of neurophysiological theory.[1] The invalidity of Newtonian time for the biologist lies in the fact that it does not point in a unique direction, and that, in principle, all motion and dynamical processes subject to Newtonian laws are reversible. The *time* of organic processes is not reversible. It is the medium in which they proceed from germination or fission to dissolution, but never vice versa.

All living things appear to have an internal clock, giving them a relationship with time more primitive than that due to perceptual or conceptual processes. Phases of living have their time-norms, compelling as a bird's impulse to migration. In primitive societies and in those ancient civilizations where change was conceived as occurring not continuously but with a discontinuous cyclic rhythm, man's journey through life was visualized similarly as a sequence of distinct stages, and the opening of each stage required appropriate ritual solemnization. These ceremonies or *rites de passage*[2] show remarkable intercultural resemblance. The internal time-clock was not concerned only with ringing in these special events. The lapse of cosmic time registers more accurately on the internal clock than in man's unaided consciousness; it is found that persons in hypnotic trance measure the hours more accurately than they do when in a normal state.

One may hypothesize that this 'internal clock' operates in the conditioning process involving reflex responses, wherein, as I have argued, no concept of cause is to be assumed. The operation of the internal clock is similarly assumed independent of any *concept* of time, but if the theory of Guyau is accepted, it may provide a foundation for time *perception*. Guyau[3] held that the idea (or percept) of time originated in the activity-filled interval

---

[1] Whitrow, p. 5: 'The absorption of time into the geometry of a hyper-space in Einsteinian theory demands circumvention of the asymmetry of past and future which characterises our temporal existence.' See also Grey Walter, in J. M. Tanner and B. Inhelder (eds), *Discussions on Child Development*, 1956, vol. 4

[2] A. van Gennep, *The Rites of Passage*, 1909

[3] M. Guyau, *La Genèse de l'idée de temps*, 1890

between desire and satisfaction: that the infant, kicking and clamouring as he awaits his food, learns to perceive differences in duration through the sensations induced by differing degrees of exertion and fatigue. Piaget[1] contends that the perception of time first occurs in the course of manipulation of objects, and is initially attributed to the object. The two views may not be irreconcilable. The percept of Piaget's subject may be of the physicist's (Newtonian) time, a function of objectively observed mass and speed, while the percept of Guyau's infant may have reference to the more primitive time of ancient civilizations, in which sequences of events are cut into periods of present, with specific affective quality, and an anticipated future of contrasted, consummatory quality.

Guyau concludes that '*Il faut désirer, il faut vouloir, il faut étendre le main et marcher, pour créer l'avenir. L'avenir n'est pas ce qui vient vers nous, mais ce vers quoi nous allons.*' Bergson, Guyau's contemporary, also stressed man's active function in the determination of the future. Guyau adds further that intention, and the effort that accompanies it, is the first source of the idea of efficient and of final cause. But the relation of cause and time is a subject (of the utmost interest) which cannot be pursued here, nor has the present writer the philosophical or mathematical expertise to do so.

It has been said of Bergson that he was representative of the nineteenth century in the view that all genuine thought is of the continuous *becoming* of things, duration being the only reality; but representative of the twentieth in the view that becoming no longer signifies *being changed* but *changing*.[2] 'To exist is to change; to change is to mature; to mature is to create oneself endlessly.' His originality, according to Poulet, lay in his affirmation that duration is something other than history or a system of laws; that it is a free creation. 'Every instant man acts, creates his action, and together with it . . . himself and the world.'

By such a belief, the anguish of helpless subjection to cruel or

[1] J. Piaget, *L'Épistémologie génétique*, 1951
[2] Poulet, *op. cit.*, p. 34 ff.

indifferent powers is overcome, but there is substituted for it the anguish of responsibility for continual creation of a self by annihilation of the determinism in the nature of things. This is the existentialist position. Pascal faced this problem and solved it for himself, in a manner characteristic of his own time in respect of the *end*, the goal, and of the present day in respect of his conclusion about how to act at the transition moment:

Each moment breaks away from the continuity conceived as . . . arranged in a line which travels from the past to the present. Each . . . must be felt, not according to the knowledge of the historical development which causes it, but according to the consciousness of a *prophetic* moment, according to an end which is God and life eternal. The tragedy and absurdity of the human condition is that man appears incapable of renouncing his present and choosing the future instead. And from all this I conclude that I ought to pass all the days of my life without thinking of what is to happen to me hereafter. . . . I want to go without forethought and without fear to try the great event, and will passively approach death in the uncertainty of my future condition.[1]

For Pascal, and indeed for Kierkegaard, the plan for freedom had as its foundation the continuity of process from past to present, from which it was to break away. Perhaps it was after the French Revolution that the *anomie* began which, as Benjamin Constant wrote in 1794, made the present seem 'so close to being nothing . . . so disconnected, so isolated, so unseizable, that it is impossible to find anything in it which would further our happiness'. And in words even more applicable to the human condition in mid twentieth century: 'We are dead ones who, as in Ariosto, have preserved of our live habits only that of fighting, which gives us an air of courage, because we bravely risk a life we no longer possess.'[2]

As men turned their thoughts from the end which Pascal had in mind they realized more acutely the death which time brings into life itself.

[1] *ibid.*, p. 92
[2] *ibid.*, p. 209 ff. quoting (a) letter to Mme de Charrière, 3.12.1794, and (b) letter to Barante, 27.7.1808

. . And when I realized that I felt no joy at the thought of her being alive, that I no longer loved her, I ought to have been more astounded than a person who, looking at his reflection in the glass, after months of travel and sickness, discovers that he has white hair and a different face . . . its message is: 'the man that I was . . . no longer exists; I am another person'.

This kind of death in life is, of course, followed by resurrection, but of a different ego. Or can a unitary, integral self be constituted by the work of memory? Can lost time be found again? 'In Proustian thought', writes Poulet, 'memory plays the same supernatural role as grace in Christian thought. Perhaps the resurrection of the soul after death is to be conceived as a phenomenon of memory.'[1]

The impulse to the integrative act of remembering is not intellectual but emotional; will-power alone is ineffectual, its effects sterile. The past is brought alive into the present only when the emotion it inspired runs like a thread unbroken through time. Following such a thread back into the past, Proust discovers a heaven in early childhood, and describes it in words strangely like those of an earlier writer whom it is most unlikely he had read:

[P.R.54.] For at that time everything which was not myself, the earth and the creatures upon it, seemed to me more precious, more important, endowed with a more real existence than they appear to full-grown men. And between the earth and its creatures I made no distinction.[2]

[P.R.55.] All appeared new, and strange at first, inexpressibly rare and delightful and beautiful. I was a little stranger, which at my entrance into the world was saluted and surrounded with innumerable joys. . . . My very ignorance was advantageous. All things were spotless and pure and glorious: yea, and infinitely mine, and joyful and precious. . . . Everything was at rest, free and immortal. . . . The dust and stones of the street were as precious as gold: the gates were at first the end of the world. . . . The Men! . . . Boys and girls tumbling in the street, and

[1] *ibid.*, p. 296
[2] *ibid.*, quoting *À la recherche du temps perdu*, vol. I

playing, were moving jewels. I knew not that they were born or should die; but all things abided eternally in their proper places. Eternity was manifest in the Light of Day.[1]

Both writers are led to the need to see the world again as they saw it in childhood, in order to recover not simply happiness but the positive value of existence; to negate the death of the perceiving self in time. In order to evaluate what is learned about time and death and their relationship, the learner returns to the period before learning began, and interprets the lesson in terms of the view he took of life before time and death were conceived at all. 'In my end is my beginning.'

[1] T. Traherne, *Centuries of Meditations*, (1908 edn) III, 3

CHAPTER 10

INEXORABLE LAW, CHANCE AND MISCHANCE

In the preceding chapter we have studied the association between concepts of death and time in the child and the adult. The measurement of time, according to the physicist, ultimately depends on our concept of universal laws of nature. The subject of this chapter is the relation between the concept of death and of the universality of natural law. Such a relationship is implied in the E-category definitions of Chapter 3, and we have observed a growth towards it in the development of the concept of cause.

In the earlier stages of conceptual development the attributes *alive* and *dead* have become separable from phenomena; the self is recognized as active centre of its own world; *dead* is not defined simply as *gone away* or *killed* or in some such limited fashion, nor is love or hate credited with efficacy to save or destroy; the biological implications of death are accepted as more essential than the ritual associations. The concept remains a source of emotion and autonomic arousal, perhaps of anxiety, of mockery, of defiant bravado, perhaps a stimulus to a perpetual search for answers. Concepts of death and cause tend to remain closely tangled. This is the relationship to be discussed first.

Piaget has written: 'Arising from the relations between personal activity and the external world, at first [causality] partakes of efficacy mixed with phenomenalism but later . . . is incorporated into a system of pure relations.'[1]

We shall be dealing, in this chapter, mainly with the transition to the later stage, definable in the terms Piaget has used here, and

---

[1] J. Piaget, *The Child's Construction of Reality*, 1955, p. 313

shall be accepting in general his account of the course of the child's intellectual development, though with reservations. In addition to the theme of the relation of the concept of death and of the universality of natural law, it will be argued that the conjunction of these concepts effects a step in intellectual development. Also that the effect of actual bereavement differs at stages of life when this step has been firmly taken and when, in childhood, it has not; and finally, tentatively, that the early associations of the death-concepts may influence the direction of major life-interests of the individual.

When the development of large samples of children is studied and norms are established, steps tend to disappear because they do not occur in every child at the same age. Average growth-curves tend to hide them. It is accepted that there are bodily changes in mode of functioning. It seems that these may bring about stages at the psychological level. Grey Walter's studies of electroencephalic records of children at different ages led him to stress the occurrence of sudden changes of individual functioning during growth, and to warn, *Mind the step!*[1] Huxley and Lorenz describe critical periods in the growth of animals, when they are especially vulnerable. The psychoanalyst Erik Erikson holds that critical events in personal life, if they occur at periods of accelerated growth, may be exceptionally traumatic, and even liable to endanger mental stability.

Distinctive stages in man's life are recognized in cultural practice and in systems of sociological theory: baptism, *barmitzvah*, school-leaving, coming of age, conclusion of apprenticeship, retirement celebrations, in practice; theoretically by reference to oral, anal, latent and genital stages; sensori-motor, egocentric, concrete-operational and logical-operational stages. Each stage, bringing new functions into play, may initially show a harking back or regressive tendency, going over old ground in a new way. Reorientation towards the future often involves some re-enactment of the past.

[1] J. M. Tanner and B. Inhelder, *Discussions on Child Development*, 1956, vol. 3, p. 161 ff. (discussion by Zazzo, Grey, Walter, Huxley, Lorenz and Erikson)

Describing mental structure at each level, Piaget posits successive conditions of equilibrium. This concept fits well with the theory of steps in development; the static or balanced character of each successive stage is seen as maintained only by its characteristic constant activity. An achievement characteristic of one stage may occur spontaneously in a moment of intellectual excitement during an earlier stage, not to reappear as a stable form of response until later. In the earlier part of a newly acquired stage, Lewis Carroll's Red Queen provides the dynamic model; much effort is required in order to stay in the same place. Poise is then achieved at the new level; there follows adaptation to an increasingly complex perception of the environment, until again a balance is tipped and a qualitative change takes place, a restructuring is called for.

Our present proposition is that stages in the conceptualization of death may initiate stages of intellectual growth. As will be shown later, this proposition has some support in Piaget's observations, but the stages we observe do not correspond closely, by age or character, to those which Piaget describes as the mode of development of the child's thought and cognitive ability, nor do we interpret as he does the relation between the concept of death and of cause at the later stage.

In the precausal thinking of the child, Piaget finds motivation as the source of all explanation. Causal and logical explanation is at this stage, in his view, confused with psychological explanation, while the idea of chance does not exist. Everything seems well regulated until the child becomes aware of the difference between life and death.

From this moment, the idea of death sets the child's curiosity in action, precisely because, if every cause is coupled with a motive, then death calls for a special explanation.[1] If the child is at this stage puzzled by the problem of death, it is precisely because in his conception of things death is inexplicable. Apart from theological ideas, which the child of six or seven has not yet incorporated into his mentality, death is the fortuitous and mysterious phenomenon *par excellence*. And in the ques-

[1] J. Piaget, *The Language and Thought of the Child*, 1926, pp. 178, 180–81

tions about plants, animals, and the human body, it is those which refer to death which will cause the child to leave behind him the stage of pure finalism, and thus acquire the notion of statistical causality or chance.

Piaget has previously classified causal explanation in five categories: (i) physical-mechanical, of which (ii) statistical or fortuitous is a special sub-division; (iii) finalist (in the Aristotelian sense, e.g. a bird has wings so that it can fly); (iv) psychological or motivational (e.g. the arrow hit the target because the archer meant it to); (v) logical-categorical (i.e. the subsuming of particular instances under general laws).

Piaget thus presents very strongly the case for functional relationship between the concept of death and the development – not the origin – of the concept of cause. Our observations would support this theory, which I believe to be of profound importance; they would not, in my view, support the whole of the exposition quoted above, to which I shall therefore refer again. Piaget refers to the functional relationship only in passing, and bases his observations on a study of questions put by a boy, obviously highly intelligent, during his sixth and seventh years of age. The idea does not reappear in the later study of the genesis of the child's concept of chance,[1] but as the earlier study was republished eight years after the work on chance, one may assume that Piaget had not revised his view about the relation between the idea of death and the development of the concept of cause.

My own researches indicate that such questioning begins at an earlier age than that at which Piaget's boy, Del, became the subject of special study, and may indeed have begun by that boy himself at an earlier age than that covered by the record. None of my reservations reduce acceptance of the first part of Piaget's statement. The relationship between the death concept, reasoning, and the concept of cause is of critical importance throughout life, and central to our theme. We must therefore pursue it further.

This will be done by reference to Piaget's statement quoted above. The reference to theological ideas need not, I think, be

[1] J. Piaget and B. Inhelder, *La Genèse de l'idée du hasard chez l'enfant*, 1951

taken too seriously, for it is evident from many records, including Rasmussen's and my own, that the young child incorporates, often very crudely and quite fantastically, such theological ideas as may be presented to him. Leaving this aside, I would differ from Piaget's exposition by maintaining: (1) that the young child begins to develop all the five concepts of causality before his seventh year; (2) that the relationship of the death and cause concepts which marks the step of prime importance in development is not that of death as a chance occurrence but (3) the relation between death and humanity as a category in which the self is logically included.

Let us consider these three points in more detail. First, that the child provides evidence of development of all Piaget's five types of causal concept at an early age; I shall argue this only with reference to that type, the logical-categorical, on which in my view the final step depends. There seems no doubt that the concept of universal laws of nature develops late in the individual and the race, and depends on the development and application of logical thinking. There is evidence, however, of development of logical thinking before and during the sixth year. Examples have been given by Sully, Nathan Isaacs, Stebbing[1] and others; the following examples come from our home records:

[H.R.55.] Ben (4:10) and his mother saw a telephone service van with an enlarged model of the receiving apparatus on the roof; they discussed how much bigger this was than the instrument in their home. M: 'Ten times?' B: 'Oh no, not more than three or four times.' (Pause.) 'Unless *times* is very little; then it might be ten times as big.'

[H.R.56.] Richard (5:1): 'Why is an orange orange?' M: 'I suppose people said, what shall we call this colour; it's like an orange; let's call it orange.' R: 'But we don't call yellow *grapefruit*; we don't call banana *yellow*.'

[H.R.57.] Richard (5:4) with M on a bus; they quietly counted the (relatively few) passengers. On another bus on the same journey, R began to do this again, alone, and then said aloud: 'There are more legs than persons.' (Pause.) 'Because persons have two legs.'

[1] L. S. Stebbing, *Thinking to Some Purpose*, 1939

[H.R.58.] Richard (5:6) lighting a splinter of wood in the fire: 'Wood burns, doesn't it? Because my bit does.'

[H.R.59.] Ben (5:10): There was a fashion among older children for mouth-organs, which they were frequently heard to play tunelessly by drawing them across the mouth as they breathed. M had bought one for her own amusement, which was picked up by B's baby brother and played in this way. M (jokingly): 'Baby can play the mouth-organ as well as the boys in the streets!' Some hours later when she was alone, B ran in and said delightedly: 'Baby can play the mouth-organ as well as the people in the streets, and I can play as well as Baby, so I can play as well as the people in the streets!' His pleasure was clearly due to having thought this out rather than to his ability to play the instrument, which he did not offer to demonstrate.

The records show that (1) Ben, under five years old, had intuitively perceived that multiplication by a fraction would reduce the product, though he could not have made the statement in accepted mathematical terms, nor would he have expressed the idea in the way he did if it had not been spontaneous. (2) Richard, barely five, protested against a class description being allocated by reference to one particular member of the class, demonstrating that this principle was not used in other similar circumstances. (3) Aged 5:6, he generalized from a particular case, making an inadequate induction,[1] but his behaviour left no doubt that he had worked from a general hypothesis that wood burns, which he had then checked empirically. (It is probable that the hypothesis was inductive initially, as he had seen tinder used for starting coal fires.) (4) Ben, at 5:10, spontaneously developed a method of rational argument.

The child's conception of causality is generally deduced from the kind of questions he asks which demand a causal form of reply, or from the answers he receives to *Why* questions. Some

[1] A faulty use of induction, like animism, is not peculiar to the immature intellect: 'Induction from particular instances occurs even in advanced scientific disciplines and is still more prevalent in the pre-scientific investigations of ordinary life.' M. Black, 'Induction and probability', R. Klibansky (ed.), *Philosophy in Mid-Century*, 1958, pp. 154, 159. See also J. O. Wisdom's 'The methodology of natural science' in the same work

questions involving the logical-categorical type of causality may not be so readily placed by this method as others involving the motivational or finalist type. At the beginning of the *Why* stage the child may be largely concerned with mapping his concepts so that they may correspond with those used in his social environment, or in other words, with the 'correct' designation of phenomena. Thus a child who is familiar with two local dogs, a dachshund and an Airedale, seeing a neighbour's white poodle, may ask, 'Why is that dog white?' and receive the answer, 'Some dogs are white.' If, however, he had asked, 'Is that a dog?' the question might not have been recognized as demanding a causal answer; and the answer would have been 'Yes'. A similar example may be given from our home records. Ben (3 :2) apparently considered that three syllables was too many for any reasonable name, and asked of things or people so named, e.g. 'Ovaltine – why 'tine?' 'Margaret [he could not pronounce this properly], why -wit?' [H.R.60.] This is the kind of absurd *Why* question which tends to go unrecorded. The impulse in this case was probably the inadmissible rejection of a baby brother who had been given a three-syllable name, which in cognitive development led to the questioning of rules of naming, which are a foundation of the logical-categorical type of causality.

The second point of my argument contra-Piaget is that the concept of death-as-a-chance-event within a system of physical-mechanical causation is a midway stage, not a peak, in the child's development of a mature concept of causality related to the concept of death. I am not sure, however, whether I rightly interpret Professor Piaget's exposition at this stage. Obviously the young child will not comprehend statistical probability concepts, or acquire such notions through curiosity about death, until adolescence, if ever. But he may, as he abandons the infantile sense of efficacy, conceive of death as a fortuitous and accidental occurrence, and as Wallon points out, he may do so without recognizing any threat to himself, even while he states or agrees that all men are mortal:

Before admitting that he too will die, the child must often pass through the stage of affirming that everyone will die. This is a syllogism, which carries with it no conviction of death. The idea of death (thus admitted) has no universal or necessary character. It represents things accidental, and individual cases.[1]

The dead and those who die are seen as a separate category of individuals. Often this category is that of the old. Old age is, of course, frequently suggested to the child as the preliminary to death. The child may come to the association of death with himself through the idea of old people dying – himself growing older – himself dying. It is a logical process, but if it actually follows forms somewhat similar to those of classical logic, it is nevertheless not usually deduction proper, but what Stern[2] called *transduction*; a form very commonly to be observed in the reasoning processes of the child. The major premise is not made. The conclusion 'I, too, shall die' is reached through 'I too shall grow old', without involving the generalization, 'All men grow old, all men die.'

The process which Stern observed as present in the early reasoning of children bears out Spearman's[3] contention about the whole process of induction as actually practised; namely, that those who use inductive processes are either basing induction on prior deduction, or else (and this he believes to occur most commonly) are reasoning not on the basis of uniformity of natural events, but on the basis of ubiquity of causation. So in the child's reasoning which educes a relation between death and the self from contemplation of the consequences of growing older, the first term is commonly not *All men are mortal* (uniformity of natural events) but *What brings death to you will bring death to me* (ubiquity of causation).

The conclusion is unpalatable. But there seems to be a loophole. Using induction based on ubiquity of causation we state as a certainty what, after all, may be only a probability. Now, true

[1] H. Wallon, *Les Origines de la pensée chez l'enfant*, 1945, vol. 1, pp. 413–14

[2] W. Stern, *The Psychology of Childhood*, 1914–27, ch. 28

[3] C. Spearman, *The Nature of 'Intelligence' and the Principles of Cognition*, 1923, p. 297

induction alone can prove nothing but uniformity based on statistical probability, which still appears to leave infinitesimal chances ever open. So induction on the causal basis is abandoned, and the child begins to ponder on the universality of natural law, which is the deduction drawn from the inductive process, not so as to accept, but in the hope of denying, the inevitability of death, his own death. (This is my third point.)

It is not suggested that the child is aware of these mental processes, but that children's thinking may follow this course is, I believe, shown by the Katz records. The conversation has already been quoted (p. 158) in which Theodor asked whether animals as well as men come to an end, then said unhappily that he did not want to die, and was told that he need not do so. A conversation recorded two months later shows that this boy had not ceased to ponder the question how death might be avoided:

[P.R.56.] Theodor (5:7): 'Was God born?' M: 'God wasn't born and God doesn't die.' T: 'If God doesn't die, then all men won't die.' M: 'I'll tell you all about that when you're bigger.' T: 'You shouldn't say things like that; it's rude.'[1]

Theodor, on the basis of a perceived non-uniformity in supposed natural events, is moved to deny the validity of a law which, as he well perceives, can only be securely founded on universality. He rightly feels it 'rude' when the maturity of his intelligence is impugned after such an intellectual achievement. For although his argument reproduces traditional theological arguments too closely to be supposed unsuggested, the logical sequence is obviously a result of his own spontaneous impulse.

The underlying form of Theodor's reasoning is deductive, though its expression is not as neat as Ben's at age 5:10 (p. 191). Theodor's thinking, however, stimulated by the desire to avoid death, shows a stronger drive to intellectual maturity in its generalization to the whole of humanity – its conception of a universal rule. In conceiving of humanity he has obviously included himself within it, abandoning egocentricity. Further, he

[1] D. and R. Katz, *Conversations with Children*, 1936, p. 120

has recognized that humanity as a whole is constrained by necessity, though this thought has been admitted only through the hope of its negation. He is aware, as Ben was, that his thinking is itself a major achievement.

American gangsters in fiction, and perhaps in fact, refer to their gun as 'the old equalizer'.[1] The concept of death fulfils intellectually the function which the weapon fulfils operationally; we might call it 'the old generalizer'. This is a dynamic function of its content, by means of which it generates a step in intellectual development. The dynamic is the individual's wish not to die.

Thinking of a kind which produces a step in individual intellectual development may be placed in the creative category. A train of thought is creative by reason of a relationship between content and generative conditions. The generalization by a six-year-old that all men must die, but if not, he himself may not, may qualify as creative, when the same statement by an adult is trite.

GERTRUDE: Thou know'st 'tis common; all that lives must die,
               Passing through nature to eternity.[2]

Queen Gertrude's words are significant by their very triteness. After the general fact has become familiar, any particular instance involving someone loved overshadows the generality by the uniqueness of the loss. The converse also holds good. If generality seems relevant, love was absent. The queen has betrayed herself. This reaches the audience, and Hamlet, if half unconsciously.

HAMLET: Ay, madam, it is common.
GERTRUDE: If it be,
             Why seems it so particular with thee?
HAMLET: Seems, madam? Nay, it is; I know not seems.

The verbal exchange subtly indicates that the queen did not love her first husband, though she had followed the coffin 'like Niobe, all tears'. Should Hamlet stress the I when he disclaims dissembling? There would then be a double irony, for he plans

[1] D. Runyon, *More than Somewhat*, 1937
[2] *Hamlet*, I. ii

to dissemble most elaborately. But the simple point is made directly, that a particular loss makes the generality of death impertinent.

We have up to this point studied normal development of the later stage of the death concept. If culturally deflected, either by unorthodox teaching or by childish misunderstanding, a logical association of death and causation may give rise to an irrational solution. Wallon reports the following conversation:

[P.R.57.] M ... in (7) said of the storm that it was [due to] a ball of fire. Q: 'Who made this ball of fire? ...' M: 'The devil. ...' Q: 'Have you seen him?' M: 'No.' Q: 'Where is he?' M: 'In heaven.' (*'Au ciel.'*) Q: 'What else does the devil do?' M: 'He makes people die.' (*'Il fait mourir du monde.'*) Q: 'If there were no devil, would old people not die?' M: 'That is so.' (*'Si.'*)

We must avoid the danger of supposing that irrational thinking of this kind occurs in the child but not in the adult, or that irrational ideas of similar content have similar origin or function in child and adult. This boy's diabolism may have been taught. The adult's reaction reported below is clearly spontaneous, and a matter of some wonder even to himself.

[P.R.58.] Three elements came together ... to make this crisis acute: an unhappy love-affair, an entirely new sense of death as nothingness in the midst of life, and an almost unendurable anxiety about a younger friend who had gone to sea in a state, I knew, of despair. ...

It was as if I were holding a thinly constructed door against a great tornado of nothingness ... the continual facing of death ... made me realize that every one of the notions of survival or restitution with which men comforted themselves was, if closely examined, a deception. ... Not merely the notions of after-life, but the notions of surviving as a part of the thought of one's friends among scenes and objects impregnated in some degree with one's personality ... one had to envisage the total destruction of a civilization. ... [I came to] the affirmation ... that even if the insistent presence of death was the trigger of the whole crisis, one could not construct any worthwhile philosophy without the experience of that presence. Demetrius [Capetanakis] ... put it exactly as I felt it ... at the end of his essay on Rimbaud: 'Nothingness might save or destroy those who face it, but those who ignore it are condemned to unreality.' [I came to] a very curious conviction, or rather, perhaps, intuition, curious, that is, for one of my sceptical and agnostic habit of mind . . . [that there were] extraneous forces that worked against love. So it was I began, in my tortured confusion, to believe in demons, spirits of evil that could capture and possess a human being, child of love, an eternal soul exposed to the cross-fire of the battle of life.[1]

Lehmann's quotation from Capetanakis might stand as the simplest possible expression of the impulse to the present work. When he says that one cannot construct any worthwhile philosophy without the experience of the insistent presence of death, he is echoing what Keats wrote, that axioms in philosophy are not axioms until we have proved them on our pulses; and Keats lived in that insistent presence.

However strange it may seem to the rational, civilized adult not living, as Lehmann was at the time he wrote, under the heavy stress of modern war, the belief in magically powerful spirits of evil is accepted today not only by primitive peoples but quite commonly by ourselves. Shortly after the above paragraph was written, a case of murder was reported from Nyasaland (now Malawi), in which the murderer claimed to have changed himself into a crocodile for the purpose, and two of the Africans on the judicial bench stated that they believed he had done so. I was briefly in hospital at the time, in London. Discussing the case with a nurse-trainee, daughter of a wealthy Hindu family of Bombay, and a capable Englishwoman, member of the cleaning staff, I found that both were prepared to credit the possibility of such a metamorphosis.[2]

Let me give another instance of autobiographical record showing that the achievement of stages in intellectual development does not result in the permanent abandonment of modes of thinking and behaviour characteristic of earlier stages, particularly in relation to concepts of death:

[1] J. Lehmann, *I Am My Brother*, 1960, pp. 136–8
[2] On the general question of spontaneous survival of folk-lore, see P. Opie, 'The tentacles of tradition', *Advancement of Science*, 1963, XX, 85, pp. 235–44

[P.R.59.] Always fearful and a prey to cruel uncertainty, I had recourse to the most laughable expedients to escape from it, for which I would unhesitatingly have anyone locked up as a madman if I saw him doing as I did. One day, while musing [*rêvant*] upon this melancholy subject [i.e. whether he would be damned] I mechanically amused myself by throwing stones against the trunks of trees with my usual good aim, that is to say, hardly hitting one. While engaged in this useful exercise, it occurred to me to draw a prognostic from it to calm my anxiety. I said to myself: 'I will throw this stone at the tree opposite; if I hit it, I am saved; if I miss it, I am damned.' While speaking, I threw my stone with a trembling hand and a terrible palpitation of the heart, but with so successful an aim that it hit the tree right in the middle, which, to tell the truth, was no very difficult feat, for I had been careful to choose a tree with a thick trunk close at hand. From that time I have never had any doubt about my salvation![1]

Rousseau, aged twenty-four, was using magic to relieve his anxiety about life after death. Piaget quotes an account of a more modern child who used magic to relieve anxiety about dying:

[P.R.60.] Every evening, from about the age of 6 to 8, I was terrified by the idea of not waking up in the morning. I used to feel my heart beating and would try, by placing my hand on my chest, to feel if it was stopping. It was undoubtedly in this way that I started counting to reassure myself. I counted very quickly between each beat and if I could succeed in passing a certain number before a particular beat or in making the beats correspond with even or with uneven numbers, etc., I felt reassured. . . . At regular intervals, from the pipes of the radiator in my room, would come a sudden, deep, rattling sound, which often used to make me jump. I used to use this as a proof of whether I should die or not; I would count very fast between one rattle and the next, and, if I passed a certain number, I was saved.[2]

The child under seven years old may painfully learn the inevitability and the generality of death, as we have seen in the records of Jane and of Theodor. The gay mockery described by the Opies may not help every child, as is clear from the account quoted above. No generalization will cover every individual case.

[1] J.-J. Rousseau, *Confessions*, I, 6
[2] Piaget, *The Child's Conception of the World*, 1929, p. 136

For many children the increased insight is not entirely painful, because when the generality of death is realized, the sense of efficacy or omnipotence is abandoned, and a burden of guilt is lifted.

This intellectual process is normally achieved during the period between six or seven and eleven or twelve years of age. During this period also, emotional relationships begin to be formed outside the family circle. The actual death of someone loved may then initiate a development of the concept more mature than those represented by the five categories illustrated in Chapter 3 above. This step may occur in adolescence, or in early adult life. It may be illustrated from a pre-Freudian autobiography in which is described the reaction to the loss of a friend when the writer was nineteen or twenty years of age:

[P.R.61.] Wherever I looked I saw only death. My own country became a torment and my own home a grotesque abode of misery. . . . I had become a problem to myself, asking myself again and again, 'Why are you so downcast? . . .' I had no hope that he would come to life again, nor was this what I begged for through my tears: I simply grieved and wept, for I was heartbroken. . . . I lived in misery, like every man whose soul is tethered by the love of things that cannot last and then is agonized to lose them. . . . This was the misery in which I lived, and yet my own wretched life was dearer to me than the friend I had lost. . . . True or not, the story goes that Orestes and Pylades were ready to die together for each other's sake, because each would rather die than live without the other. But I doubt whether I should have been willing, as they were, to give my life for my friend. I was obsessed by a strange feeling, quite the opposite of theirs, for I was sick and tired of living and yet afraid to die. I suppose that the great love which I had for my friend made me hate and fear death all the more, as though it were the most terrible of enemies, because it had snatched him away from me. I thought that, just as it had seized him, it would seize all others too without warning.[1]

This recorded reaction differs greatly from records of childish or 'primitive' sorrow. Grief has made death seem the normal condition. The sufferer longs to leave his own home and people

[1] Augustine of Hippo, *Confessions*, IV, 4 (1962 edn)

(which indeed he actually did). Yet in this case we find no pathological symptoms. With complete frankness the mourner records
that he himself had no wish to join his friend in death, and would
even have been unwilling to die for him. He realizes that his grief
was mingled with a general fear of death not due to the immediate
loss alone. The depth and sincerity of his emotion can hardly be
doubted. He further records thoughts that mourners constantly
echo:

[P.R.61 cont.] I wondered that other men should live when he was
dead, for I had loved him as though he would never die. Still more I
wondered that he should die and I remain alive, for I was his second
self. I felt that our two souls had been one, living in two bodies, and
life to me was fearful because I did not want to live with only half a
soul. Perhaps this, too, is why I shrank from death, for fear that one
whom I had loved so well might then be wholly dead.[1]

We have not found in the child's thought the idea (to which
Lehmann also referred in the quotation above) of defeating mortality through survival in the memory of the living, still less the
idea of cherishing one's own life because it enshrines the memory
of another. Such thoughts, stimulated by actual loss, are those of
a mature individual, and create new social values.

The grief which marks the stage here under consideration is
typically aroused by a death outside the parental family circle.
Within this circle the passions of the child have developed, the
anxieties arising from them have normally been resolved, distress
anticipated and in some degree disarmed. Sex relationships,
through their unconscious re-enacting of family associations, may
be similarly safeguarded against such grief in its most acute form.
The sex relationship being functionally concerned with procreation, essentially provides a form of defence against death-anxiety.
In relations between persons of the same sex there is no such
defence. One might suppose that the difference would be felt
during the living association, rather than in the grief after death,
but the evidence in literature offers little support for this view.

[1] *ibid.*, IV, 6

The note of passionate grief is to be heard as keenly and as often –
perhaps more often – in elegies such as the passage quoted from
St Augustine, as in memorials of a dead wife or mistress.

To suppose for this reason that this stage is passed through, or
such grief suffered, only by men or women not normally heterosexual is demonstrably erroneous. St Augustine, by his own
confession, had strong heterosexual impulses, unrestrained during
adolescence and exercised within a permanent (though not legal-
ized) union during the greater part of his life before he entered
the Church. It is, of course, true that some of the most moving
elegiac utterances have been made by individuals cut off, by
choice, circumstance or personal development, from procreative
activity, or whose life was passed in a culture where the companionship of the sexes was qualitatively restricted, and that they
write of the death of a person of their own sex. But their reactions
do not differ in keenness or elegiac quality from those of individuals such as Augustine, whom his confessions show to have been
fully heterosexual.

Neither Lehmann's diabolism, Rousseau's magic nor Augustine's acute distress were permanent. Augustine, entering the
Church some twelve years later after profound intellectual conflict, came to believe that death would be for him the gateway to
a life compared with which his life in the world was a kind of
death. Rousseau was, however intermittently, a child of the
Enlightenment. Lehmann's evaluation of nothingness places him
with the existentialist philosophers, but for English thinkers,
anguished existentialism does not seem to offer a long-term
resting place. They return to a travelling ark of philosophy,
bringing back hope that the wilderness of anguish will subside
and ground more solid and fruitful emerge.

Augustine's reversal of the values usually attached to life and
death is illuminated by Freud's dream analysis in his essay on the
Shakespearian theme of the three caskets. The third, leaden,
casket, which held the key to joy, represented, he said, death, and
so also did Lear's most loved, quiet, third daughter. The three
sisters are the Fates, and the third is Atropos, the inevitable end.

The Graces and the Hours are related to the Fates. The Hours were originally goddesses of the waters of the sky, thence of the seasons, thence of divisions of time, thence 'of the law of Nature, and of the divine order of things, whereby the constant recurrence of the same things in unalterable succession in the natural world takes place'. The aspect of the Hours as goddesses of destiny found expression in the Moerae, who watch over human life.

The implacable severity of this law, the affinity of it with death and ruin . . . its full solemnity was only perceived by mankind when he had to submit his own personality to its working. Man struggles against recognition of subjection to death . . . it is only with extreme unwillingness that he gives up his claim to an exceptional position. The Goddess of Death is therefore replaced in his myth by the Goddess of Love. The Goddesses had originally been the same. And choice is substituted for necessity.[1]

In studying the records made in childhood of children now grown up, it has seemed to me that their early interest in the discovery of death may have had some connection with their major interests in later life. Here no claim can be made for a firm hypothesis; the facts may be recorded, but are no more than suggestive. And it would seem that such special interest may lead either to avoidance or approach in respect of activities emotionally associated with the idea of death. From her hypothesized fear of death Dr Sterba's young patient (p. 162 above) developed first a fear of dogs and then an inability to learn elementary mathematics. Thus in her case, anxiety led to withdrawal and inactivity in a particular learning situation. The relationship between anxiety and learning, or anxiety and achievement more generally, has of late years been the subject of many experimental studies. In some of these, *manifest* anxiety is measured by verbal responses, in others anxiety is inferred from psychomotor behaviour. It has been found in association with reduction of activity in some cases, increase of activity in others.[2]

[1] S. Freud, *The Theme of the Three Caskets*, 1913 (1953 edn, vol. 12)
[2] See S. B. Sarason, *Psychological Bulletin*, 1960; I. Sarnoff *et al.*, *British Journal of Psychology*, 29, 1959

INEXORABLE LAW, CHANCE AND MISCHANCE

Our records provide an example of a child's reaction to the thought of death which had quite a different sequel to that observed in the case of Dr Sterba's patient. Stephen's conversation with his schoolfellows and, two months later, with his mother, show that a train of thought has been followed on the subject of the association of death-age-number (see [H.R.45.] above). His grandmother had died; he asked what age she was when that happened. He then expressed expectation that his own mother would die at the same age. He also expressed the hope and intention to live longer than he expected his mother to live; he sets his own term at ninety-nine, having previously heard that everybody will be dead by the time they are 100. His interest in age-as-number, however, did not cease at this point. Shortly after his fifth birthday he was having tea with some other children and the present writer, when it was discovered that he could immediately give the day of the week for any date for months back. According to the record made at the time, 'he did so at the tea-table, casually, about the birthday of one of the other children present, although he had not known the date of the birthday till that moment; and he was confirmed in what he said, and in other dates we tried him with'. [H.R.61.]

Now, some twenty-four years later, it is possible to add that Stephen subsequently won a mathematical scholarship to Cambridge, took a first-class degree, and has held university teaching posts in pure mathematics and cybernetics. Neither of his parents are mathematicians or teachers.

The case of Stephen and the little patient have one thing in common; the concept of death has been deeply associated with the idea of number. They have one significant point of difference; in the case of the neurotic child the whole complex has been repressed, being brought to light only in the analytic situation, and indeed after a false start even then; whereas Stephen's freedom from repression is remarkable, and deserves some further analysis. (It may be added that the children probably differed considerably in intelligence level, but the fact is here only of importance in making it easier to demonstrate the deep and permanent effect of

203

the early form taken by the concept in the non-neurotic child, by opening for him a direct line of activity through to manhood, which might otherwise have been closed at an earlier stage.) In the conversation with his mother reported on p. 154 above, the thought which might have been repressed may be crudely stated as 'I don't mind who dies as long as I don't'. Certainly this is too crude, for Stephen does not as yet appear to accept or deny, consciously, the certainty of his own death. It is still an event relative to that of his mother. He considers whether she is replaceable. Aware that there is a part of his life that he cannot remember, he wonders whether she may actually be a replacement, and puts the point to her. He is mastering separation-anxiety. Anxiety about annihilation of self is only on the horizon. About this, the comforting thought is its distance; the measured size of this distance is the defence. The record illustrates an intensification of interest in number through its association with the deep, normal anxiety aroused by the development of the concept of death not unduly repressed. The child's intellectual development might, we believe, have been blocked or deflected by repression either of anxiety about loss of the mother or about his own desire to outlive her.

In the records of Francis, the association of the death-concept with age as number did not occur, but the following conversation gains significance in the light of subsequent events:

[H.R.62.] F (4:11), out for a walk with his mother and the baby, had picked some holly. F: 'Flowers die and we die, don't we, Mummy?' M: 'Yes.' F: 'Who kills us in the night; does Jesus?' M: 'We die when we are old and ill, or if some sudden accident occurs.' F: 'Like lepers, for lepers are diseased, aren't they? They go white, with spots on their legs.' (See [H.R.4.] above.)

Francis, twenty-five years later, is medically qualified and occupied in medical research. Neither of his parents studied medicine, nursing or any allied discipline.

Thirdly, in the records of Richard extensively quoted in Chapter 5 above, the predominant interest in animals in connection with the development of the death concept appeared very clearly. His subsequent educational record included pre-university work in biology and zoology, and a doctoral thesis based on experimental work with rats and ferrets. The experiments did not involve the injury or sacrifice of the animals. Neither of his parents held biological qualifications or had worked with animals.

So it is suggested that the way death is represented in the early thinking of the child may influence the direction of his major interests through life. But the direction of interest may be the independent common factor in both, and our observations simply support the statement of Claude Bernard: *'Le commencement et la fin nous tourmenteront toujours et nous tourmenteront surtout.'*

CHAPTER 11

MORTALITY THE SPUR TO SCIENTIFIC INQUIRY

The development of science is perhaps the most striking and characteristic phenomenon of the present age. The change which has occurred during the past 300 years in men's ways of thinking affects every concept of wide range and generality. In this chapter the aim is to illustrate how the concept of mortality grew and changed, swept along in the great current of scientific progress, and to suggest that it had itself a generative function in respect of that progress. Concepts function only through the activities of individual men; the demonstration will be attempted by tracing successive records of scientific thought in which either a concept of mortality demonstrably activated the worker, or generally accepted concepts of mortality were modified or enlarged through his work.

In London, bills of mortality began to be regularly printed and published towards the end of the sixteenth century. Men wanted to know whether the plague was increasing or diminishing; the bills also provided ephemeral material for tavern gossip. In the seventeenth century, John Graunt, a London shopkeeper, collected and studied them. Realizing (perhaps through contact with Sir William Petty) that they had value as scientific material he addressed himself to the newly founded Royal Society:

The Observations which I happened to make (for I designed them not) upon the Bills of Mortality, have faln out to be both Political and Natural. . . . All which (because Sir Francis Bacon reckons his Discourses of Life and Death to be Natural History. . . .) I am humbly bold to think Natural History also. . . .[1]

Graunt was elected a Fellow of the Society. His modern editor notes that he

was permeated with the spirit of that new philosophy which bade curiosity turn for satisfaction rather to observation than to speculation. He was the first to note (a) the constant proportion of incidence of certain types of casualty (e.g. suicide) to the total number of burials, (b) the excess of male over female births, (c) the approximate numerical equality of the sexes, (d) the high infant mortality rate, and (e) the excess of urban over rural death rates.[2]

Mortality, previously the concern of the mourner, the beneficiary, the physician, the lawyer, the priest and the sexton, now provided material also for the natural historian and the statistician.

Halley, astronomer, mathematician and later Secretary of the Royal Society, applied Graunt's[3] discovery of the regularities of mortality to the calculation of life insurance premiums, and found useful data in the registers maintained at Breslaw (Breslau, now Roclaw or Wroclaw). In January 1693/4 he presented to the Society a paper entitled 'An Estimate of the Degrees of Mortality of The City of Breslaw, With an Attempt to Ascertain the Price of Annuities Upon Lives'.[4] Today we are struck by the high infant mortality rate recorded in all such early tables: 31 per cent of those born had died within seven years of birth. Halley makes the curious observation that 'from the Age of seven years, the Infants being arrived at some degree of Firmness, grow less and less Mortal'. Of his material in general he points out, first, that:

the Contemplation of the Mortality of Mankind has besides the Moral,

[1] C. H. Hull, *Economic Writings of Sir W. Petty together with the Observations* . . . *More Probably by Capt. J. Graunt*, 1899, vol. 2, p. 322

[2] *ibid.*, vol. 1, lxxvi ff.

[3] Halley ascribed to Petty the *Observations* of Graunt

[4] E. Halley, in *Philosophical Transactions*, 196, vol. 17, pp. 596–610, 1693/4; or see A. Wolf, *History of Science, Technology and Philosophy in the Sixteenth and Seventeenth Centuries*, 1950

its Physical and Political Uses . . . [and, as examples of the latter, that the numbers show] the proportion of Men able to bear arms in any Multitude, and the Odds that a Person of any particular Age will die in a Year – and if it be enquired at what number of Years it is an even Lay that a Person of any Age should die, this Table readily performs it . . .

In using the language of wagers to discuss annuities and life insurance, Halley was following the practice of his time and earlier. In the earliest recorded cases of monetary insurance against risks – marine, fire, life, or the chance of the unborn being a boy – the transaction was looked upon as a gamble. Gambling, however, was a serious matter, particularly when games of chance were, as in seventeenth-century France, one of the main occupations of the aristocracy. For a noble chevalier Pascal and Fermat worked out probability theory with reference to gaming.

Marine and fire insurance became general before there was any intelligent study of the risks by statistical or mathematical methods, but life insurance waited until the theory of probabilities had become a recognized part of the common stock of ideas.[1] In America there was no such study until the end of the eighteenth century, largely because legislation forbade the taking of interest, gambling and betting, and because life insurance was looked upon as a dangerous gamble.[2] Marine, fire and accident insurance are commonly so regarded today.[3] The present relation between actuarial practice and probability theory may be matter for debate,[4] but there is no doubt that the chances of disease and death have provided classic demonstrations of particular laws of probability. Poisson's theory (1837) of the distribution of small chances was classically demonstrated from data on the mortality of Prussian soldiers from horse kicks during the twenty years preceding 1895. Halley's assumption that mortality and wagering, dying and dicing, have features in common is a pointer to the history of probability theory before and since his time.

[1] C. T. Lewis and T. A. Ingram, 'Insurance', Encyclopedia Britannica, 11th edn.
[2] A. Manes, 'Insurance', E. Seligman (ed.), Encyclopedia of Social Sciences, 1930
[3] A. Sampson, Anatomy of Britain, 1962, p. 398
[4] See L. Hogben, Statistical Probability, 1957, p. 96

Two months after his first paper on this subject, Halley presented to the Society further considerations on the Breslaw tables.[1] In this second paper, after demonstrating the value of logarithms in the calculation of multiple life interests, he drew from the vital statistics the inference

how unjustly we repine at the shortness of our Lives, and think ourselves wronged if we attain not Old Age; whereas it appears hereby, that the one half of those that are born are dead in Seventeen years time. . . . So that instead of murmuring at what we call an untimely Death, we ought with Patience and unconcern to submit to that Dissolution, which is the necessary Condition of our perishable Materials; and of our nice and frail Structure and Composition . . .

Statistical observations thus provided a novel foundation for a counsel of resignation to mortality which many of Halley's contemporaries would have based on acceptance of divine will, or hope of after-life. The progress of science was later to lead to rejection of Halley's basis for resignation on other grounds, namely, the power of science itself to increase man's expectation of life. Indeed progress in this field depended on refusal of resignation to mortality, particularly that of others, either on religious grounds or on those here advanced by the freethinker, Halley. In his day the mortality pattern was regarded as a constant.

It was as natural history that Graunt had commended his observations on the bills of mortality to the consideration of the Royal Society. Halley realized that Nature, in the ordinary sense, was not solely responsible for the ratio of births to deaths:

The growth and Encrease of Mankind is not so much stinted by anything in the Nature of the Species, as it is from the cautious difficulty most People make to adventure on the state of *Marriage*, from the prospect of the Trouble and Charge of providing for a Family. Nor are the poorer sort of People herein to be blamed, since their difficulty of subsisting is occasion'd by the unequal Distribution of Possessions, all being necessarily fed from the Earth, of which yet so few are Masters.

[1] E. Halley, 'Some further considerations . . .', *Philosophical Transactions*, 198, vol. 17, March 1693/4

So that besides themselves and families, they are yet to work for those who own the Ground that feeds them; And of such does by very much the greater part of Mankind consist; otherwise it is plain, that there might well be four times as many Births as we now find.

He suggests that the national interest is promoted by increase of population – 'the Strength and Glory of a King being in the multitude of his Subjects' – and therefore

Celibacy ought to be discouraged ... And those who have numerous families of Children to be countenanced and encouraged ... especially by an effectual Care to provide for the Subsistence of the Poor, by finding them Employments whereby they may earn their Bread, without being chargeable to the Public.

The last half-dozen words provide an ominous clue to the social history of the period that followed. The economic insecurity and widespread poverty of the peasantry and the landless labourer during the eighteenth and nineteenth centuries has been amply documented, together with the reluctance of ruling sovereigns, parliaments or landed gentry to support or even consider measures for a more equal distribution either of the material sources of wealth or the product of industry. Premature death of the breadwinner left many women and children destitute. At about the period when Halley reported to the Royal Society, small groups of tradesmen began to organize mutual assistance against sickness or loss of the breadwinner. Through lack of knowledge of sound actuarial practice, and indeed lack of adequate basis for correct calculation, many of these societies failed. By mid-eighteenth century, 'The various societies for the benefit of age and widows which were continually rising up to allure and to defeat the hopes of the ignorant and distressed, were become an object of serious concern.'[1] The matter was of particular interest to the clergy, who had inherited from early Christian doctrine and from the traditional practice of the great medieval Church foundations a sense of obligation to relieve distress, without retaining in Protestant lands the financial means or adminis-

[1] W. Morgan, Introduction to *The Works of Richard Price*, D.D., F.R.S., 1816

trative status required to fulfil it on a national scale. An Anglican cleric, Derham, saw in the constant proportion of births to burials a divine ordinance; a German theologian who had been an army chaplain sought to demonstrate this by collecting data on large populations.[1] A Welsh nonconformist divine, Richard Price,[2] tried to promote the provision of annuities for widows and orphans by collecting more satisfactory data for life insurance calculations, and gained the ear of Pitt, then Chancellor of the Exchequer. Unfortunately Price calculated the number of births from registered baptisms, including those of the city of Northampton, where many parents did not hold with the baptism of infants; consequently his birth-death ratios were faulty, and he is said to have involved the Exchequer in the loss of two million pounds.[3] This, and his sympathy with American and French revolutionaries, made Price many enemies in his own day. In our own, his attempts to promote life insurance have been interpreted as a move to strengthen nonconformity at a period when relief was largely in the hands of the established Church,[4] but the evidence that he was more a sectarian than a humanitarian appears slight.

Price was a friend of Hume, Franklin and Priestley, and a founder member of the Unitarian church. This circle was deeply influenced by the French *philosophes* of the Enlightenment. The belief was widely held among them that an ideal state of society was obtainable by sweeping away obscurantist and illiberal traditions in Church and State. Frequently associated with this belief was the view that men should be left to seek each his own advantage without hindrance, and that where *laisser-faire* policies prevailed men were in actual fact becoming more prosperous.

---

[1] J. Süssmilch, *Die göttliche Ordnung in den Veränderungen des menschlichen Geschlechts, aus der Geburt, dem Tode, und der Fortpflanzung desselben Erwiesen,* 1st edn 1742

[2] R. Price, *Observations on Reversionary Payments; on Schemes for Providing Annuities for Widows . . . and on the National Debt. Works,* Morgan, *op. cit.,* vol. 2

[3] Lewis and Ingram, *op. cit.*

[4] Hogben, *op. cit.,* p. 115

This Price did not concede. Daniel Malthus, also of the liberal circle, was of the optimistic persuasion. His son Robert, though educated in the views of Godwin and Condorcet at home and by Unitarians at school, rejected both anti-clericalism (by taking Anglican orders) and philosophical optimism (in the arguments of his first *Essay on Population*).[1] It was vain, he wrote, 'to dream of a society, all the members of which should live in ease, happiness, and comparative leisure, and feel no anxiety about providing the means of subsistence for themselves and families', for man's reproductive urge – 'the passion between the sexes' – which does not appear to diminish with the progress of civilization, leads by a geometric rate of increase to over-population of the land from which man must draw his food, and thence to misery through starvation, disease or war. By a high mortality rate, human increase is then reduced to match the lesser rate of increase of agricultural production.

The power of population is so superior to the power in the earth to produce subsistence for man, that premature death must in some shape or other visit the human race. The vices of mankind are active and able ministers of depopulation. They are the precursors in the great army of destruction; and often finish the dreadful work themselves. But should they fail in this war of extermination, sickly seasons, epidemics, pestilence and plague advance in terrific array, and sweep off their thousands and ten thousands. Should success be still incomplete, gigantic inevitable famine stalks in the rear, and with one mighty blow levels the population with the food of the world.[2]

As an alternative to the positive checks of vice (the diseases associated with promiscuity) and natural disaster, Malthus, like Halley, recognized the preventive check of prudence in the form of deferment of marriage. Contraception he does not explicitly mention; he later made known that he disapproved of 'artificial and unnatural modes of checking population, both on account of their immorality and their tendency to remove a necessary

[1] T. R. Malthus, *Essay on Population* (first published anonymously in 1798), K. Boulding (ed.), 1959
[2] *ibid.*, ch. 7

MORTALITY THE SPUR TO SCIENTIFIC INQUIRY

stimulus to industry'.[1] He differed from Halley in that he wished to encourage 'prudence', but he showed himself well aware that poverty does not promote it. *Laisser-faire* principles he supported to the extent that he thought direct legislation could not do much to encourage 'prudence' but that the assurance of civil liberty, the security of property and earnings by just laws impartially administered, and the spread of education 'tend to encourage [those] prudential habits among the lower classes of society' upon which depend the desire and the ability to secure for themselves and their children 'the means of being respectable, virtuous and happy'.[2] When Malthus is represented as a heartless ogre, it is well to remember that he favoured repeal of the laws preventing trade unionism, on the grounds that they weighted the bargaining scales against the workers.[3]

The theory that the ratio of births to deaths is divinely ordained Malthus discussed only to reject. He showed how in Europe the ratio increased in periods following pestilence, and how it ranged higher in a newly settled country such as America than in lands longer invaded.

Great and astonishing as this difference is, we ought not to be so wonder-struck at it, as to attribute it to the miraculous interposition of heaven. The causes of it are not remote, latent and mysterious; but near us, round about us, and open to the investigation of every inquiring mind. It accords with the most liberal spirit of philosophy, to suppose that not a stone can fall, or a plant rise, without the immediate agency of divine power. But we know from experience, that these operations of what we call nature have been conducted almost invariably according to fixed laws. And since the world began, the causes of population and depopulation have probably been as constant as any of the laws of nature with which we are acquainted.[4]

In his later work, Malthus carries this argument a step further.

[1] See D. V. Glass, *Introduction to Malthus*, 1953, p. 29
[2] T. R. Malthus, *A Summary View of the Principle of Population*, 1830. Reprinted in *On Population: Three Essays*, 1956, p. 40
[3] See J. L. and B. Hammond, *The Town Labourer*, 1917
[4] Malthus, *First Essay*, ch. 7

With reference to the relatively stationary population of different districts of Switzerland, he showed how the differing death rates affected not the rate of increase but the way of life of the people. A Swiss commentator, Muret, had conjectured (Malthus translates):

> In order to maintain in all places a proper equilibrium of population, God has wisely ordered things in such a manner as that the force of life in each country should be in the inverse ratio of its fecundity. . . . Leyzin, a village in the Alps, with a population of 400 persons, produces but a little above 8 children a year. The Pays de Vaud, in general, in proportion to the same number of inhabitants, produces 11, and the Lyonnais 16. But if it happen that at the age of twenty years, the 8, the 11, and the 16 are reduced to the same number, it will appear that the force of life gives in one place what fecundity does in another. But [observes Malthus] if the positive checks to population [in Leyzin] had been unusually small, the preventive checks must have been unusually great. . . . Except in extreme cases, the actual progress of population is little affected by unhealthiness or healthiness [of district]; but these circumstances show themselves most powerfully in the character of the checks which keep the population down to the level of the means of subsistence . . .[1]

Here we have in early outline a human social ecology, brought to light out of a hazy theology, by clarification of the function of mortality.

Malthus's work still excites both admiration and criticism. His arguments have been riddled, not destroyed, by developments he did not foresee or only doubtfully conjectured. Triumphs of agricultural and medical science have tended to cancel out in their effect upon his argument; social dissemination of contraceptive techniques, lowering of class barriers, spread of education have all had effects which he would have assessed justly. In those who read his work in the original, admiration is inspired not only by the power of his argument but also by the spirit in which he conducts it: the concern for suffering, the lack of sentimentality, the refusal to identify national wealth or glory with the happiness

[1] *A Summary View* (1956 edn, pp. 48–50)

of a people or to rate them more highly; the courage in facing distasteful facts and theological odium. 'The most baleful of mischiefs may be expected from the unmanly conduct of not daring to face the truth because it is unpleasing.' The gist of his argument and philosophy may, for our purpose, be stated thus: mortality has a necessary function in the social life of man, as it has for all 'animated nature'; if we would master and control our economy we must learn to understand this function. It effects a balance between a species and the environment by means of which it subsists. For mankind, this means living under the constant and inevitable pressure of distress and anxiety, yet this may be the means of exciting the activity by which 'mind is formed out of matter'.[1]

With such speculations Malthus, it has been said, stands at the portal of nineteenth-century evolutionary thought. When Darwin returned in 1836 from his long voyage in the Beagle he brought with him a mass of material, but no unifying theory by which to interpret it. Two years later, after much industrious study, he wrote:

I perceived that selection was the keystone of man's success in making useful races of animals and plants. But how selection could be applied to organisms living in a state of nature remained for some time a mystery to me. [Then] I happened to read for amusement 'Malthus on Population', and being well prepared to appreciate the struggle for existence which everywhere goes on from long-continued observation of the habits of animals and plants, it at once struck me that under these circumstances favourable variations would tend to be preserved, and unfavourable ones to be destroyed. The result of this would be the formation of new species. Here then I had at last got a theory by which to work.[2]

In the final chapter of On the Origin of Species, Darwin summed up his observations and the details of his argument; the final sentence is the kernel of this summary, and the clearest link between the concept of death's function, transmitted by Malthus,

[1] First Essay, last chapter
[2] F. Darwin (ed.), The Life and Letters of Charles Darwin, 1888, vol. 15, p. 83

and the concept of evolution as a process by which species originated through natural selection:

Thus, from the war of nature, from famine and death, the most exalted object which we are capable of conceiving, namely, the production of the higher animals, directly follows. There is grandeur in the view of life, with its several powers, having been originally breathed into a few forms or into one; and that, while this planet has gone cycling on according to the fixed laws of gravity, from so simple a beginning endless forms most beautiful and most wonderful have been, and are being, evolved.[1]

The *Origin* is probably one of the most influential books ever written. Darwin, it has been said, opened up a whole new world. It is in the nature of science that a century later, Darwin's theory should have been substantially modified.

Muret, attributing the 'proper equilibrium of population' to God, spoke of the force of life being inversely proportionate to fecundity; thus he avoided attributing the mortality of the innocent to divine ordinance. Neither Malthus nor Darwin used such euphemisms and inversions, but an unconscious reluctance to speak or think of death may appear even in the behaviour of these, the most gentle of men, who were determined in their conscious thinking 'to face the truth however unpleasing'. Francis Darwin in his reminiscences of his father noted: 'He sometimes combined his metaphors in a curious way, using such a phrase as *holding on like life* – a mixture of *holding on for his life* and *holding on like grim death*.'[2] This *lapsus linguae* suggests that Darwin would if alive today welcome the view of Hogben, as reported and modified by Julian Huxley,[3] that natural selection by mortality, or the survival of the fittest, is a destructive agency, creative only in conjunction with mutation. The *exalted object* does not, in the view of Darwin's scientific successors, *directly* follow from famine and death alone.

[1] C. R. Darwin, *On the Origin of Species* (reprint of 1st edn. C. D. Darlington (ed.), 1950, p. 415)
[2] F. Darwin, 'Reminiscences', *op. cit.*, vol. 1, ch. 3, p. 141
[3] J. S. Huxley, *Evolution, a Synthesis*, 1942, pp. 23–8

Darwin, ignorant, as were his fellows, of Mendel's contemporary work on mutation, and unable to explain how new favourable variations were not swamped in later crossings, fell back, in his later work, on the principles of Lamarck, and the view that environmentally induced changes in the parent might be inherited by the progeny. Only after the death of both Darwin and Mendel was it made generally known, through the discovery of Mendel's researches, that new characters are not swamped by crossing. Geneticists who reject Lamarckian theory therefore represent a development from early Darwinism by incorporating Mendel's findings, while scientists who work on a theory of inheritance of characters environmentally modified may claim to represent the later views of Darwin. Freud belonged to the latter group.

In *The Descent of Man* Darwin dealt more fully than in the *Origin* with intraspecific, sexual selection as an evolutionary factor. In the extensive development of theories of evolution at this period, man's social evolution was treated as analogous to the biological evolution of species. Intraspecific competition was assumed to be a major factor in the process. Hobbes was frequently cited, without regard for the need for zoological or anthropological confirmation of his view that in man's natural or savage condition each was at war with each, and mutual behaviour wolfish (traducing the wolf, which does not fight within the pack). The authority of both Malthus and Darwin was used in support of views they did not express, and practices which were contrary to the temper of both. Charitable behaviour was deprecated on the grounds either that the miseries of the poor could not ultimately be alleviated by it (citing Malthus), or that it was 'dysgenic' and opposed to the best interests of the 'race' (citing Darwin). Clough expressed the conflict aroused in the individual between traditional morality and the current philosophy, in his *Later Decalogue*:

> Thou shalt not kill; but need'st not strive
> Officiously to keep alive.[1]

[1] A. H. Clough, *Poems, Etc.*, 1869, vol. 2, p. 186

Unwilling to participate in the competitive struggle either of individuals or of groups, Clough himself was led to spend much of his time doing odd jobs for Florence Nightingale, who never ceased to strive to keep the British soldier alive. Charitable behaviour might be dysgenic, but war was believed to be eugenic. There was 'a monstrous over-emphasis on conflict as *the* dynamic factor in all social change. Struggles between individuals, groups, social strata, tribes, states, races and so on were all confused with one another, and a crude Darwinismus was mingled with cruder versions of classical economics to produce what men believed to be evolutionary sociology, but was actually mere ideology'.[1] The Russian aristocratic anarchist, P. A. Kropotkin, argued that many animal species and living primitive men developed systems of mutual aid, which was therefore a factor in evolution.[2] His work also served an ideological purpose; he was concerned to demonstrate that authoritarian systems of law are superfluous in the organization of civil society. J. B. S. Haldane was among the geneticists who hold that intraspecific selection is a biological evil not conducive to the adaptation of a species to its environment, but a potential cause of species-mortality;[3] he found his spiritual home in India.

Evolutionary theories for which Darwin provided a factual basis and a mechanism in the *Origin* in 1859 were in the forefront of many men's thinking for years before that date. Comte published in 1830 his law of three stages of human intellectual development. Herbert Spencer, lone survivor of his parents' nine infants, published *The Development Hypothesis* in 1852. Gobineau's *Essai sur l'inégalité des races humaines*, which has been called the Bible of racist theory, also appeared shortly before the *Origin*; and the *Communist Manifesto*, which proclaimed the virtue and historical necessity of the class struggle came out in the year of European revolutions, 1848. Marxists hold that the *Manifesto* anticipated and completed the view of the total world of nature

[1] D. G. Macrae, *Ideology and Society*, 1961, pp. 143–4
[2] P. A. Kropotkin, *Mutual Aid: a Factor in Evolution*, 1902
[3] Huxley, *op. cit.*, p. 483

presented in the *Origin*, and Marx wished to dedicate the first volume of *Capital* to Darwin.

Thus human antagonisms were endowed with new sanctions, and attempts were made to base them on new human groupings. The evidence for the evolution of species by natural selection, *scientifically considered*, 'turned out to be not a law but a litany – sung over the graves of those who were not fit ... [where] *fitness* merely means *survival*'.[1] Until the upshot of a struggle is known, no criterion of fitness is available. The ranks can only be closed for human conflict on the basis of fantasy and hope, faith and pseudo-science. In such a pseudo-scientific humanism, the superman of Nietzsche and Shaw was begotten as an ideal, beyond good and evil. Russell tells us that Nietzsche never mentions Darwin except with contempt. 'Nietzsche ... likes the contemplation of pain ... the men whom he most admires are conquerors, whose glory is cleverness in causing men to die.'[2]

Darwin's concept of mortality and its function, though applied more widely than that of Malthus, did not essentially differ from it. His exposition, however, was used in support of ethical transvaluations in consequence of which men fought with new fervour under the old national banners and also found new reasons for killing millions of their fellow citizens, many of whom had or would have fought by their side under the old dispensation. Murderous conflict was sanctioned between old and new groupings; both the sanction and the groupings claimed scientific authority in Darwinism.

Enthusiasm for the work of Darwin led Freud to study biology and medicine rather than law. His biographer, Ernest Jones, is surprised at the rare allusions to Darwin's work in the master's correspondence, conversation or writings, and the fact that Freud remained 'from the beginning to the end of his life ... an obstinate adherent of the discredited Lamarckism'.[3] Freud's acceptance of Lamarckian doctrine, however, is not inconsistent with Darwin-

[1] H. T. Pledge, *Science Since 1500*, 1939, p. 158
[2] B. Russell, *A History of Western Philosophy*, 1940, pp. 800, 808
[3] E. Jones, *The Life and Work of Sigmund Freud*, 1955, vol. 3, pp. 332–7

ian influence, though he carries it into realms where it is doubtful that Darwin would have joined him. In his last work, *Moses and Monotheism*, Freud attributes the excessive consciousness of guilt in Jewish history and religion to inherited unconscious memory of their forefathers having slain the father of the race, Moses. 'I wished him,' says Jones, 'to alter a sentence in which he expressed the Lamarckian view in universal terms . . . since no responsible biologist regarded it as any longer tenable. All he would say was that they were all wrong.'

Freud's view of the evolution of man differed from Darwin's not in retention of Lamarckism but in general temper, and in his theory of death, both of which appear to have been deeply influenced by Nietzsche. His views are set out for lay readers in the open correspondence with Einstein published under the auspices of the League of Nations in 1932.[1] In respect of war, mortality and evolution these views may be summarized as follows:

(a) Intraspecific conflict is natural to man and animals, biologically healthy and practically unavoidable.

(b) A death instinct operates in every animate organism, impelling it to revert to inert matter. It reacts against this by extraversion of the process, i.e. by aggression against foreign bodies. There is also a constructive instinct. The two may operate in fusion. Neither is to be considered good or evil.

(c) In the process of civilization the death process may turn inwards. This is a morbid development, less natural than its extraversion. It gives rise to conscience and dislike of war.

(d) The violence of the primitive strong individual was originally curbed by a numerically superior alliance of weaklings. Right [*recht*, law] may be defined as the might of a community of this type when permanently established.

(e) Men, innately and irremediably unequal, are divided into leaders and led (the majority). The latter usually bow without demur to the decision of the former.

[1] A. Einstein and S. Freud, *Why War?*, 1932. (J. Frosch and N. Ross have briefly surveyed Freud's views on death in a review of K. Eissler's *The Psychiatrist and the Dying Patient*, in *Annual Survey of Psychoanalysis*, 1955, vol. 6)

(f) The process of civilization involves the progressive rejection by the cultured individual of natural instinctive ends [e.g. (c) above], changing his organic and psychic constitution and making him necessarily pacifist. This does not occur with the masses.

(g) Although leaders are necessary, it is utopian to hope that a superior class of men will be chosen to lead, or that among the masses men will subordinate their instinctive life to the dictates of reason.

Since Freud lived to suffer two world wars, it is possible to consider not only his theories but also his reactions to war. In his biography we are told that at the outbreak of war in 1914, he found himself an enthusiastically patriotic citizen of Austria-Hungary, though somewhat later he transferred his love and loyalty to Germany as the more efficient member of the military alliance. Pacifism played no part in his reactions throughout the war.

In the open letter, he asks Einstein, 'Why do we protest against war, for it seems a natural thing enough, biologically sound and practically unavoidable?' Then, answering the question, he says, 'We cannot do otherwise than hate it. Pacifists we are, since our organic nature wills us thus to be.' Yet in the light of his own earlier behaviour, this argument is strange. He can hardly be suggesting that his organic nature and psychic constitution had radically changed between 1914 (when he was in his fifties) and 1932.

To labour this point would give an impression different from what is intended. If Freud was moved by patriotic belligerent emotion in 1914, he behaved as the great majority were behaving in his own country and also in Germany, France, Britain, Russia and other civilized communities, with little distinction of cultural level. As a pacifist in 1932 he was again one with a wide fellowship of Europeans and Americans, the majority of whom ceased to act or think as pacifists within the next decade. If he showed himself politically neither profound nor prophetic, that is no matter for surprise or reproach. Only one aspect of his behaviour demands comment here, because of its bearing on his argument: the attribution to organic nature, psychic constitution and cultural level of a pacifism so clearly the reverse of the attitude he had taken some eighteen years earlier.

Although Freud's attitude to war changed, in most respects his *Weltanschauung* remained constant;[1] he was a child of the Enlightenment, in so far as this was consistent with conformity to the outlook of the Viennese bourgeois male of his time – except in respect of his psychoanalytic work. The conforming pressure and response seem to have been largely unconscious. To them may be attributed his successive militarism and pacifism, and to his unconsciousness of this, his attribution of his belated pacifism to his own cultural level and psychic constitution. His theory of the political relationship of leaders and led, if ultimately derived from Plato, is surely that of the contemporary Germany he admired. His admiration was strengthened by distaste for Austrian inefficiency, which was largely responsible for the transfer of his loyalty to Germany during the First World War. Imagination boggles at the thought of the rewriting of history which would be necessary if Englishmen transferred their national loyalties when their government was inefficient.

In Freud's final theory two basic instincts provide the drive of human action, one towards love and integration, the other towards disintegration and destruction. The theory of the death instinct is rejected by many of Freud's followers, including his biographer, Ernest Jones. Jones describes the way the theory developed.[2] Observing the tendency of children and some neurotics to repeat forms of behaviour obsessionally, Freud interpreted this as an instinctive desire to restore a previous condition, and concluded that the fundamental aim is to cause the organism to revert to an earlier state, hence ultimately to inorganic matter; hence the final aim of life must be death. This death instinct was assumed to operate through the whole of living nature, and even to invade the realm of the inanimate. Aggression was an extra-

[1] See Jones, *op. cit.*, vol. 3, p. 376; also E. Fromm, *Sigmund Freud's Mission*, 1959

[2] Jones, *op. cit.*, vol. 3, p. 292 ff.

version of the death instinct; dying in one's own way and time was secured by killing others first.

Jones raises two objections to the death instinct theory; first, that Freud used as basis for it a theory of recapitulation of the embryo since discredited, and secondly, that he confuses *telos* and *finis* (aim and end). The fact that the body is composed of matter which ultimately was and again becomes inorganic provides no support for an argument that this is the aim of the organism. Unable to accept the theory, Jones suggests that it is the product of subjective preoccupation rather than scientific observation.[1] From personal knowledge he observes:

> In the world of reality, Freud was an unusually courageous man. But in fantasy there were other elements. As far back as we know anything of his life he seems to have been prepossessed by thoughts about death. ... Even in the early years of our acquaintance he had the disconcerting habit of parting with the words, 'Goodbye; you may never see me again.' There were the repeated attacks of what he called *Todesangst* (dread of death). He hated growing old ... and once said he thought of it every day of his life, which is certainly unusual.[2] On the other hand there was a still more curious longing for death. ... He often said that his chief fear was the haunting thought that he might die before his mother. ... When it came about that she died first, he did not mourn, but felt a deep sense of relief at the thought that now he could die in peace (and be reunited?) ... Thus Freud always had a double attitude of phantasy about death, which I may well interpret as dread of a terrible father alternating with desire for reunion with a loved mother.

Thus Jones dismisses Freud's later theory by interpreting it in the light of the master's earlier system with the Oedipus complex as its foundation. Freud has been hoist with his own petard, but maybe that instrument was overvalued. When Freud derives religious systems or Jones derives Freud's later theories from

---

[1] Jones, *op. cit.*, p. 300
[2] Jones's certainty may not be justified; Freud's behaviour may be compared with that of Benjamin Constant: 'I have ... the misfortune never to be free of the idea of death', and of Proust: 'I think each day is the last of my existence.' Quoted by G. Poulet, *Studies in Human Time*, 1956, pp. 209, 295

infantile family relationships, the validity and value of religion and of instinct theory are not overthrown.

Freud's later theory placed death in a more primary position biologically than his earlier theory did. This makes it more credible, since the desire to continue in one's own being is biologically more general than dread of the father. All men, indeed all animate beings, die, but not all fear, or even know, their fathers. Jones demonstrates the undoubted weakness of arguments on which the theory was based, but there are also arguments in its favour. In magical thinking, death is an event imposed on the organism; in rational thinking it is also an internal biological process operating throughout life. The metabolism of the living matter of the body gradually becomes less efficient. The metabolism of the body cells involves anabolic and katabolic processes – assimilation-growth-repair and dissimilation-breakdown. Output of energy is associated with the latter. The same biological process which is associated with breakdown of body cells is paramount in exteriorized aggression.

Actually death by failure of the general metabolism process, which by Freudian theory would appear the most natural form, seldom occurs. It is, we are told, usually the result of the failure of some one of many complex mechanisms, while the majority of the tissues are still able to maintain their existence if supplied with proper conditions of nourishment. Death is normally, so to speak, accidental rather than natural. Before heart transplants had been attempted, textbooks of physiology informed us:

From our knowledge that all men and animals are mortal, it has been supposed that the somatoplasm (that part of the body which is not germ-plasm) is subject to senescence and natural death from some intrinsic peculiarity of its structure; but this conclusion has been found too sweeping. Strains of some of these cells may be kept living in artificial cultures for many years (after the death of the organism).[1]

A main objection to a theory of drive of the organism towards inorganic matter is that animals, including man, do not necessarily

[1] W. H. Howell, *Textbook of Physiology*, 1933, pp. 1,087–9

die as a whole naturally. Then what is death? The germ-plasm is potentially immortal. The heart, the liver, the eyes may continue to live after the man is seen and heard no more. Death is the cessation of *rapport* between physiological and psychical processes which previously operated in concert. The concepts of life, death and psyche are inseparably interrelated. 'All the physiological phenomena – organization, assimilation, respiration, the discharge of energy, growth, reproduction and death itself – are bound up in our conception of life. We cannot operationally define death without reference to psyche, or life without reference to death.'[1]

The physiologist's definition of death as cessation of *rapport* between processes which previously acted in concert, raises another much older question than that of the moment at which life ceases. Apart from disagreement about whether brain and consciousness act in concert or interact – whether consciousness is an epiphenomenon – there is the ancient question, *can they act separately*? Nowadays such questions arise, as Antony Flew writes, most typically in a scientific and secular context, but more often in the past they have arisen out of a religious concern, or in a context which, though secular, could not be characterized as scientific. 'Indeed it would be fair to say that in the past most enquirers have had at least half an eye, and sometimes both eyes, on the implications which the various possible views of the status of mind hold for the question of a future life.'[2]

Many psychologists banish from the realm of science the question of the existence or survival of the soul (in translated Platonic terms) or of consciousness (in Cartesian systems) or of personality (in F. W. H. Myers's conception) or mind, as used in the above quotation. Empirical evidence has been sought, however, over the past century by increasingly refined and generally undoubtedly conscientious methods, for the occurrence of psychic phenomena such as those classified as extrasensory perception, psycho-

[1] C. Lovatt Evans and B. Hartridge (eds.), Starling's *Principles of Human Physiology*, 1956, p. 3
[2] A. Flew, *Body, Mind and Death*, 1964, p. 3

kinesis, telepathy, precognition, etc. The question of communication between the living and the dead has played a part in these inquiries, and cannot be entirely separated from the problem as a whole; it has often spurred them on.

Professor Burt, on the basis of recent physiological studies of brain function in relation to consciousness, postulates that the structural basis of the brain may possess the characteristics of a psychic field; that the time-honoured issue raised by Cartesian dualism, whether mind really has a location and extension in space, as commonly conceived is a meaningless pseudo-problem; that a 'psychic factor' might conceivably persist after the death of the present body; and that the empirical evidence is strong enough to keep the issue open, but not sufficient to outweigh the antecedent probabilities against such a notion, at any rate so long as we remain within the framework of natural science.[1]

The psyche maintains *rapport* with the physiological functions of the organism mainly through the nervous system; the autonomic nervous system, with centres in the brain, regulates, for instance, heart-beat, breathing, body-temperature; the central nervous system regulates, for instance, sensory functions by which external phenomena are perceived. The problem of distinguishing the living from the dead has become more difficult since some of the functions of the psyche can, under favourable conditions, be taken over mechanically after brain damage and cessation of spontaneous *rapport*. The line between life and death may have to be drawn anew with reference to the expectation of re-establishment of spontaneous *rapport*.

The increasing value of uninjured parts of the corpse as spares for the living has made this problem more acute, but it is only one of many which the advance of medical science has presented to the profession in relation to death, and presented also to the potential corpses, the general public. With the increased availa-

[1] C. L. Burt, (a) 'Brain and consciousness', *British Journal of Psychology*, 59, 1, 1968, and (b) 'Brain and consciousness', *Bulletin of British Psychology and Sociology*, 22, 74, 1969, pp. 34, 36

bility of pain-lessening drugs, the problem of euthanasia for relief of pain diminishes, while that of the criteria for resuscitation looms larger. It is commonly assumed to be unwise to discuss his death with the patient. Studies of the prevalence, quality and effect of anxiety about death among the seriously ill may help those serving them to decide whether, and if so when, this matter should be broached. For many a hope of dying with dignity in peace may override a wish to lengthen briefly a life whose near end is already known. The doctor is professionally committed to maintain the patient's life, but the patient, when not temperamentally suicidal, may also be permitted some responsibility in the matter.

In a sister profession also with long traditions (the law), the agent of death rather than the patient has been a stimulus to scientific research. The operations of the law provide the data for the work of criminologists. A psychopathologist observes:

Punishment of criminals is believed to have the effect of deterring others from committing crimes. This is an empirical question. In the absence of controlled experimentation, the only source of evidence lies in the study of changes in the crime rate following changes in the punishments assigned to a given class of crime, or in the comparison of societies where a crime is punished lightly with other societies where the same crime is punished heavily. *Almost the only crime-punishment relationship that has been studied in this way is capital punishment.*[1] [My italics.]

In the extensive scientific literature on crime there is, of course, much use of the statistical records of many countries and cultures, but comparisons are often difficult.[2] Legal definitions differ; sentences and penalties apparently similar tend in effect to press very differently on the accused; even murder is differently defined in

[1] B. A. Maher, *Principles of Psychopathology*, 1966, p. 231
[2] See M. Wolfgang and F. Ferracuti, *The Subculture of Violence*, 1967; also *Excerpta Criminologica* as general guide to international statistical publications; also reports of the U.S. Presidential Commission on Violence set up in 1969

different codes of law.[1] But everywhere a death is a death, despite all we have said above, and this makes the study of capital punishment relatively simple compared with that of other penalties. So concern with death in the form of homicide – as prohibited act and as socially sanctioned penalty – has cleared the way for the study of crime, both in relation to punishment and to insanity.

Dr Nigel Walker[2] has remarked on the difficulty of studying the relation between crime and insanity scientifically until, in the nineteenth century, the age of reason gave place to the age of statistics. From 1834 onwards it becomes possible to discover, from the fates of persons committed for trial in England and Wales, the number who were acquitted or found unfit for trial because of their mental condition. In making a table of the latter as a percentage of the former, Dr Walker has excluded offences other than murder because the probable penalties attached to them varied during the period covered. To be admitted insane might be a doubtful advantage:

But murderers had the strongest possible incentive throughout to plead insanity, with one or two minor exceptions (the infanticidal mother or the very young murderer, who have been able to count on a reprieve for the last three-quarters of a century, and those covered by the new category of non-capital murderer which was created in 1957).

In 1964 the death penalty for all murders was suspended in Britain and subsequently abolished. The murder rate in this country, though varying from year to year as a percentage of the total population, is relatively low (under four per million). In a considerable number of cases, murder is followed by suicide.[3] The later act then appears to be usually due not to a desire to escape arrest but to the same distress and mental disorder as motivated the murder. Many of the victims of these dual incidents are

[1] The difficulties which may arise in classifying murder when the penalty is not capital are illustrated by the study by E. Gibson and S. Klein, *Murder 1957 to 1968*, 1969

[2] N. Walker, *Crime and Insanity in England*, 1968, vol. 1, pp. 85–8

[3] D. J. West, *Murder Followed By Suicide*, 1965. (The statistics are brought up to date by Gibson and Klein, *op. cit.*)

children under sixteen years old, and more of the adult victims are women than men, neither of which characteristics are so marked when murder is not followed by suicide.

Homicide contributes relatively little to the total record of criminal offences, though it looms so large in the news-reporting of crime, and in fiction. Even crimes of violence falling short of manslaughter – in many cases very far short – form a relatively small proportion of all recorded male crimes in the United Kingdom, and even less of female.

The relative rarity and immense fascination of homicide in most human communities has doubtless many reasons. It was, I think, Macchiavelli who wrote that men would rather lose their parents than their patrimony. It is perhaps partly a result of early uncertainty whether we want to kill our parents, or they us, that the prohibition *not to kill* appears to be so deeply rooted in the conscience. The emotional conflict involved in taking life, much more powerful than that involved in taking property, shows its other side in the heroic status and historic glory granted to men who transgress the prohibition on a grand scale.

In nineteenth-century Russia, what was called the Napoleonic complex developed around this ethical knot. Tolstoy in *War and Peace* tried to reduce the immense reputation of Napoleon, whom he saw as responsible for the slaughter of thousands of his own countrymen. Dostoyevsky, uncannily perspicacious, shows Raskolnikov as for a time obsessed with the thought that '*the extraordinary man* has a right to permit his conscience to step over obstacles' in pursuit of his idea of a better future for mankind, although this stepping over obstacles might involve 'wading through blood', eliminating a dozen or a hundred people, which such a man (but only such a man) is absolutely entitled to do in accordance with the dictates of his conscience. Raskolnikov's friend counters:

Well, old chap . . . of course this isn't new – we've heard and read about it a thousand times, but what is really original . . . is that you permit the shedding of blood in accordance with the dictates of one's conscience. . . . I think [that] is more awful than any official, legal sanction to shed blood.[1]

It was indeed not a new theory, as Razumikhin said. Within the conventions of war, it was not even a new practice; many conquerors have 'waded through blood' in order to secure a better future for mankind, or some section of it. But two things give the idea a novel twist in its context, and make it predictive rather than backward-looking at the time Dostoyevsky wrote: Raskolnikov, having persuaded himself that freedom from the trammels of conscience (as formerly interpreted) is a mark of superiority, commits murder partly to assure himself of his inclusion in the class of the free; and the elimination of other men is seen as permissible within the great man's own society, for they are not social or personal enemies but simply objects which, by denial of value of ordinary human beings, permit the exercise and expression of his power. In this respect Hitler and Stalin exemplified the new ethic, and differed from Napoleon.

The process of reassuring oneself of one's personality by committing murder, which Raskolnikov followed in his deranged condition, is shown at a further psychological stage in the novels of Gide and of Camus, where the heroes, in order to establish any assurance of personality at all, murder a man indifferent to them; the murderer and the victim are both depersonalized, as the tale is told. Then only death seems to have any reality, and that is little enough; life is 'a tale told by an idiot, signifying nothing'.

Dostoyevsky through the mouth of Raskolnikov, and Freud in his correspondence with Einstein refer to the part played in war by the masses who are led. It is of course the latter who in war perform the actual homicidal function. Science has scarcely begun to study personality variation in respect of this function. We find the conforming Eichmann at one end of the scale and the deviant Siegfried Sassoon at the other. Within a scientific framework, a foundation for such studies has first to be laid down. No direct reference to death or war is necessary. A primary question is: are

[1] F. Dostoyevsky, *Crime and Punishment*, 1870, pt 3, ch. 5 (1951 edn)

men generally (in democratic and in more authoritarian societies) ready, as Freud stated to Einstein in 1932, 'to bow without demur to the decisions' of those they accept as having authority, the leaders.

Men who are prepared to obey authority in administering severe pain may, by hypothesis, be prepared to go further. Milgram,[1] wielding the authority of a Yale University scientist, made a study of obedience among adult men, sampling across educational level, occupational status and age. In a laboratory experiment on learning and punishment they were told to administer (bogus) electric shock of increasing intensity to (stooge) adult pupils if the 'learners' gave incorrect answers to a series of questions. The 'teachers' were told that the shock, though causing no permanent tissue damage, could be extremely painful, and on the press-button display panel, intensity up to danger level was indicated. At a given stage of the experiment the 'learner', in a separate cell out of sight, having been given supposed intense shock, pounded on the wall and then ceased to respond at all. If the 'teacher' then asked what to do, he was told to go on giving increasing shock unless correct answers were received, which they were not.

When the experiment was planned, it was expected by a number of psychologists that only an insignificant minority would persist in giving shocks to the end of the series, when their press-button panels showed the shock to be dangerously severe. The tension of the 'teachers' during the experiment was observably extreme – men trembled, stuttered, groaned, and dug their finger-nails into their flesh. This surprised the experimenters; but what surprised them more was that 65 per cent of the sample persisted beyond the point where the shock was *shown* as intense and dangerous.

The fourteen men who defied the authority of the experimenter were frequently in a highly agitated and even angered state, or

[1] S. Milgram,(a) 'Behavioral study of obedience', *Journal of Abnormal and Social Psychology*, 67, 2, 1963; (b) 'Some conditions of obedience and disobedience to authority', *Human Relations*, 18, 1, 1965

sometimes they simply got up and went out of the lab. Some of the obedient subjects remained calm throughout.

If this cross-section of the male community represented those whom Freud called the masses (and if we accept a dichotomy of leaders and led, it would seem that they did), one notes that only about two-thirds were 'led' the whole way to what seemed like the torture of fellow men for scientific purposes. The experimenter, however, was surprised at 'the sheer strength of obedient tendencies manifested, when these countered what men have learned from childhood, that it is a fundamental breach of moral conduct to hurt another person against his will'. The results of this series of experiments should prevent any psychologist referring to *social conditioning* – the process by which, theoretically, moral conformity is instilled into the child – as standardized or straightforward. It seems that if civilization is not to founder, obedience *and* disobedience must be instilled, conformity *and* nonconformity. The evidence that most of these American men were not potential Eichmanns is given by the fact that they showed acute stress, but those among them who remained calm while administering (bogus) torture might under other orders have been prepared to torture or kill, without contravening the dictates of their conscience, which, as Razumikhin said, is awful.

The mortality which may seem the most obvious spur to scientific inquiry is that which is suffered in war. Death is then the means by which one nation or group of nations forces another to submit by the slaughter of thousands, or indeed millions, of men, women and children. This is the most terrible and prospectively the most terrifying phenomenon in the experience of mankind. But the aim to kill the enemy of one's social group involves no new development of the concept of mortality or of its social function. New developments may emerge from the more fervent, agonized desire not to have to kill or be killed, resultant upon the much increased probability that the effects of new methods of destruction cannot be limited to the intended victims with any assurance.

Towards preventing war, man tries to understand his own

aggressiveness. Is it biologically determined? Assumptions about human aggressiveness are often drawn from observation of the behaviour of animals. The theory that there is an aggressive drive in man, assumed by many psychologists, including Freud, instinctive in nature as the drives of sex and hunger, is denied by some workers, including J. P. Scott.[1] Within animal societies (i.e. within a species) outbreaks of destructive violence seldom occur except when they are disturbed by man. Such outbreaks may resemble the violence of juvenile gangs deeply alienated from the community in control; it is doubtful, however, whether this type of behaviour is closely related to the causes of war.

Young animals can be trained (conditioned) to be *more* or *less* aggressive, and bred to aggressive or non-aggressive behaviour, but with reduction in aggressiveness it seems that there is also reduction not in sexual[2] but in exploratory behaviour. Eibl-Eibersfeldt has said 'that is one reason why it is probably dangerous to try, by education, to cure man of his aggression ... [but] courtesy is an aggressivity buffer ... a unifying religious symbol [may also be useful]. Whether we identify ourselves with man ... is a question of education.'[3] This means conscious education, not the sort of training or conditioning given to the caged animal.

Crowding of animals tends to suppress reproductive activity; chemical processes delay puberty and reduce fertility in other ways. Fertility is not thus controlled in man. But both animal and human aggressiveness is related to population density. This observation has been developed in detail in a recent work by C. and W. M. S. Russell.[4]

The animal's aggressiveness may not lie dormant until population density impels a break-out. His constant activity may consist

[1] In discussion, C. D. Clemente and D. B. Lindsley (eds.), *Aggression and Defense*, Nov. 1967
[2] K. M. J. Lagerspetz, 'Aggression and aggressiveness in laboratory mice', S. Garattini and E. B. Sigg (eds.), *Aggressive Behaviour*, 1968
[3] In discussion, Clemente and Lindsey (eds.) *op. cit.*, p. 88
[4] *Violence: What are its Roots?*, 1968

of defensive patrol of territory or announcement of his claim. The discovery of the importance of territory in the determination of animal behaviour is relatively recent in scientific research; it is a new idea that the song of the skylark or the nightingale is not an outpouring of joy in living, or a love serenade or aubade, but an announcement of local proprietorship. But the discovery has obvious relevance also to the behaviour of man. The intense emotion felt by men for a particular part of the earth's surface, often expressed by poets, has been illustrated by spontaneous actions of men of different cultures from early to modern days: the London *Times* reported, with a photograph, on 15 June 1963, how Greeks repatriated after over ten years spent as hostages in Albania lay down and kissed the soil of Greece as they set foot on it again. Similar behaviour was recorded much earlier of Scots repatriated after many years' military service in Ireland; the reporter remarked that this was irrational, since western Scotland was originally populated from Ireland! The ritual of burial may partly derive from man's love of the ground that supports him. The call of governments to their people to fight for their country arouses deep and irrational sentiments which men share with non-human species. And where there is irrational love of one's own land, there may also be a longing to own more, especially where boundaries are not clearly set geographically.

The curious reason given by the historian for judging the Scots' behaviour irrational points to the fact that love of soil is indeed of territory *belonging*; that is, it is bound up with a sense of community, and wells up most strongly after long sojourn among people felt to be alien. When men are prepared to die for their country, it is indeed for that, but much more for those they feel not alien to them. They are in effect denying the sentiment of the Roman who said that as a man he considered no human being alien to him.

That was a noble sentiment, but the sentiment of the volunteer prepared to die for a country or a cause is not ignoble. Indeed in seeking to prevent war it is necessary to take into account the fact that men, aware of mortality, may seek something to die for, and aim to use death, since they cannot escape it. The desire to give a purpose to life may involve the enlistment of death in the same cause. Such we may see as the motivation of Jan Palach in Czechoslovakia, of Buddhist monks in Vietnam, of Emily Davidson, the suffragette who threw herself under the horses at the Derby race in England. Such cases demonstrate conscious individual *anomie*, the reaction against disorganization or ill-organization of society which Durkheim judged the social source of suicide. The volunteer in war, or indeed the conscientious objector who suffers for refusal to fight, may be less extreme examples of a very similar motivation, to use life for a cause, though when the social group calls for such service, the only *anomie* consists in the fact that what is founded to protect men should instead endanger them.

So ready have most men been in the past to respond to the call to defend their country or aggress on its behalf that governments have been able to count on support if they plan to make or resist attack. The nature of modern war may reduce the response and the assurance, for there is no decorum about such death today; it tends to be shared with too many who have even less claim to glory than the military rank and file.

It may be the more necessary to recognize the existence of the normal wish to have something to die for. Over thousands of years, adventure and war have given men this opportunity, and childbirth has given it to women. Now if warfare is to be prevented and childbirth to become less frequent and safer, since *living for* and *dying for* are part of the same complex, other ways must be found.

The absolute opposite is the motiveless murder described by Gide and by Camus, done by the man who has no purpose in life and kills only to show that even murder may be committed without purpose. The positive direction, then, is towards the establishment and social recognition of the individual personality of every man. The problem is not ephemeral but of all time. The Homeric Greek solution made very clear the link with the idea of death.

This unchangeable identity of the person (*eudaimonia*), though disclosing itself intangibly in act and speech, becomes tangible only in the story of the actor's and speaker's life; but as such it can be known . . . only after it has come to its end. . . . Therefore whoever consciously aims at being 'essential' . . . must not only risk his life but expressly choose, as Achilles did, a short life and premature death. . . . Even Achilles . . . remains dependent upon the storyteller, poet, or historian, without whom everything he did remains futile . . .[1]

In many ways the motivation of the action of Jan Palach resembles that of the Homeric Greek: in the need for publicity, in the need to die, and in the blessedness (as Arendt says, without necessarily religious overtones) eternally established by the action. But the Homeric solution was completely individualistic; courage was involved, but not a cause. The Periclean solution was that the existence and quality of the *polis*, the civil community, guaranteed the permanent identity, the immortality, of those who by their actions contributed to it. Essentially this resembles the solution of Isaiah and the Hebrew prophets: individual identity and permanent value is given by membership of a divinely chosen people with laws to be obeyed and social activities to be undertaken. The Christian solution resembles the Periclean in suggesting the vicarious component of the sacrifice; it takes this idea further back in time, to the buying back of the ritual human victim by the substitution of another life; but, as in Athens, links the sacrifice with the safety of a whole people – indeed mankind. The actions of the Buddhist monks show that in other traditions also there must be historic motives for such behaviour, which may be signposts to ways to strengthen personality without supporting aggression, but by giving positive social aim to life.

[1] H. Arendt, *The Human Condition*, 1958, pp. 192–4

CHAPTER 12

RETROSPECT AND ANTICIPATION

THE impulse to study and write on the discovery of death came from observation of children's behaviour; children not ill or in distress but leading lives otherwise unreported for any purpose but family affection. The problem that arose first was, how to explain the expression by the young of thoughts about death which echo those of cultures far distant from their own. Some half-century ago, many psychologists would have answered this question in terms of individual recapitulation of human cultural stages. Such an answer is not acceptable today. How then do we account for such behaviour? It is suggested that for children the phenomena on which are built up concepts of time, death, etc., may lead to ideas over the whole range available to man, from which normally as they grow up they eliminate from their conscious repertory those not acceptable in their own culture.

This rather vague hypothesis followed from a suggestion made by Onians in discussion of a problem that seemed allied to our own: how explain the widespread similarity of the early thought of European peoples about the body, the mind, the soul, the world, time and fate. Onians holds that although influence cannot be excluded, it is more probable that the same phenomena led to the same conclusions. A phenomenon has been defined as the data of experience at any given moment.[1] It is useful to think of phenomena as having objective and subjective sources. When in widely separated cultures men develop similar ways of interpretation of and response to phenomena, it is to be inferred that there is a general human propensity to such behaviour. This appears to be so in respect of early ways of thinking about the

[1] J. Drever, *A Dictionary of Psychology*, 1952

body and the soul, fate (which includes death) and time, though perhaps of these time is the most subject to variations in early human ways of thinking.[1]

The intelligent adolescent's concept of death refers to mortality as physically ascertainable. In the child's earliest conception, physical observations of this kind play only a small part. They are the keystone rather than the foundation of the final structure. A young child sees a dead animal, or kills one, and may regard the inanimate object not as exhibiting a condition new to him but as asleep. Again, the recurring presence and absence of persons is a condition of infant experience; the non-appearance of a recently deceased relative may objectively signify to the young child a departure, and departure be indistinguishable from death. These phenomena are subjectively interpreted in terms of things familiar. Yet the interpretation carries with it a question; a matching process is involved, with a query about the goodness of the match. It was recorded of the two-year-old who killed a fly and thought it asleep, that a doubt remained; the child who thinks a deceased relative has gone away is conditioned from infancy to conceive of disappearance as temporary, but he may show uncertainty or displaced distress. In referring to the dead as asleep or departed an adult will consciously employ metaphor. The child, on the other hand, is attempting an objective description of a phenomenon. Upon the accompanying questioning attitude depends the gradual differentiation and enlargement of the individual's conceptual scheme as he matures.

Asleep and *departed* are but two of many interpretations which we have received from young children as equivalent to *dead*. Their concepts of death and of life are often erroneous and always incomplete. The former may signify, for instance, asleep, gone away, bodiless, buried, in heaven, waiting to be born, in hospital or killed. Many of these interpretations would, we hypothesize, be given by young children in other cultures. Similar objects and

[1] On this point see the work of B. L. Whorf, and discussion by C. Kluckhohn, 'Culture and behavior', G. Lindzey (ed.), *Handbook of Social Psychology*, 1954, vol. 2, ch. 25

situations seem to contribute everywhere to the phenomenal world of the infant, and this environmental similarity is a major factor in the similarity of non-verbal symbols described by analytic psychologists, and of the ways of thought of early European peoples as shown by Onians.

Two problems remain. If the similarity of symbols of death, time, etc., are to be thus accounted for, how can we explain cultural differences in these fields? And how is it that children echo the thoughts expressed in cultures other than their own, particularly in respect of death and allied themes?

Let us consider these questions in turn. We have found that young children in our own culture tend to differ between themselves in their concepts of life and death. The conscious concepts of adults in any one culture show less simplicity, but also less diversity. Although some inconsistency is commonly tolerated in civilized and (according to anthropologists) in primitive communities, there is a general pressure towards consistency and conformity, attributable to the need for social action in the face of death. Such action has the function of organizing the physical disposal of the corpse, and of reconciling survivors to the loss and the disposal. The continued integration and stability of the group may depend upon such action being in accord with conceptions held in common. In a situation involving personality so deeply, the outlook and attitude of the child will necessarily contribute to the adult social formulation, but the need for consistency prohibits the inclusion in any one system of every interpretation arising in childhood. A consistent formulation rejects over-divergent immature conceptions in order to lay down a pattern for ritual action, and to canalize the flow of emotion. In the mythology of different cultures, different childhood conceptions are therefore elaborated and standardized.

Children spontaneously interpret in various ways the objective sources of phenomena, whereas a culture develops an interpretation relatively consistently. Children do not echo concepts from distant cultures. They offer, in every culture and every generation, a variety of potential foundations for religion, philosophy and myth, relatively independent of the selection made by their own society.

Why should the apparent echoing occur, particularly in respect of death and allied themes? The answer is to be found in the psychology of the adult, not of the child. A supremely repugnant phenomenon tends to evoke regressive impulses. A mature interpretation reached unemotionally may then be repressed in favour of an earlier one less mature.

The early Egyptians concentrated interest on permanent, material things to ease the encounter with death, somewhat as Jane valued the cotton poppy because it would not die. To suppose that everything that dies has been killed by evil powers is another regressive solution of a problem posed in an intolerably frustrating situation. On occasions when inactivity is personally distressing and may be socially dangerous, men's effort may be harnessed to the performance of programmes founded on such regressive thinking. Thus concepts typical of the immature have determined the form of products of genius memorializing the dead, and communal aggressions may have been largely due to the immature tendency to seek foreign animate objects upon which to wreak anger after defeat and loss.

The child's conceptual scheme is built up on subjective interpretations of objects in terms of familiar things and functions, plus queries. In this process social communication as well as independent sensory perception plays a part. It was found, however, that the maturity of children's concepts of death was related more closely to mental than to chronological age, irrespective of the distinctive content of what they had been told. Social teaching independent of experience was swallowed whole, as it were, undigested. Children would believe that a worm or rabbit after burial would go up into the sky and be no longer bodily present in the ground. There seemed to be so strong a tendency to encourage regressive impulses in the contact between adult and child on the subject of death that communication frequently confuses rather than clarifies the child's conception. On the other hand, an educational theory which encourages a fully mature objectivity among young children by the dissection of dead animals may when put into practice show that many of them have a prior need to work through a stage of preoccupation with social reaction to the death of human beings. They may join in dissections with enthusiasm and scientific interest, but if there has been an emotional relationship with an animal, they may choose to bury it with ceremony rather than dissect it.

Somewhat later, the young tend to dispel solemnity and sentimentality in group mockery of death, and at the same age many of them undertake daring exploits in active derision of it. In these practices an element of defence against anxiety may lie hidden, which may persist in many people through life, so that without the opportunity to dare, life seems to them hardly worth living.

Freud noted that the child does not inhibit expression of thoughts about death as adults do, but develops them directly and in fantasy.[1] The observation has been confirmed by subsequent researches in Switzerland, England, Hungary and America. It would be a mistake, however, to suppose that the child's behaviour is normally entirely free from anxiety. The infant's belief in the efficacy of his own wishes involves the small child in guilt and fear about the effect of his aggressive impulses towards those on whose ministrations his welfare depends, so it would appear. Such impulses are expressed in fantasies in which the urge to aggression oscillates with an urge to reparation. The anxiety typical of this stage is normally reduced by the gradual acceptance of the limitations of psychic power when divorced from bodily action. Magic becomes the matter of fairy tales, consciously fantastic, rather than one of the dangerous facts of life.

The normal reduction of anxiety may be promoted or obstructed. A question frequently debated is the advisability of telling the child traditional 'fairy tales'. The Katz parents, who 'tried in every way to keep from our children the idea of the death of people', thought that 'in fairy tales there is a great deal – indeed too much – about striking dead, burning to death, hanging and

[1] S. Freud, *Thoughts for the Times on War and Death*, 1915 (1953 edn, vol. 14)

other methods of causing the transition from life to death'.[1] In their view the child does not comprehend what reality lies behind this. 'For the child, death in fairy tales probably means nothing more than *not playing any longer*, the withdrawal of the person concerned.' In their intelligent preoccupation with the problem of the child's discovery of death, the Katz parents seem to have overlooked the essential difficulty in 'what really lies behind' the fairy tales they refer to, which are evidently those traditionally offered to Central European children during the century 1840–1940 – the *märchen* collected by the brothers Grimm. (French children were probably more generally brought up on the more civilized and witty collection of Perrault, from which English children selected as favourite Puss-in-Boots.) The Grimm brothers, admirable scholars, faithfully recorded folk tales told by illiterate adults, some of whom provided versions unashamedly sadistic. The fact that the stories frequently treat of death does not in itself make them unsuitable for children, for death also enters frequently into children's own fantasies. The unsophisticated enjoyment of cruelty which is often apparent bears witness to the authenticity of the collection. Nor is such cruelty, in immature forms, alien to the world of childhood. But the adult who offers such material for the child's enjoyment is actively encouraging a sadistic disposition in the child, and may increase anxiety in those who appear either to accept or to reject the tale. A writer of the 1930s described how Grimm's fairy tales encouraged sadistic attitudes in the child of a Nazi family:

Always Trudi was having her hands smacked at meals for putting them on the table, and then she had to be told a fairy story, and all the time it was . . . 'The Wolf and the Seven Little Kids', and when it ended up *'Der Wolf ist tot, der Wolf ist tot, Hurra, Hurra, Hurra'*, the blood lust and ferocity on the infant face of the infant neurotic was something more than I could stand. And there was another one she would allow sometimes to be told . . . about Snowdrop and her cruel stepmother. . . . So eventually Snowdrop . . . grows right up and marries her prince. And the wicked stepmother? Ah well, this is what happens to her. She

[1] D. and R. Katz, *Conversations with Children*, 1936, p. 251 ff.

falls in with the happy wedding-party and they take her by force and make her dance in red-hot shoes until she is dead: '*Da musste sie in die rotglühenden Schuhe treten und so lange tanzen, bis sie tot zur Erde fiel.*' See the idea? Well, try it on the baby.[1]

The view that, in general, folk tales are suitable material for the young imagination is, however, surely based on sound psychology. They have a positive value through their employment of simple symbols which the child is able to understand. The sophisticated adult tends to use such symbols, if at all, with a self-conscious or false simplicity. An instance may be found in that common theme of the folk tale, metamorphosis, the changing of one thing into another of different form, not explained but treated as simple fact. They are not to be believed, still less disbelieved; they are for amusement and excitement, and if one wants a moral, to suggest that appearances may be deceptive. They may add excitement to scientific observations of metamorphosis, as when one of our subjects, Richard, aged 5:5,

[H.R.63.] had enquired about the nature of steam, and after a simple explanation said: 'It's water-air; the frog prince was a frog that changed into a prince, so steam is water-air.' He proceeded to enumerate other things that changed their form, such as caterpillars.[2]

Ultimately, however, the defence of folk tales in the nursery is not that they excite to the learning of or pleasure in scientific fact, but that they communicate ways of thinking, symbols, concepts and attitudes that enrich and humanize life. It is much the same defence as that of poetry against Plato. They do this by handling the whole natural range of human activity with cultural singleness and simplicity. The case against the sadistic fantasy holds nevertheless, so long as the child is offered the material by the adult. When he can read himself, he may be left free to choose or leave, though as with other activities, the adult may need to be alert to the child's reactions.

[1] S. Smith, *Novel on Yellow Paper*, 1936 (1951 edn, p. 85)
[2] W. Grimm, '*Der Froschkönig oder der eiserne Heinrich*', *Märchen*, vol. 1, 1, Berlin, 1843. In English translations, *The Frog Prince*

The Katz parents also raised another question. They refused for a time to let their children know that the meat they ate came from animals which had been killed. Later they found that this knowledge did not disturb the children. The unconcern appears normal, but there are children who react somewhat in the way the Katzs expected. Such an instance occurred in mild temporary form in one of the subjects of our research:

[H.R.64.] Ben (6:0) asked what animals the different kinds of meat came from, pitied the sheep, pigs and calves, and expressed the view that we ought not to eat meat. M told him that there were adults who held this view and acted on it, and that if he wished he might be a vegetarian. Dinner was served soon after, with pork sausages, which was one of Ben's favourite dishes. While eating them he asked about the animal they came from. He had a second helping.

The child's reaction to the killing of animals may be more profound and long-lasting than this. It may determine behaviour through life. If vegetarianism is presented to the child as the family norm and voluntarily maintained by him in other milieux, the psychological significance of his behaviour is, of course, different. One possible source of conflict is avoided; another is substituted. The avoidance of sources of conflict is, however, not the main aim of those concerned for the welfare of children. In the process of personal adjustment to a complex culture, choosing between conflicting impulses is unavoidable. The aim is to strengthen the decision-making process, so that its results may be profoundly satisfying and relatively stable.

The significance of animals in the emotional development of the child was noted by Freud, and has been demonstrated in a number of subsequent researches. In childish fantasy large animals generally represent parents and small or young ones self or siblings. These identifications throw light upon actions or passionate reactions such as distress or enjoyment at the killing of animals for food, sport, or human protection; the beating or killing of a small animal by a child, or the expression of affection for animals because they are killed. In a society in which humanitarianism is expressed most fervently with reference to animal welfare, adult reaction to children's behaviour towards animals may be particularly ill-conceived. The adult's refusal to countenance active cruelty, either from sympathy with animal suffering or in order to teach the child the social *mores* for his own future comfort, is clearly wise. To suppose or suggest that the cruelty is prognostic of perversion is not. The idea appears to be without foundation, and the suggestion may be harmful. Observation, supported by biographical record such as that of Darwin, which has been quoted, indicates that the child who beats a puppy, stamps on a goldfish or kills a kitten is not necessarily or probably an abnormal child, nor more likely than the next to evince sadistic, masochistic or any other form of perversion in later life.

The child's identification of himself with the immature of other species has a basis in reality, the strength of which has been more fully understood in recent years owing to researches into the nature and effects of anxiety. The young child tends to think of death in terms of either aggression or separation, or a combination of the two. From either of these associations, anxiety may follow. Psychiatric researches into the effect upon infants of separation from the mother or her substitute have indicated how profound such effects may be. These investigations led zoologists to study the effect of stressful situations upon immature animals when accompanied by or separated from their dams. The striking results of these experiments demonstrate how deep-seated biologically may be anxiety about death conceived in terms of separation from parent-figures.

The analogy between the lamb and the child is not to be carried too far. Anxiety about separation from the mother appears to be most acute at the age when there is no concept of death. At the period when the concept is emerging, society provides safeguards against such anxiety. The human infant does not depend so exclusively upon its mother as do the young of animals. Under favourable conditions the child spreads his dependence. Unfortunately, opportunities for doing so tend to be reduced in modern industrial societies. Mobility of labour, family limitation, and housing projects which result in the removal of young

families from the neighbourhood of the senior parental generation may all tend to operate against the maintenance of an
extended intimate group around the child, and so increase the
incidence of immature anxiety associated with death as separation.

In children under seven years old, it may happen that conscious
acceptance of the inevitability of their own death is eased through
a process of denial. One instance has been recorded in which this
was a blissful process. Three instances were quoted of anxiety
connected with it, overcome with the help of a mother who
encouraged or assented to the denial. In one case, more doubtfully
interpreted as falling within this category, psychiatric treatment
was required. The process of acceptance through negation has
been described by Freud and Ferenczi. Its foundation is seen in
the reversal to which Freud[1] testified from one of his own dreams,
in which love was substituted for death and choice for necessity.
The process is enshrined in language; in Greek, for instance, the
words for joy and death differ only in stress and gender, and the
word for joy resembles the Italian for beloved-woman. Unconscious displacement and denial, evidently general, may become
temporarily conscious in childhood; this negation may be accepted as a means of reducing stress in a process, which, although
not pathological is, like childbirth, often painful.

In some cases concern for the child's future mental health is
justified. Dr Sula Wolff[2] considers that 'childhood bereavement
alone . . . does not appear to predispose an individual to develop
a depressive illness, as Bowlby has suggested. It may, however,
contribute to abnormal personality development.' She points out
the disadvantageous effects for children of having only one
parent, and quotes Marris as showing that even financially better-
off widows have to rear their families on a much-reduced income.

The immediate psychological effect of loss of a parent or sibling
was observed in several cases in my earlier research; some notes

[1] S. Freud, *The Theme of the Three Caskets*, 1913 (1953 edn, vol. 12)
[2] S. Wolff, *Children under Stress*, 1969, p. 80, quoting (a) J. Bowlby, 'Childhood
mourning and its implications for psychiatry', *American Journal of Psychiatry*,
118, 1961, and (b) P. Marris, *Widows and their Families*, 1958

on a younger child can now be added. Reference has been made to the eight-year-old Bernard, whose father's death was found to set up in the child strong feelings of guilt, obscuring his ability to interpret situations at the intellectual level otherwise normal to him. In a girl of about the same age, the father's death had apparently induced a state resembling incipient mania. In a younger school child, the mother's pregnancy following the death of younger siblings seemed to be responsible for a condition of neurotic anxiety. In a child of three and a half who had not yet begun to ask *Why* questions but showed an intense desire to play a part in every adult domestic activity, the father's death was followed by a brief period in which he whimpered 'I can't do it' of actions which he had previously performed with ease and pleasure. [H.R.65.]

In our earlier study it was suggested that the child should not be deprived at such a time of adult companionship and conversation. This applies particularly to schoolchildren, who will normally spend much of their day with children of their own age-group, or in formal relationship with the teacher. The attitude of the adult in a freer relationship, rather than the companionship of other children, reminds the child of his relative impotence. This frees him from a sense of responsibility for the distressful event. The encouragement given to the child to recognize the reality of his impotence may, however, support an impulse on his part to regress to earlier patterns of behaviour, unless accompanied by encouragement of the exercise of his actual abilities.

Reassured that he is not guilty by the evidence of what he actually can and cannot do, the child may then accept without repression the memory of his antagonistic as well as his loving impulses towards the deceased. The manner of the adult's reference to the loss may influence this process. Suggestions of constant affection or of pity – 'your poor dear mother', 'your darling little brother', 'your poor granny' – are not likely to reduce anxiety.

Although there is evidence of a common factor in the way human beings react to bereavement, the relative weight of general human and specific cultural factors may be very difficult to assess. Margaret Mead has written that in Bali the expression of grief was almost entirely banned, but might be enacted on the stage, when its representation 'would be recognized by a European as a beautiful, deep grief'.[1] This suggests the existence both of a general human factor and a culturally determined inhibiting of its expression without severe control. Such inhibition – 'the stiff upper lip' – is also greatly admired in cultures remote from Bali. A mourning process whose expression is so severely controlled may induce neurotic reactions in personalities not capable of conforming without deep stress to the social code. Lindemann has said that one typical failure of the mourning process in America is that 'the image of the deceased disappears from consciousness and . . . will only be recalled with great reluctance and difficulty during waking hours'.[2] A British woman recently bereaved informed the writer that in order to maintain control she had to drive out all thought of the deceased, even at the funeral service. Another whose elder brother was killed in the 1914–18 war when she was adolescent, wrote: 'I could find no comfort for years after R died. It hurt so much that I had to thrust every thought of him away.' [H.R.66.] These women drove away the image consciously, and recalled it only too easily, whereas the neurotic patient barred the thought unconsciously and recalled it only with difficulty, yet the similarity is evident. The form of reaction is a function of the cultural code which demands absence of public physical expression of grief. Such codes are developed as methods of mastering stress and containing group hysteria. It follows, as Lindemann says, that 'many of the stress responses labelled neurotic or psychosomatic, which might previously have been viewed as personal psychological failure of mastery of a problem, turn out to be . . . ways of solving problems typical of some particular ethnic group'.

It was suggested by Piaget some forty years ago that the child's

[1] M. Mead, in J. M. Tanner and B. Inhelder (eds.), *Discussions on Child Development*, 1956, vol. 1, p. 213

[2] E. Lindemann, in J. M. Tanner (ed.), *Stress and Psychiatric Disorder*, 1960, pp. 14, 15

encounter with the idea of death plays a special part in intellectual development. The idea of death, he wrote, sets the child's curiosity in motion because if, for him at an early age, every cause is coupled with a motive, then death calls for a special explanation. In my researches, mentally retarded children were found to continue to couple cause and motive in adolescence, so that such children might define *dead* as *killed* or *murdered*; a response normally only likely to be given at an earlier age. According to Piaget, the fact that human mortality represents a limitation of adult power over events, because death cannot be explained in terms of motive consistently with *decus*, the right ordering of society, leads the child to the conception of physical causation and chance – unless the issue is confused by theological explanations, in which case one may find the logical child deducing, as one of Wallon's small subjects did, that if it were not for the machinations of the devil no one would die.

It is sociologically interesting that Piaget's theory should have been put forward by a Swiss citizen, whose people have for centuries recognized by neutrality the futility of human aggression and maintained a most decorous society. Would the argument still hold for little boys in Colombia, where homicide is the leading cause of death among men between fifteen and forty-five years of age, according to the study of Wolfgang and Ferracuti?[1]

The encounter with the thought of one's own death marks a separate stage in intellectual growth. Wallon, discussing the nature of children's thinking at the approach of this stage, finds that the apparent acceptance of general mortality may be conjoined with a concept of death as essentially accidental, not inevitable. Stern and Spearman have independently shown how the processes of children's thought involve deduction by other sequences than those of classical logic. One of the Katz conversations with children illustrates how the desire to escape the application of death to the self leads a child to develop valid methods of verbal argument: 'If God doesn't die, all men won't die.' The intellectual process has been stimulated by the desire to avoid

[1] M. E. Wolfgang and F. Ferracuti, *The Subculture of Violence*, 1967

death, previously expressed by this boy. The reasoning might seem to echo an earlier Jew, St Paul, whose arguments this child would not have been taught.

In social communication between adult and child on this subject there is generally a continuous tradition. The persistence of the practice of baptism in countries where other church services are comparatively sparsely attended bears similar witness. Lightly to assume that participation in this ceremony has no influence on the subsequent development of the child is to misunderstand the psychology of the adult. The motivation in arranging for the baptism, and the recollection that the event has occurred, necessarily affect the manner in which the parent responds to the child's later questions. The discrepancy between the baptismal and the attendance figures suggests – as do also the results of a number of researches among college and high school students – that changes in religious attitude in adolescence are frequently not reflected in the subsequent teaching of offspring. Consideration of ecclesiastical statistics in the light of socio-psychological researches suggests that whereas the adolescent of Protestant background has for at least a quarter-century tended towards agnosticism, younger children continue to be taught along traditional lines at home. If this is so, the parental behaviour may represent various attitudes. The agnostic may intend to offer the child a *Weltanschauung* consciously modified to suit an immature mentality or to encourage cultural conformity. He may consider it unwise to suggest that the child should respond to the age-old cry of the Protestant: 'Dare to be a Daniel, dare to stand alone!' The parent's behaviour may, on the other hand, represent a less rational process such as Eliade[1] has described:

> Individuals who no longer have any religious experience properly speaking, reveal in their behaviour a whole camouflaged mythology, and fragments of a forgotten or degraded religion. [Their] religion has become unconscious.

Without specific intent, this is what they then pass on to their

[1] M. Eliade, *Birth and Rebirth*, 1958, p. 127

children. Or, thirdly, the demand to teach a child a considered view of life and death may reawaken in the young adult an active interest in problems laid aside in adolescence.

In the development of any concept profoundly significant to all men, sex is necessarily implicated, in the Freudian connotation of the word. The unconscious identification of love and death to which Freud testified appears to set up sometimes interaction and sometimes alternation between them in consciousness. When there is alternation, excitation of the one theme assists repression of the other. In a recent novel the hero is shown using this as a technique for the relief of anxiety:

[P.R.65.] Just nerves, he said to himself. Nothing to do with dying. And anyway, men must endure their going hence even as their coming hither, mustn't they? Ah, but men weren't given the tip in advance about their coming hither, were they? Anyway, nothing to do with dying. Perhaps a little bit to do with going mad. That would be unusual, because he was pretty sound these days on the bonkers question. Meditations on the last end were giving him a good deal more trouble. Well, thinking about sex as much as possible was the only way to lick that.[1]

In nineteenth-century English-speaking society when references to sex were more strictly taboo than they are today, particularly in literature provided for the young, references to death were relatively acceptable. Today the situation is reversed. A sociologist observer in the U.S.A. has written:

Whether through fear of the emotional depths or because of a drying up of the sluices of religious intensity, the American avoids dwelling on death or even coming to terms with it: he finds it morbid, and recoils from it . . . with a word-avoidance . . . and various [other] taboos. . . . American culture cuts away the sensitivity to death and grief, to suicide and immortality.[2]

This was written before the murder of President Kennedy. It may be that the deepest effect of the deaths of John and Robert

[1] K. Amis, *Take a Girl Like You*, 1960, p. 69
[2] M. Lerner, *America as a Civilization*, 1958, p. 618

Kennedy on the mentality of their country will prove to be a change in American sensitivity to death and grief.

Another American, Hannah Arendt, has written that modern man differs from men of all previous ages in having become accustomed to the notion of absolute mortality, 'so that the thought of it no longer bothers us'.[1] Of modern man in general, I cannot accept this observation as valid, and am surprised to read it in the work of so sensitive an observer. Concern with absolute mortality appears to me patent in the work of writers such as Sartre, Heidegger, Marcel, Pasternak, C. S. Lewis, H. A. Wolfson and many others – though perhaps it does not 'bother' them. Further, when we examine the appeals made to the man in the street by exponents of rival philosophies, we find similarities which point to a common origin, in the effort to provide a programme for harnessing anxiety about absolute mortality. An eminent Marxist[2] tells us that there must be 'faith in the future establishment of what materialist theologians have called the kingdom of God on earth', which the present individual participates in by assisting in its foundation. A Christian historian[3] argues that

the purpose of life is not in the far future . . . but the whole of it is here and now as fully as ever it will be on this planet. It is always a 'Now' that is in direct relation to eternity . . . always immediate experience of life that matters in the last resort.

The traditional roles and message of the communist and the Christian seem to have been reversed, the former stressing the importance of the hereafter, the latter of the now. Both appeal to men's desire to live time-transcendently. Both aim to harness man's anxiety about mortality to the wagon of current action, the one by faith and hope in establishing communism as the kingdom of God, the other by insisting that every present moment is related to eternity.

[1] H. Arendt, *Between Past and Future*, 1951, p. 74

[2] J. Needham, review of P. Teilhard de Chardin, *The Phenomenon of Man*, in the *New Statesman*, 7 November 1959

[3] H. Butterfield, *Christianity and History*, 1957, p. 89

Again, when we compare men of the present day with men of earlier times we find in each period variations of manner of concern, but no lack of it in any age, nor lack of resemblances in attitude to mortality. Compare, for instance, Pascal and Sartre: the former urges men to make each moment prophetic in the sense of freely exercising choice towards a chosen end, and then to cease thinking about what may happen after death; the latter writes: 'I am not *free in order to die* (as Heidegger would hold) but a free being who dies; it is the exercise of freedom, not the death, which gives meaning to personal existence.'[1]

In the calm recording of observations or in dispassionate attempts to account for observed behaviour, we may forget the intensity of the anxiety and anguish men, women and children suffer, some somewhere every day, from the actuality of loss or the expectation of the near ending of life, their own or another's. 'The world of the happy is quite other than the world of the unhappy.' All men in the course of time pass through both. Protestant cultures deprecate their uncontrolled expression. Excess of either reduces industrial efficiency. Cultures which deplore the expression of grief tend thereby to reduce sympathy with it and sensitivity to it. They may in so doing reduce hypocrisy too, for grief is not always keenly felt where convention requires it, and where it is acute and long-lasting it may choose to remain hidden. But surely reduction of sensitivity to grief does not ultimately increase happiness, and may be a source of danger to civilization.

The development of the child's concept of death seemed to have reached intellectual maturity when the word *dead* was defined logically and physiologically. But for the adolescent and the adult this is only the beginning of the meaning of death, which in the most literal sense (that required for medical purposes) is very difficult to pin down. The idea is developing continually, linking with the concepts of time and cause in ways philosophers and physicists must unravel, and with the concept of man himself, which is the concern of us all. The links between birth and death

[1] H. J. Blackham, on J.-P. Sartre, in *Six Existentialist Thinkers*, 1952–61, pp. 135–6

take on new, grim meaning as, throughout the world, population increases. Preparations for defence against large-scale human-produced disaster are not distinguishable from preparation to produce such disaster; the synthesis of offensive and defensive manoeuvres was made long before their scale reached its present proportions.

Under the menace of mortality, the only hope is in natality, death's counterpart; that new life will draw from the past new powers of perceiving, of communicating concepts and conclusions drawn from phenomena without reference to irrelevant differences of culture, and of organizing afresh the endless struggle for the survival of humanity, in all senses of the word.

APPENDIX

THE relation between definitions of *dead* and age
   (a) chronological,
   (b) mental,
calculated by Terman-Merrill test of intelligence.

TABLE AI: *Meaning given to 'dead' by age and concept-category*
(Educationally subnormal entered separately, bracketed)

Category	A	B	C	D	E	Total
Age						
Under 5:0	1	3	–	–	–	4
5:0–5:11	1	3	6	–	–	10
6:0–6:11	1	1	6	–	–	8
7:0–7:11	–	–	14	–	–	14
8:0–8:11	–	1	6	1	1	9
9:0–9:11	(1)	–	8	1	1	10 + (1)
10:0–10:11	–	–	4 + (1)	3	3	10 + (1)
11:0–11:11	–	–	2 + (3)	1	2	5 + (3)
12:0–12:11	–	–	– (3)	–	–	– (3)
13:0–13:11	–	–(1)	– (3)	–(1)	–	– (5)

Average age   5:6(6:6)   5:8(6:6)   8:0(8:9)   10:2(10:6)   10:4   8:1(8:9)
(including subnormal)

Total no.   3 + (1)   8 + (1)   46 + (10)   6 + (1)   7   70+(13)
   Per cent   4·8   10·8   67·6   8·4   8·4   100·0

TABLE A2: *Meaning given to 'dead' by mental age and concept-category*

Category	A	B	C	D	E	Total
Mental age						
Under 5:0	3	I	I	–	–	5
5:0 –5:11	I	5	2	–	–	8
6:0 –6:11	–	3*	15	–	–	18
7:0 –7:11	–	–	13	–	–	13
8:0 –8:11	–	–	9	I*	–	10
9:0 –9:11	–	–	5	2	I	8
10:0 –10:11	–	–	6	3	2	11
11:0 –11:11	–	–	3	I	I	5
12:0 –12:11	–	–	2	–	I	3
13:0 –13:11	–	–	–	–	2	2
Average mental age	4·9	5·9	8·2	10·1	11·8	8·2
Total no.	4	9	56	7	7	83

* Notes. (1) The highest mental age in B-category was 6:7; the lowest in D-category was 8:9

(2) The correlation ratio (η) between age and concept-category as shown in Table A1 is 0·47; between mental age and category as shown in Table A2 is 0·67. Both coefficients are statistically significant

BIBLIOGRAPHICAL REFERENCES

THE following list includes, with very few exceptions, references only to works mentioned in the text. These restrictions are set by the design of the book and the ignorance of the author, but not without awareness of the wealth of material, new and old, which is omitted. Readers are invited to write between the lines below – unless, of course, the book is borrowed.

H. B. Adams, *The Education of Henry Adams*, Boston: Houghton Mifflin, 1918

Aeschylus, *The Choephori* in *Prometheus Bound and Other Plays*, trans. P. Vellacott, Penguin Books, 1961

W. F. Albright, *The Archaeology of Palestine*, Penguin Books, 1949

I. E. Alexander and A. M. Adlerstein, (a) 'Is death a matter of indifference?' *Amer. J. Psychol.*, 43, 1957

   (b) 'Affective responses to the concept of death in a population of children and early adolescents', *J. Genet. Psychol.*, 93, 1958

L. B. Ames, 'The development of the sense of time in the young child', *J. Genet. Psychol.*, 68, 1943

K. Amis, *Take a Girl Like You*, Gollancz, 1960

S. Anthony, (a) *The Child's Discovery of Death*, Routledge & Kegan Paul, 1940

   (b) 'The child's idea of death', T. Talbot (ed.), *The World of the Child*, Doubleday, 1967; Penguin Books

M. H. Appley and R. Trumbull (eds), *Psychological Stress*, P. Appleton-Century-Croft, 1967

H. Arendt, (a) *Between Past and Future*, 1951

   (b) *The Human Condition*, University of Chicago Press, 1958

M. Argyle, *Religious Behaviour*, Routledge & Kegan Paul, 1958

J. A. Arlow, 'Fantasy systems in twins', *Psychoanal. Quart.*, 29, 1960

Magda Arnold, 'Stress and emotion', M. H. Appley and R. Trumbull (eds), *q.v.*

St Augustine of Hippo, *Confessions*, trans. R. S. Pine-Coffin, Penguin Books, 1962

J. Baillie, *The Belief in Progress*, Oxford University Press, 1950

H. Becker, 'The sorrow of bereavement', *J. Abn. Soc. Psychol.*, 27, 1932

H. Belloc, *Cautionary Tales*, Eveleigh Nash, 1908

C. Bernard, *Philosophie (MS inédit)*, J. Chevalier (ed.), Paris: Boivin, 1937

M. Black, 'Induction and probability', R. Klibansky (ed.), *Philosophy in Mid-Century*, Florence: Nuova Italia, 1958

H. J. Blackham, *Six Existentialist Thinkers*, Routledge & Kegan Paul, 1952–61

F. Borkenau, 'The concept of death', *Twentieth Century*, clvii, 1955

K. Boulding, *see* T. R. Malthus

P. Bovet, *The Child's Religion*, trans. G. H. Green, Dent, 1928

J. Bowlby, (a) *Maternal Care and Mental Health*, Monograph Series 179, Geneva: World Health Organization, 1951

(b) *Child Care and the Growth of Love*, Penguin Books, 1953

(c) 'Separation anxiety', *Internat. J. of Psychoanal. and Psychiat.*, 41 and 42, 1961

(d) 'Childhood mourning and its implications for psychiatry', *Amer. J. Psychiat.*, 118, 1961

S. G. F. Brandon, (a) *Time and Mankind*, Hutchinson, 1951

(b) *Man and his Destiny in the Great Religions*, Manchester University Press, 1962

O. Bratfös, 'Parental deprivation in childhood and type of future mental disease', *Acta. Psychiat. Scand.*, 43, 4, 1967

J. H. Breasted, *The Dawn of Conscience*, New York: Scribners, 1922

M. E. Breckenridge and E. L. Vincent, *Child Development*, 4th edn, W. B. Saunders, 1960

P. W. Bridgman, (a) *The Intelligent Individual and Society*, Macmillan, 1938

(b) *The Way Things Are*, Harvard University Press, 1959

C. Brontë, *Jane Eyre*, 1st edn, 1847

R. Brooke, *1914 and Other Poems*, Sidgwick & Jackson, 1917

F. Brown, 'Childhood bereavement and subsequent psychiatric disorder', *Brit. J. Psychiat.*, 112, 1966

L. H. Brown, 'A study of religious belief', *Brit. J. Psychol.*, 53, 3, 1962

J. Bunyan, *The Pilgrim's Progress*, vol. 1: 1st edn, 1678; vol. 2: 1st edn, 1684

C. L. Burt, (a) 'Brain and consciousness', *Brit. J. Psychol*, *59*, 1, 1968
  (b) 'Brain and consciousness', *Bull. Brit. Psychol. and Sociol.*, *22*, 74,
  1969
H. E. Butler, *Introduction to Aeneid VI*, Blackwell, 1920
H. Butterfield, *Christianity and History*, Fontana, 1957
N. G. G. Byron, 'The destruction of Sennacherib', *Poems*, 1815
M. C. Caplan and V. I. Douglas, 'Incidence of parental loss in children
  with depressed mood', *J. Ch. Psychol. Psychiat.*, 10, 1969
J. Cary, *A House of Children*, Michael Joseph, 1941
L. Carmichael (ed.), *Manual of Child Psychology*, J. Wiley & Sons,
  1954
Lewis Carroll (C. L. Dodgson), *Alice Through the Looking Glass*,
  Macmillan, 1876
G. M. Carstairs, *The Twice-Born*, Hogarth Press, 1957
E. Cassirer, *An Essay on Man*, Yale University Press, 1944
R. H. Charles (ed.), *The Apocrypha of the Old Testament in English*, 2
  vols, Oxford: Clarendon Press, 1913 (*see also* Old Testament
  below)
Church of England, *Book of Common Prayer*
C. D. Clemente and D. B. Lindsley (eds), *Aggression and Defense*,
  University of California Press, 1967 (Conference on Brain Func-
  tion, November 1965)
A. H. Clough, *Poems*, Macmillan, 1869
S. Cole, *The Prehistory of East Africa*, Penguin Books, 1954
C. Connolly, *The Unquiet Grave*, Arrow Books, 1961
F. C. Conybeare, *et al.*, *The Story of Ahikar from the Aramaic, Syriac,
  Arabic, Armenian, Ethiopic, Old Turkish, Greek and Slavonic Versions*,
  Cambridge University Press, 1913
S. A. Cook, (a) 'The Semites', *Cambridge Ancient History*, vol. 1
  (b) 'Israel before the Prophets', *Cambridge Ancient History*, vol. 3
  (c) *An Introduction to the Bible*, Penguin Books, 1945
F. Harvey Darton, (a) 'Children's Books', *Cambridge History of Literature*,
  vol. II, 1932–53
  (b) *Children's Books in England*, Cambridge University Press, 1958
C. R. Darwin, (a) *On the Origin of Species*, C. D. Darlington (ed.),
  1950 (reprint of 1st edn)
  (b) *Autobiography*, F. Darwin (ed.), *q.v.*, vol. 1, ch. 2
F. Darwin (ed.), *The Life and Letters of Charles Darwin*, 3 vols, J.
  Murray, 1888

W. Dennis, (a) 'Historical notes on child animism', *Psychol. Rev.*, 45, 1938
(b) *see* R. W. Russell
J. Deutsche, *The Development of Children's Concepts of Casual Relations*, University of Minnesota Press, 1937
J. Donne, 'Satire III', *Poems*, E. K. Chambers (ed.), Routledge
F. Dostoyevsky, *Crime and Punishment*, 1st edn, 1870; trans. D. Margashack, Penguin Books, 1970
J. Drever, *A Dictionary of Psychology*, Penguin Books, 1952
A. Einstein, *see* S. Freud (h)
K. Eissler, *see* J. Frosch
M. Eliade, (a) *Birth and Rebirth*, trans. W. R. Trask, Harvill, 1958
(b) *Myths, Dreams and Mysteries*, Harvill, 1960
D. Elkind, 'The child's conception of his religious denomination', *J. Genet. Psychol*, 99, 1961
E. Erikson, (a) *Childhood and Society*, Imago, 1950
(b) *see* J. M. Tanner (b)
C. Lovatt Evans and B. Hartridge (eds), *Starling's Principles of Human Physiology*, Churchill, 1956
J. H. Ewing, *Jackanapes, the Story of a Short Life*, 1885
F. W. Farrar, *Eric, or Little by Little*, 1858
H. Feifel, (a) (ed.), *Freud and the Twentieth Century*, Meridian, 1957
(b) (ed.), *The Meaning of Death*, McGraw Hill, 1959
S. Ferenczi, 'The problem of the acceptance of unpleasant ideas', *Further Contributions to Psychoanalysis*, 1926
M. Finley, *The Greek Historians*, Chatto & Windus, 1959
R. Firth, (a) *The Fate of the Soul*, Cambridge University Press, 1955
(b) (ed.) *Man and Culture*, Routledge & Kegan Paul, 1957
A. Flew, *Body, Mind and Death*, Macmillan, 1964 (the Bibliographical Notes repay special study)
J. C. Flugel, Introduction to S. Anthony, *The Child's Discovery of Death*, Routledge & Kegan Paul, 1940
G. A. Foulds, 'Characteristic projection test responses in a group of defective delinquents', *Brit. J. Psychol.*, 40, 3, 1950
H. and H. A. Frankfort, J. A. Wilson and T. Jacobsen, *Before Philosophy*, University of Chicago Press, 1946; Penguin Books, 1949
J. G. Frazer, (a) *The Golden Bough*, 12 vols, 1890
(b) *The Belief in Immortality*, 1913
(c) *The Fear of the Dead in Primitive Religion*, Macmillan, 1933

A. Freud, (a) and D. Burlingham, *War and Children*, Imago, 1943
  (b) *The Psychoanalytic Treatment of Children*, Imago, 1946
S. Freud, *Standard Edition of Psychological Works*, 21 vols, J. Strachey
  (ed.), Hogarth Press, 1953
  (a) *Analysis of a Phobia in a Five-year-old Boy*, vol. 10, 1909
  (b) *The Theme of the Three Caskets*, vol. 12, 1913
  (c) *Thoughts for the Times on War and Death*, vol. 14, 1915
  (d) *Mourning and Melancholia*, vol. 14, 1917
  (e) *The Uncanny*, vol. 17, 1919 (1953 edn)
  (f) *Negation*, vol. 19, 1925
  (g) *The Future of an Illusion*, vol. 21, 1933
  (h) and A. Einstein, *Why War*, League of Nations, 1932
  (i) *Moses and Monotheism*, 1939
E. Fromm, *Sigmund Freud's Mission*, Harper, 1959
J. Frosch and N. Ross, review of K. Eissler, *The Psychiatrist and the Dying Patient*, Annual Survey of Psychoanal., 6, International University Press, 1955
D. A. E. Garrod and D. M. A. Bate, *The Stone Age of Mount Carmel*, vol. 1, Oxford: Clarendon Press, 1937
A. van Gennep, *The Rites of Passage*, 1909; trans. M. B. Vizedom and G. L. Caffee, Routledge & Kegan Paul, 1960
A. Gesell, 'Child psychology', E. Seligman (ed.), *Encyclopedia of Social Sciences*, 1930
E. Gibbon, *History of the Decline and Fall of the Roman Empire*, 1776 (also the anonymous Introduction to 1808 edn)
E. Gibson and S. Klein, *Murder 1957 to 1968*, H.M.S.O., 1969
E. Gilson, *History of Christian Philosophy in the Middle Ages*, Sheed & Ward, 1955
D. V. Glass, *Introduction to Malthus*, Watts, 1953
J. W. Goethe, *Faust*, I, trans. P. Wayne, Penguin Books, 1969
G. S. W. Gorer, *Death, Grief and Mourning in Contemporary Britain*, Cresset Press, 1965
E. Grosse, *Father and Son*, Heinemann, 1906
H. Graham, *Ruthless Rhymes for Heartless Homes*, E. Arnold, 1909
J. Graunt, *see* C. H. Hull
R. Griffiths, *A Study of Imagination in Early Childhood*, Kegan Paul, 1935
W. Grimm, *Märchen*, Berlin, 1843 (numerous English translations)
M. Grotjahn, 'The representation of death in the art of antiquity and

in the unconscious of modern men', C. B. Wilbur and W. Muensterberger (eds), *Psychoanalysis and Culture*, International University Press, 1951

M. Guyau, *La Genèse de l'idée de temps*, Paris: Alcan, 1890

F. J. Hacker, contribution to H. Feifel (ed.), *q.v.* (a)

G. Stanley Hall, *et al.*, *Aspects of Child Life and Education*, Appleton, 1921

E. Halley, (a) 'An estimate of the degrees of mortality of mankind . . .', *Philosophical Transactions*, *196*, vol. 17, 1693/4
 (b) 'Some further considerations . . .', *Phil. Transs.*, *198*, vol. 17, 1693/4 (*or see* A. Wolf *below*)

J. L. and B. Hammond, *The Town Labourer*, Longmans Green, 1917

S. I. Harrison, *et al.*, 'Children's reactions to bereavement: adult confusions and misperceptions', *Arch. gen. Psychiatry*, *17*, 5, 1967

J. Hastings, 'Death', *Encyclopedia of Religion and Ethics*, 1908

A. Heidel, *The Gilgamesh Epic and Old Testament Parallels*, University of Chicago Press, 1946

W. Henderson, *Folklore of the Northern Counties*, Satchell, Peyton, 1879

I. Hermann, 'A study of G. T. Fechner', abstract in *Psychoanal. Rev.*, *24*, 1937

Herodotus, *The History*, trans. G. Rawlinson, annot. A. W. Lawrence, Nonesuch Press, 1935 (*see also* trans. A. de Selincourt, Penguin Books, 1954, IV, 26)

G. Highet, *Poets in a Landscape*, Penguin Books, 1959

O. W. Hill, 'The association of childhood bereavement with suicidal attempt in depressive illness', *Brit. J. Psychiat.*, *115*, 1969

F. H. Hilliard, 'The influence of religious education upon the development of children's moral ideas', *Brit. J. Ed. Psychol.*, *29*, 1, 1959

L. T. Hogben, *Statistical Probability*, Allen & Unwin, 1957

S. Holmes (ed.), 'The Wisdom of Solomon', R. H. Charles (ed.), *q.v.*

Homer, *Iliad*, trans. E. V. Rieu, Penguin Books, 1950

G. M. Hopkins, *Poems (1876–1889)*, 2nd edn, Oxford University Press, 1930

Horace (Quintus Horatius Flaccus), *Odes*, I, 28

W. H. Howell, *Textbook of Physiology*, 12th edn, W. B. Saunders, 1933

I. Huang, (a) 'Children's conceptions of physical causality', *J. Genet, Psychol.*, *63*, 1943

(b) and H. W. Lee, 'Experimental analysis of children's animism', *J. Genet. Psychol.*, 66, 1945

C. H. Hull, *Economic Writings of Sir W. Petty together with the Observations . . . more probably by Capt. J. Graunt*, Cambridge University Press, 1899

D. Hume, (a) *An Inquiry Concerning Human Understanding*, IV, 2
(b) *A Treatise of Human Nature*, quoted D. G. C. McNabb, *q.v.*

J. S. Huxley, (a) *Evolution, a Synthesis*, Allen & Unwin, 1942
(b) *see* J. M. Tanner (b)

E. Hyman, 'Psychoanalysis and the climate of tragedy', H. Feifel (ed.), *q.v.* (a)

B. Inhelder, *see* (a) J. Piaget (k), and (b) J. M. Tanner (b)

N. Isaacs, 'Children's why questions', in S. Isaacs, *q.v.* (b)

S. Isaacs, (a) *The Social Development of Young Children*, Routledge, 1930
(b) *Intellectual Growth in Young Children*, Routledge, 1931

G. Jahoda, 'Child animism: a critical survey of cross-cultural research', *J. Soc. Psychol.*, 47, 1958

W. James, *Principles of Psychology*, Macmillan, 1890

J. Janeway, *A Token for Children: being an Exact Account of the . . . Exemplary Lives, and Joyful Deaths of several young Children*

E. Jones, (a) 'The significance of the grandfather', *Papers on Psychoanalysis*, 4th edn, 1938
(b) *The Life and Work of Sigmund Freud*, 3 vols, Hogarth Press, 1955

C. G. Jung, (a) *The Psychology of the Unconscious*, 1915, trans. B. Hinkle, 1951
(b) *The Development of Personality*, trans. R. F. C. Hull, Routledge & Kegan Paul, 1954
(c) *Collected Works*, trans. R. F. C. Hull, Routledge & Kegan Paul.

A. Kaldegg, 'Responses of German and English secondary school boys to a projection test', *Brit. J. Psychol.*, 39, 1, 1948

D. and R. Katz, *Conversations with Children*, trans. H. S. Jackson, Kegan Paul, Trench & Trubner, 1936

S. Kierkegaard, (a) *Journals*, trans. A. Dru, Collins, 1958
(b) *The Concept of Dread*, trans. W. Lowrie, Oxford University Press, 1944

H. D. F. Kitto, *The Greeks*, Penguin Books, 1951

G. Klingberg, 'The distinction between living and not-living among 7- to 10-year-old children', *J. Genet. Psychol*, 90, 1957

W. F. Jackson Knight, *Cumaean Gates*, Blackwell, 1936

A. Koestler, 'The age of discretion', *The Listener*, 1960

P. A. Kropotkin, *Mutual Aid*, Heinemann, 1902

R. G. Kuhlen and M. Arnold, 'Age differences in religious beliefs and problems during adolescence', *J. Genet. Psychol.*, 64, 1944

K. M. J. Lagerspetz, 'Aggression and aggressiveness in laboratory mice', S. Garattini and E. B. Sigg (eds), *Aggressive Behaviour*, Milan, May, 1968

R. S. Lazarus, *Psychological Stress and the Coping Process*, McGraw Hill, 1966

E. R. Leach, 'The epistemological background of Malinowski's empiricism', R. Firth (ed.), *Man and Culture*, Routledge & Kegan Paul, 1957

J. Lehmann, *I Am My Brother*, Longmans Green, 1960

M. Lerner, *America as a Civilization*, Jonathan Cape, 1958

C. T. Lewis and T. A. Ingram, 'Insurance', *Encyclopedia Britannica*, 11th edn

H. S. Liddell, 'Experimental neuroses in animals', J. M. Tanner (ed.), *q.v.* (a)

E. Lindemann, 'Psycho-social factors as stressor agents', J. M. Tanner (ed.), *q.v.* (a)

K. Lorenz, *see* J. M. Tanner (b)

St Luke, *see* New Testament

D. McCarthy, 'Language development in young children', L. Carmichael (ed.), *q.v.*

E. McCormick, 'Last, loneliest, most loyal', K. Sinclair (ed.), *Distance Looks our Way*, University of Auckland, New Zealand, 1961

T. D. McCown and A. Keith, *The Stone Age of Mount Carmel*, vol. 2, Oxford: Clarendon Press, 1939

D. G. C. McNabb, *David Hume*, Hutchinson, 1951

D. G. Macrae, *Ideology and Society*, Heinemann, 1961

B. A. Maher, *Principles of Psychopathology*, McGraw Hill, 1966

B. Malinowski, (a) *Magic, Science and Religion* Glencoe, Illinois: Free Press, 1948

(b) *see* E. R. Leach

T. R. Malthus, (a) *Essay on Population*, 1st edn, 1798; K. Boulding (ed.), University of Michigan Press, 1959

(b) *A Summary View of the Principle of Population*, 1st edn, 1830; reprinted in *On Population: Three Essays*, New American Library, 1956

(c) *see* D. V. Glass

A. Manes, 'Insurance', E. Seligman (ed.), *q.v.*

R. R. Marett, *Faith, Hope and Charity in Primitive Religion*, Oxford: Clarendon Press, 1932

P. Marris, *Widows and their Families*, Routledge & Kegan Paul, 1958

K. Marx and F. Engels, *The Communist Manifesto*, 1st edn, 1848

M. Mead, (a) 'Research on primitive children', L. Carmichael (ed.), *q.v.*

(b) 'An investigation of the thought of primitive children', *J. Roy. Anthrop. Institute*, 62, 1932

(c) and M. Wolfenstein, *Childhood in Contemporary Cultures*, University of Chicago Press, 1955

F. K. and R. V. Merry, *The First Two Decades of Life*, Harper, 2nd edn, 1958

S. Milgram, (a) 'Behavioural study of obedience', *J. Abn. Soc. Psychol.*, 67, 2, 1963

(b) 'Some conditions of obedience and disobedience to authority', *Human Relations*, 18, 1, 1965

N. Miller, 'Learning of visceral and glandular responses', *Science*, 163, 1969

J. Mitford, *The American Way of Death*, Hutchinson, 1963

M. de Montaigne, *Essais*, III, 12, trans. J. Cohen, Penguin Books, 1958

E. Morante, *Arturo's Island*, Italian edn, 1957; Collins, 1959

W. Morgan, Introduction to *The Works of Richard Price*, D.D., F.R.S., 1816

S. Morgenstern, 'La pensée magique chez l'enfant', *Revue franç. de psychoanal.*, 7, 1, 1937

O. H. Mowrer, (a) 'A stimulus-response analysis of anxiety and its role as a reinforcing agent', *Psychol. Rev.*, 45, 1939

(b) *Learning Theory and Personality Dynamics*, 1950

N. L. Munn (ed.), *The Evolution and Growth of Human Behaviour*, Boston: Houghton Mifflin, 1955

A. Munro and A. B. Griffiths, 'Further data on childhood parent-loss in psychiatric normals', *Acta Psychiat. Scand.*, 44, 4, 1968

G. Murphy, discussion in H. Feifel (ed.) *q.v.* (b)

F. W. H. Myers, *Human Personality and its Survival of Bodily Death*, Longmans Green, 1919

M. Nagy, 'The child's theories concerning death', *J. Genet. Psychol.*, 73, 1948

J. Needham, (a) *Time, the Refreshing River*, Allen & Unwin, 1943
   (b) *Human Law and the Laws of Nature in China and the West*, Oxford University Press, 1951
   (c) review of P. Teilhard de Chardin, *The Phenomenon of Man, New Statesman*, 7 November 1959
New Testament, Books of: St Luke, Revelations
Old Testament, (a) Books of, canonical: II Chronicles, Daniel, Deuteronomy, Exodus, Ezekiel, Genesis, Isaiah, Jeremiah, Job, Judges, II Kings, Micah, Psalms; Authorized Version (King James). On Job, *see also* (b)
   (b) Books of, apocryphal: II Maccabees, Tobit, Wisdom of Solomon; Authorized Version, and R. H. Charles (ed.), *q.v.* On Enoch, *see* R. H. Charles
R. B. Onians, *The Origins of European Thought about the Body, the Mind, the Soul, the World, Time and Fate*, Cambridge University Press, 1954
I. and P. Opie, *The Lore and Language of School Children*, Oxford: Clarendon Press, 1959
P. Opie, 'The tentacles of tradition', *Advancement of Science*, 20, 85, 1963
F. T. Palgrave (ed.), *The Golden Treasury*, 1st edn, 1861
B. Pascal, *Pensées*, quoted by G. Poulet, *q.v.*
B. Pasternak, (a) *Doctor Zhivago*, trans. M. Hayward and Manya Harari, Collins & Harvill, 1958
   (b) *An Essay in Autobiography*, Collins & Harvill, 1959
I. P. Pavlov, *Lectures on Conditioned Reflexes*, 2 vols, trans. W. H. Gantt, New York: International Publishers
W. Petty, *see* C. H. Hull
J. Piaget, (a) *The Language and Thought of the Child*, trans. M. Gabain, 3rd edn, Routledge & Kegan Paul, 1959
   (b) *The Child's Conception of the World*, trans. J. and A. Tomlinson, Kegan Paul, 1929
   (c) *The Child's Conception of Casuality*, trans. M. Gabain, Kegan Paul, 1930
   (d) *Play, Dreams and Imitation in Childhood*, trans. C. Gattegno and M. M. Hodgson, Heinemann, 1951
   (e) *The Child's Conception of Number*, Routledge & Kegan Paul, 1955
   (f) *The Origin of Intelligence in the Child*, trans. M. Cook, Routledge & Kegan Paul, 1953

(g) *The Child's Construction of Reality*, trans. M. Cook, Routledge & Kegan Paul, 1955

(h) *Logic and Psychology*, with an Introduction by W. Mays, Manchester University Press, 1953

(i) *La Genèse des structures logiques élémentaires*, Delachaux & Nestlé, 1959

(j) *L'Épistémologie génétique*, Presses Universitaires de France, 1950

(k) and B. Inhelder, *La Genèse de l'idée de hasard chez l'enfant*, Presses Universitaires de France, 1951

(l) *see also* J. M. Tanner (b)

Plato, (a) *The Republic*, trans. H. Spens, Everyman, 1908

(b) *The Symposium*, trans. P. B. Shelley, Everyman, 1905

H. T. Pledge, *Science Since 1500*, H.M.S.O., 1939

Plutarch, (a) *Lives*, A. H. Clough (ed.), Everyman, 1910

(b) *Roman Questions*, trans. H. J. Rose, Oxford: Clarendon Press, 1924

Polybius, quoted by M. I. Finley, *q.v.*

P. Poppleton and G. W. Pilkington, 'The measurement of religious attitudes in a university population', *Brit. J. Soc. Clin. Psychol.*, 2, 1963

G. Poulet, *Studies in Human Time*, trans. E. Coleman, Baltimore: Johns Hopkins Press, 1956

R. Price, *see* W. Morgan

Propertius, trans. G. Highet, *q.v.*

M. Proust, quoted by G. Poulet, *q.v.*

O. Rank, (a) 'The *Doppelgänger*', *Imago*, III, 1914

(b) *The Trauma of Birth*, Kegan Paul, 1929

V. Rasmussen, (a) *Diary of a Child's Life*, trans. M. Blanchard, Gyldendal, 1919

(b) *Child Psychology*, trans. D. Pritchard, Gyldendal, 1921

S. Reinach, *Orpheus*, French edn, 1929; trans. F. Simmons, Owen, 1960

J. Renard, *Poil de Carotte*, 1895; *Carrots*, trans. G. W. Stonier, Grey Walls Press, 1946

D. E. Roberts, *Existentialism and Religious Belief*, Oxford University Press, 1957

S. Rosenzweig, (a) 'Sibling death as a psychological experience with special reference to schizophrenia', *Psychoanal. Rev.*, 30, 1943

(b) and D. Bray, 'Sibling deaths in the anamnesis of schizophrenic patients', *Arch. Neur. Psychiat.*, 49, 1943

J.-J. Rousseau, *Confessions*, Everyman, 1931

D. Runyon, *More than Somewhat*, E. C. Bentley (ed.), Constable, 1937

B. Russell, *A History of Western Philosophy*, Allen & Unwin, 1940

C. and W. M. S. Russell, *Violence: what are its Roots?*, 1968

R. W. Russell, (a) and W. Dennis, 'Studies in animism. I', *J. Genet. Psychol.*, 55, 1939

  (b) 'II. The development of animism', *J. Genet. Psychol.*, 57, 1940

  (c) and F. E. Ash, 'III. Animism in feeble-minded subjects', *J. Genet. Psychol.*, 57, 1940

  (d) 'IV. An investigation of concepts allied to animism', *J. Genet. Psychol.*, 57, 1940

A. Sampson, *Anatomy of Britain*, Hodder & Stoughton, 1962

S. B. Sarason, 'The measurement of anxiety in children', ch. 3 in *Anxiety and Behaviour*, C. D. Spielberger (ed.), New York and London: Academy Press, 1966

I. Sarnoff and S. M. Corvin, 'Castration anxiety and fear of death', *J. of Personality*, 27, 1959

P. Schilder, (a) and D. Bromberg, 'Death and the dying', *Psychoan. Review*, 20, 1933

  (b) and D. Wechsler, 'The attitudes of children towards death', *J. Abn. Soc. Psychol.*, 45, 1934

H. Selve, *The Stress of Life*, Longmans, 1937 (*see also* J. M. Tanner (a))

W. Shakespeare, *Works*, C. J. Sisson (ed.), Odhams, 1953

  (a) Sonnet 12

  (b) *King John*

  (c) *Coriolanus*

  (d) *Macbeth*

  (e) *Henry IV*, Part One (Hotspur)

  (f) *Henry IV*, Part Two (Henry V)

  (g) *Hamlet*

  (h) *The Merchant of Venice* (the three caskets)

  (i) *King Lear* (the same theme, in Freud's paper)

A. J. Simmons and A. E. Goss, 'Animistic responses as a function of sentence contexts and instructions', *J. Genet. Psychol.*, 91, 1957

D. C. Simpson (trans. and ed.), The Book of Tobit, *see* R. H. Charles (ed.)

H. Shelton Smith, *Changing Conceptions of Original Sin*, New York: Scribners, 1955

M. W. Smith, 'Different cultural concepts of past, present and future', *Psychiatry*, 15, 1952

Stevie Smith, *Novel on Yellow Paper*, 1936; Penguin Books, 1951

Sophocles (a) *Oedipus at Colonus*, and (b) *Antigone*, in trans. E. F. Watling, Penguin Books, 1947

C. Spearman, *The Nature of 'Intelligence' and the Principles of Cognition*, Macmillan, 1923

L. S. Stebbing, *Thinking to Some Purpose*, Penguin Books, 1939

W. Stekel, *Conditions of Nervous Anxiety*, trans. R. Gabler, Kegan Paul, 1923

E. Sterba, '*Analyse d'un cas de phobie des chiens*', *Revue franç. de psychoanal.* 7, 4, 1934 (trans. from *Z. f. Psychoan. Päd.*, 1933)

W. Stern, *The Psychology of Childhood*, 1914–27; trans. A. Barwell, Allen & Unwin, 1930

M. D. Stocks, *Eleanor Rathbone*, Gollancz, 1949

G. F. Stout and C. A. Mace, *Manual of Psychology*, 4th edn, 1932

J. Sully, *Studies of Childhood*, Longmans Green, 1895

J. Süssmilch, *Die göttliche Ordnung in den Veranderingen des menschlichen Geschlechts, aus der Geburt, dem Tode, und der Fortplanzung desselben Erwiesen*, Berlin, 1742

J. M. Tanner, (a) (ed.), *Stress and Psychiatric Disorder*, Blackwell, 1960
   (b) and B. Inhelder (eds), *Discussions on Child Development* (with contributions from Bowlby, Erikson, J. S. Huxley, Inhelder, Lorenz, Mead, Piaget, Grey Walter and Zazzo), Tavistock, 1956

L. Terman, (a) *The Measurement of Intelligence*, Harrap, 1917
   (b) and M. Merrill, *Measuring Intelligence*, Harrap, 1932

M. Thomas, '*Méthode des histoires à compléter pour le dépistage des complexes enfantins*', *Arch. de Psychol.*, Geneva, 1937

L. Tolstoy, *War and Peace*, Penguin Books, 1970

T. Traherne, *Centuries of Meditations*, Dobell, 1908

E. B. Tylor, *Primitive Culture*, 1871

Virgil (P. Vergilius Maro), *Aeneid*, VI

C. W. Wahl, 'The fear of death', H. Feifel, (ed.), *q.v.* (b)

N. Walker, *Crime and Insanity in England*, Edinburgh University Press, 1968

H. Wallon, *Les Origines de la pensée chez l'enfant*, 2 vols, Presses Universitaires françaises, 1945

W. Grey Walter, *see* J. M. Tanner (b)

E. Waugh, *The Loved One*, Chapman & Hall, 1948

D. J. West, *Murder Followed by Suicide*, Heinemann, 1965

G. Whitrow, *The Natural Philosophy of Time*, Nelson, 1961

B. L. Whorf, 'An American Indian model of the universe', *Int. J. Amer. Linguistics*, 16, 1950 (*or see* J. B. Carroll (ed.), *Language, Thought and Reality*, Massachusetts Institute of Technology, 1956)

R. L. Williams and S. Cole, 'Religiosity, generalized anxiety and apprehension concerning death', *J. Soc. Psychol.*, 15, 1968

J. O. Wisdom, 'The methodology of natural science', *Philosophy in Mid-Century*, R. Klibansky (ed.), Florence: Nuova Italia, 1958

S. L. Witryol and J. E. Calkins, 'Marginal social values of rural school children', *J. Genet. Psychol.*, 92, 1958

L. Wittgenstein, *Tractatus Logico-Philosophicus*, Routledge, 1922

A. Wolf, *History of Science, Technology and Philosophy in the Sixteenth and Seventeenth Centuries*, 2nd edn, Allen & Unwin, 1950

M. Wolfenstein, (a) *see* M. Mead (c)

(b) and G. Kliman (eds), *Children and the Death of a President*, 1965

S. Wolff, *Children under Stress*, Allen Lane The Penguin Press, 1969

M. Wolfgang and F. Ferracuti, *The Subculture of Violence*, Tavistock, 1967

H. A. Wolfson, *Religious Philosophy*, Harvard University Press, 1961

W. Wordsworth, *Works*, E. de Selincourt and H. Darbishire (eds), Oxford: Clarendon Press, 1947

R. Zazzo, *see* J. M. Tanner (b)

HOME RECORDS

Francis
  and death
    associated with birth, 21, 33
    interest in manner of as pictured, 52
    killing assumed cause of, 25
    and medical associations of, 204

G
  death of mother anticipated without dismay, 145

Jane
  and death
    and age, 139, 153
    anguish about, 139, 144, 145, 157, 160, 198
    anxiety caused by separation due to, 139, 145, 147
    of animals, 139, 140, 151
    and material object not subject to, 175, 240
    and renewal of life after, 139
    repression of thought of, 154
    sequence of discovery of, 138–40, 148
    worry of mother about J's reaction to discovery of, 139, 140, 153, 157, 160

Jeremy
  and anxiety about death
    caused by separation due to, 145
    reduced by anticipating company of loved object, 20

Judith
  and death
    of animals, 107
    interest in ritual of, 116
    of self, hoped with father and mother, 150
    -wishes, 114

Philip
  death of father induces expression of impotence, 227

Richard
  and death
    and angels' assistance, 45
    of animals, 107–10

INDEX OF NAMES

The pseudonyms of children for whom home records were kept by parents are listed separately, with subject references (see pp. 271–3).

Butler, H. E., 26
Butterfield, H., 252
Byron, N. G. G., 129

Cain, 117, 127
Calkins, J. E., 164
Camus, A., 230, 235
Capetanakis, D., 196, 197
Cary, J., 164, 165
Carmichael, L., 18
Carnot-Clausius, 177
Carroll, Lewis, 127, 188
Carstairs, G., 40
Cassirer, E., 174, 177, 178
Charles, R. H., 40, 122, 178
Charon, 38
Churchill, W. S., 15
Clemente, C. D., 233
Clough, A. H., 217, 218, 233
Cole, S., 23, 136
Coleridge, S. T., 126
Commodus, 39
Comte, A., 17, 180, 218
Condorcet, M. J. A. N., 212
Connolly, C., 43
Constant, B., 183, 223
Conybeare, F. C., 41
Cook, S. A., 23
Corvin, S., 87
Creon, 39, 40

Dante, 128, 130, 179
Darbishire, H., 134
Darton, F. H., 126, 127
Darwin, C., Darwinism, 113, 130, 215, 216
Darwin, F., 216
David, King, 117
Davidson, E., 235
Demeter, 26
Dennis, W., 55-7, 62, 67

Derham, W., 211
Descartes, René, Cartesian, 225, 226
Deutsche, J., 56
Dickens, C., 119
Diderot, D., 34
Donne, J., 42
Dostoyevsky, F., 229, 230
Drever, J., 237
Durkheim, E., 235

Edward VIII, 27
Edwards, J., 119
Eibl-Eibersfeldt, 233
Eichmann, ., 230, 232
Einstein, A., 180, 181, 220, 221, 230, 231
Eissler, K., 220
Electra, 34
Eliade, M., 250
Elijah, 134, 178
Eliot, T. S., 174
Elisha, 39, 134
Elkind, D., 120
Enoch, 134, 178
Epicurus, 123, 133
Erigena, see John Scotus
Erikson, E., 159, 187
Evans, C. I., 225
Ewing, J. H., 127
Ezekiel, 23, 26

Farrar, F. W., 127
Fechner, G., 33
Feifel, H., 10, 11, 136, 137, 161
Feldman, M. J., 11
Ferenczi, S., 16, 156, 246
Fermat, P. de, 208
Ferracuti, F., 227, 249
Finley, M., 121
Firth, R., 45
Flew, A., 225